WRITING THE SHORT FILM, SECOND EDITION

WRITING THE SHORT FILM, SECOND EDITION

Pat Cooper
and
Ken Dancyger

Focal Press
Boston Oxford Auckland Johannesburg Melbourne New Delhi

Focal Press™ is an imprint of Butterworth-Heinemann.
All trademarks found herein are property of their respective owners.

Recognizing the importance of preserving what has been written, Butterworth-Heinemann prints its books on acid-free paper whenever possible.

Butterworth-Heinemann supports the efforts of American Forests and the Global ReLeaf program in its campaign for the betterment of trees, forests, and our environment.

Library of Congress Cataloging-in-Publication Data

Cooper, Patricia.
Writing the short film / Pat Cooper and Ken Dancyger.
p. cm.
Includes bibliographical references and index.
ISBN 0-240-80369-8 (alk. paper)
1. Motion picture authorship. 2. Short films. I. Dancyger, Ken.
II. Title.
PN1996.C814 1999
808.2'3—dc21
99-27623
CIP

British Library Cataloguing-in-Publication Data
A catalogue record for this book is available from the British Library.

The publisher offers special discounts on bulk orders of this book.
For information, please contact:
Manager of Special Sales
Butterworth–Heinemann
225 Wildwood Avenue
Woburn, MA 01801-2041
Tel: 781-904-2500
Fax: 781-904-2620

For information on all Focal Press publications available, contact our World Wide Web home page at: http://www.focalpress.com.

10 9 8 7 6 5 4 3 2 1

Printed in the United States of America

To the memory of Richard Protovin,
dear friend and colleague
—P. C.

For Gerald and Perry Charles,
my brothers
—K. D.

CONTENTS

ACKNOWLEDGMENTS

PAT COOPER

I would like to thank Ken Dancyger for his provocative ideas, easy wit, and exemplary patience throughout our partnership on this project. He is a most gracious collaborator and a valued friend. I would also like to thank Mary Carlson for her perceptive comments on the first draft.

KEN DANCYGER

The notion of writing a book about scripting short films began with Pat Cooper. I have to thank her for her enthusiasm, her insights, and her commitment to students. And I thank her for bringing me into this project. She is a great friend and collaborator. At New York University, I'd like to thank Christina Rote and Delliah Bond, who assisted me in the preparation of the manuscript. Finally, I'd like to thank my wife, Ida, for her intelligent critiques of the manuscript at all phases.

INTRODUCTION

The aim of this book is to reach independent filmmakers and film or video students who are faced with the necessity of writing a short script. We hope to dispel many misconceptions about the short film, and also to articulate a definition. The most common misconception is that a short film is a fragment of a long or feature-length film; more subtle misunderstandings compare the short film to its analogues in other arts—the short story, the one-act play, the photograph, or the painting. Although the short film is related to other arts, it is unique in its length, and in that it is a film narrative, that is to say, a narrative told through images, whereas a play or short story is a narrative told through language.

WHAT IS A SHORT FILM?

We consider a short film to be one that is thirty minutes long or less. Its narrative may be based in dramatic, documentary, or experimental genres; it can be live-action or animated.

We specify a certain length because films longer than thirty minutes tend to take a different approach to character and plot: films of thirty to sixty minutes often include a secondary, or minor, plot line. This is most apparent in the structure of telefilms, where even the half-hour shows include a minor plot line, while a singular approach to character and a simplified plot are characteristic of the short film.

Every genre has its own narrative form, and each tells a story. Although the main focus in this book will be on the dramatic short film, we will also show how that short form has borrowed freely from the other genres. It is important for the young or less-experienced writer to realize that, although scripting of the documentary and the experimental film may proceed in an informal manner, these types of films do need a narrative purpose and a narrative shape. Particular stories may be concerned with form, may be struggling or playing with form as context, as is the case in many postmodern, experimental films, and this too is a narrative strategy. In the documentary, it may be the narration that gives the narrative shape, or it may be an onscreen narrator acting as a guide. These third-person approaches provide a formal narrative strategy for the filmmaker, although they often don't work in dramatic films, which tend to have more story than experimental short films. Also, the documentary film tends to have a more pronounced editorial purpose than the dramatic short film.

THE EVOLUTION OF THE SHORT FILM

At the outset of film as an art, all films were short. Indeed, until 1913 all films were fifteen minutes long or less. Only after the Italian film epics had influenced D. W. Griffith to produce *Judith of Bethulia* did the longer form come to be the norm.

Although the feature film eventually became the predominant form, comedy shorts, from Mack Sennett to the Bowery Boys, were produced until the success of television in the 1950s. Serialized films were also essentially shorts, characterized by an incident or catalytic event, which led to a character responding and other characters resisting that response. The films presented melodramatic protagonists and antagonists: the *Battle at Elderbrush Gulch*, by D. W. Griffith, and *The Tramp*, by Charlie Chaplin, illustrate the common characteristics of these short films. An ordinary character caught up in extraordinary events succeeds in overcoming those events and antagonists, in an exciting, incredible fashion. One of the most famous short films ever made was both a response to the conventions of narrative film in the twenties and an experiment influenced by ideas being explored in the visual arts (surrealism) and in the particulars of Spanish Catholic theology. That film, *Un Chien d'Andalou*, was the product of a collaboration between Salvador Dalí and Luis Buñuel. No other short film still succeeds in shocking and confusing audiences as does the Buñuel-Dalí collaboration, and no other film has shown such shocking individual images paired with so little concern for overall meaning.

But for our purpose in this book, *Un Chien d'Andalou*—because it is so challenging to the narrative conventions often associated with film—remains an experiment in form rather than a case study for scripting the successful short film. Nevertheless, the audacity of the film cemented a relationship between film and the visual arts and ideas closely tied to art (for example, surrealism and the growing importance of psychotherapy in the visual arts); this has become a continuing source of short films, from the work of Man Ray and Maya Daren to the more contemporary work of Stan Brakhage, Michael Snow, and Joyce Wieland.

Other developments in the short film coalesced around the documentary work of John Grierson and his colleagues Basil Wright and Edgar Ansty at the Empire Marketing Board in England, and around the work of Pare

Lorentz and Willard Van Dyke in the United States. The films these filmmakers produced were issue driven, encouraging government intervention in the economy in the United States or promoting the benefits of government policy in the United Kingdom. None of these films revolved around a particular event or used a protagonist or an antagonist. The drama of real-life issues close to a particular political consciousness motivated these filmmakers, and their films were often labeled propaganda.

Yet another offshoot of the short film, this time from the commercial work of Walt Disney, was the animated short, intended to be shown with feature films in theaters. These five-to-eight-minute films had a protagonist (often a mouse, a rabbit, or a wolf) with a strongly defined character and a particular goal. The story would unfold when the character's efforts to achieve a goal were thwarted by a situation or antagonist. The character's struggle to achieve the his/her goal made up the story of the film. These films abounded in action and conflict, the dramatic values yielding laughs rather than sympathy for the main character and his or her struggle.

They were very successful, and their pattern of narrative plotting and the development of character set the tone and pace for an even shorter film form—the commercial. Whether they last three minutes or thirty seconds, commercials tell a story based on the pattern established in the animated short films, which used established narrative forms—the tale, the fable, the journey—to convey, and at times to frame, the narrative. By 1960, filmmakers in Europe had begun to use the short film as a means of entry into the production of longer films. In Poland, Roman Polanski directed *Two Men and a Wardrobe* (1958). In England, Lindsay Anderson directed *O Dreamland!* (1954), and Richard Lester directed *The Running Jumping and Standing Still Film* (1959). In France, Jean-Luc Godard directed *All Boys Are Called Patrick* (1957), and François Truffaut directed *Les Mistons* (1958). In this period, Alain Resnais directed his remarkable *Night and Fog* (1955), about Auschwitz; Federico Fellini directed *Toby Dammit* (1963); and Norman McLaren directed his classic antiwar short *Neighbors* (1952). Only McLaren did not proceed into feature films; all the others moved on to distinguished careers as international filmmakers and continued their work in the long form.

This transition from short film to the longer form also seems to be the pattern for students in American film schools. Since the 1960s, the schools have produced distinguished alumni who began their work in the short form and then moved to the long: Oliver Stone, Martin Scorsese, Susan Seidelman, and Martin Brest on the East Coast, and Francis Coppola and George Lucas on the West Coast are among the most successful graduates of the film schools. Lucas's *THX 1138* (1966) and Scorsese's *It's Not Just You, Murray!* (1964) are among the best student films ever made, though their work in the short film was no more than apprenticeship for the long film.

This apprenticeship is the major reason for short film production in North America today, and while it is true that there are filmmakers in the experimental and documentary area who continue to work in the short form more and more filmmakers in these areas are moving to the long form as well

(Bruce Elder or Su Friedrich in the experimental film genre, or the work of Ross McKelwee and Barbara Kopple in the documentary, for example).

The short film, at least in North America, is increasingly a form of economic necessity for the student filmmaker and the recent professional, and while there are still short films produced in the educational corporate sectors, they are far fewer than in the past.

In Europe, however, the short film remains a viable form of expression, one supported in large part by cultural ministries. Magazines devoted to short films, as well as festivals devoted exclusively to the short film assure, at least for the medium term that the form will continue to thrive in Europe. Internationally, film schools have provided continuing support for the short film. The international organization of film schools, CILECT, has held a biannual student film festival focused on the European schools, and an annual student festival has been sponsored by the Hochschule in Munich. Another important biannual festival is the Tel Aviv Film Festival. All of these festivals are related to the CILECT organization and focus on the work of students in member schools. The Oberhausen Festival in Germany and the Clement-Ferrand Festival in France are devoted to short films, including fictional, experimental, documentary, and animated films.

Besides CILECT, a growing number of film festivals worldwide have short film categories. Chicago, Toronto, even Cannes show short films, and all of these festivals have been important launching points for the careers of the filmmakers. But both the CILECT-sponsored festivals and the larger international ones highlight short films as a path to the production of longer films, an apprenticeship experience rather than as an end in itself. Unlike the short story, which continues to be a lively, viable form, the short film is not widely and internationally recognized as something to which artists devote their careers.

However, during the time filmmakers devote their energies to short films, there is considerable opportunity for screening them, although their commercial viability is at best modest, except in those countries where considerable public subsidies are available to support their distribution.

Nevertheless we believe that, just as the short story has experienced a renaissance in the past ten years, so too it is possible that a new and longer-term interest in the short film may develop; recent cable programming initiatives and specialty market developments suggest that it may experience a renaissance.

THE RELATION OF LONG TO SHORT FILM

The long-form, or feature-length film, has a definite set of qualities beyond its physical length. There are particular expectations of character, complexity of plot, presence of a subplot, or secondary story line, and a particular structure (generally called a three-act structure). There are numerous secondary characters, and often particular genre forms are used, such as the gangster film or film noir.

Are the characteristics of the short film variations of those of the long film? In most cases, no. It is true that the two forms rely on visual action for exposition and characterization, as well as on the illusion of reality inherent in the use of film as a visual medium. Beyond these two characteristics, however, the short film proceeds in both a simpler, and a potentially freer, manner.

The simplicity lies in the restricted number of characters, often no more than three or four, and the level of plotting, which is usually a simple story. This does not mean that the main character is necessarily simple in the short film, but it does mean that an economy of style is employed to create that character. There is no time in the short film for the kind of pauses for elaboration of character so often deployed in the long film.

The freedom of the short film relative to the long film lies in the possibilities of using metaphor and other literary devices to tell the story, a luxury not available in the commercially driven, realism-oriented long film. Indeed, one of our major points about the short film is its linkage to literary forms such as the short story, the poem, the photograph, and the one-act play.

THE MYTH OF THE SHORT STORY AND THE SHORT FILM

Rust Hills characterizes the short story as a "story that tells of something that happened to someone. Second, the successful contemporary short story will demonstrate a more harmonious relationship of all its aspects than will any other literary art form excepting perhaps lyric poetry."[1] He also suggests that the story is dynamic, that the character is moved in the course of experience of the story, and that there are few secondary characters and no subplot. Often the story will unfold around a choice that presents itself to the character, who never returns to his or her former state; closure is attained by virtue of making or avoiding that choice.[2] Rust Hills's observations about the short story could be as readily applied to the short film.

However, not all short stories are suitable material for short films. In some, the level of narrative is more appropriate for a long-form film. The suitability of some short story material for long films is illustrated in a number of well-known feature-length films. Joseph Mankiewicz's *All About Eve*, John Sturges's *Bad Day at Black Rock*, Michelangelo Antonioni's *Blow-Up*, Fred Zinnemann's *High Noon*, Frank Capra's *It's a Wonderful Life*, Alfred Hitchcock's *Psycho*, and Stanley Kubrick's *2001: A Space Odyssey* are all based on short stories.[3] These feature films are among the most famous films ever made.

An example of largely successful use of short story material in the sixty-minute teleplay is the PBS series entitled *The American Short Story*.[4] This

1970s series was an effort to produce dramatic films based on a number of American classic short stories. One of the most impressive was the one-hour teleplay adapted by Joan Micklin Silver from F. Scott Fitzgerald's "Bernice Bobs Her Hair."

Again, the amount of narrative in these one hour stories transcends the scale of the short film, and the result confirms the danger of assuming that all short stories are suitable for the creation of short films: the writer should be aware of the prerequisites of simplicity of plot and a small number of characters.

Although many books have been written about screenwriting, with few exceptions they are concerned with writing the long film. Most recent books have focused on structure and have moved away from the Aristotelian concerns of their predecessors. Consequently, the relevance of these books to the writing of the short film posits an analogy between the structure of the short film and the long-form film, in essence a three-act structure. This relationship between short and long film, both in proportion and in form, is at best tenuous. The long-form act-length proportion is 1:2:1 (thirty minutes, Act I; sixty minutes, Act II; thirty minutes, Act III). In a short film of fifteen to thirty minutes, it is doubtful that this proportion would hold. The catalytic event that would begin the action of the film, which could be viewed as the beginning of Act II, must come much more quickly than a quarter of the way into the film. Indeed, in the short film, if we use the long-form act proportion or three-act structure, we find that both Act I and Act II are very short, because the setting up of the story (Act I) must be fast. Without the characterization and relationships of Act II, the conventional conflicts of the long-form Act II also move quickly, which leaves the largest proportion of the short film for the character to find a resolution. In many short films, a two-act structure might be a more productive writing device. The upshot is that much of what has been written about screenwriting in general is not very helpful for the writing of short films.

THE SHAPE OF THIS BOOK

We have broken down the structure of the book into three sections, the first dealing with the underlying fundamental character of the short screenplay; the second moving the writer from the fundamentals to strategies for storytelling, visualization, dramatization, character, and dialogue; the third dealing with forming the story.

Since the process of writing the short film is essentially organic, we begin with the idea and move the writer through the various phases of the actual writing and rewriting of the script. Where relevant, chapters will include exercises intended to guide the writer in writing the best script possible.

We acknowledge that writing is a mix of talent and technique. We can teach you the technique and provide exercises to elicit creative solutions to writing problems, but in the end, it is your unique voice that will make your film story different from every other film story.

NOTES

1. Rust Hills, *Writing in General and the Short Story in Particular* (New York: Houghton Mifflin, 1977), 1.
2. Ibid., 1–11.
3. D. Wheeler, ed., *No, But I Saw the Movie: The Best Short Stories Ever Made into Film* (New York: Penguin, 1989).
4. Calvin Scaggs, ed., *The American Short Story* (New York: Dell, 1977).

PART I

FUNDAMENTALS: BREAKING GROUND

The story resembles a wind filtering through the cracks in a wall: it gives evidence of the vastness. It provides a mobility through time and space. . . . To enter a story, one must give up being oneself for a while. Self-abandonment to a story is probably one of the crucial forms of human experience, since few cultures have been discovered which did not value it.

PAUL ZWEIG, *The Adventurer*

1
STORYTELLING IN GENERAL

Anyone who has ever been confronted by a small child's searching gaze or seen an infant gulp down its surroundings with its eyes (Where am I? Who are you? What's going on here?) will recognize that from early in their lives human beings have an intense need to understand the world around them, to make sense of things. Inventing and embellishing stories are ways to satisfy that need; the first stories human beings told themselves and one another were about how everything in the world came into being, how things came to be the way they are.

A WORKING DEFINITION

For the purposes of this book, which deals with writing the short screenplay of thirty minutes' length or less, we will define a story as any narration of events or incidents that relates how something happened to someone. The "someone" will be considered the main character of a story, and if the element of causality is added to the telling of how something happened to that character, the story will be considered to have a plot. In his book *Aspects of the Novel*, novelist E. M. Forster gives a succinct example of this process: "'The king died and then the queen died' is a statement. 'The king died and then the queen died of grief' is a plot."[1] In general, the short screenplay, like the short story, works best when its plot is uncomplicated, when we are given a glimpse of someone at a particular—very likely pivotal—moment in his or her life, a moment when an incident or a simple choice sets in motion a chain of events.

WHAT STORIES CAN DO

From early on in our history, stories have offered us alternative ways of experiencing the world. Huddled in the dark about a fire or in the heat of a marketplace, seated at a great lord's table or in the darkness of a movie theater, we drink up stories about the marvelous or terrifying or comical experiences of other human beings. We participate in the adventures of heroes and heroines, whether they are called Achilles or Michael Corleone, Little Red Riding Hood or Dorothy of Kansas. The most important factor in making it possible for a narrative to entertain, as well as to instruct or inspire us, is our ability to project ourselves into characters, whether imaginary or "real." It is to this ability that Paul Zweig refers when he writes, "To enter a story one must give up being oneself for a while."[2]

A universal longing to hear about the lives of others seems to be as strong in our own time as in the past. In industrialized countries, at least, it is no longer the oral or printed word that is the primary medium for storytelling, but the film or television screen. At home, we catch bits and pieces of other people's lives as they are offered on newscasts and two-minute "in depth" portraits; we find ourselves held captive to the relentlessly predictable narratives of situation comedies, police procedurals, or search-and-rescue docudramas. Although, as an educated audience, we complain about the dull and repetitive scriptwriting, the exaggerated acting, and the lack of variety in programming, we continue to watch faithfully week after week, even year after year, in our hunger for stories.

In *The Poetics*, his great manual on how to write a play, the philosopher Aristotle said, "Objects which in themselves we view with pain, we delight to contemplate when reproduced with minute fidelity. . . . The cause of this again is that to learn gives the liveliest pleasure, not only to philosophers but to men in general."[3]

A biologist as well as a philosopher, and a close observer of human behavior on stage and off, Aristotle was interested not only in the Greek tragedies themselves but in the reactions of their audiences. He goes on to say that for an audience, the pleasure of recognition is to "grasp and understand." Like those Athenian audiences twenty-three centuries ago, audiences today long to grasp and understand something of the human condition.

FAIRY TALE, MYTH, AND GENRE IN FILM

The early myths of any tribe usually tell about ways in which human beings are affected by the actions of a god or gods, while its fairy tales and legends are apt to describe ways in which human beings are affected by more earthy aspects of the supernatural—say witches, giants, trolls, talking animals, or magical objects. In both, feelings and thoughts are externalized and given substance, which is undoubtedly why mythmaking of a sort has been an important part of narrative filmmaking from its early days until the present.

Just as oral myths and fairy tales changed over the years in the process of being passed from one storyteller to the next, so the myths in genre film have gradually been transformed by writers and directors. It can be instructive to trace the line of descent from a one-dimensional hero like Tom Mix in crude early westerns to the comical, reluctant hero played by Clint Eastwood in *Unforgiven*; or the gradual transformation of the pint-sized innocent played by Charlie Chaplin in *Modern Times*, struggling with a machine as ruthless and powerful as any giant, into the scrawny sophisticate played by Woody Allen in *Annie Hall*, trying to master an evil-looking lobster; or the evolution over the years of the rigorous, if unconventional, code of honor of private-eye Sam Spade in *The Maltese Falcon* to the code of resolute self-interest practiced by private investigator Jake Gittes in *Chinatown*. In most cases, the archetypal form of the story remains, while the meaning of the underlying myth changes in response to the pressure of changes in society.

To reflect such changes successfully, screenwriters need to be familiar with the classic films of the genre in which they choose to work. This is as true of writing parody—a favorite of film students—as it is of using any other style that deals with inherited material.

It happens that the two archetypal structures that have proved most useful in shaping material for a short screenplay are those considered by scholars to be the very oldest of narrative forms: the *journey*, and what we call the *ritual occasion*. If you have a main character clearly in mind, a good idea of what that character's situation is and of what it is that he or she is after, you can often get a script off to a good start simply by choosing one or the other of these as a structure for your story line and seeing where it takes you.

EXAMPLES OF THE JOURNEY STRUCTURE

Two award-winning student shorts from New York University that use this structure to very different ends are *Going to Work in the Morning from Brooklyn*, written and directed by Phillip Messina, and *Champion*, written and directed by Jeffrey D. Brown.

Going to Work in the Morning from Brooklyn tells the story of a man who absolutely does not want to go to work, although he knows he must. We follow him in his anguished, comical struggle to get out of bed, into a suit and tie, out the door, and onto the Manhattan-bound subway. We feel his despair while we laugh at his actions: the film successfully walks a fine line between comedy and drama.

At one point the main character, standing miserably in the packed train, glances about him and meets the eyes of an attractive woman sitting opposite. When she looks away, he surreptitiously studies her. She catches him at it, tosses her head, and frowns; he shifts his eyes, muttering a protest to himself. They both get out at the next stop and wait on the subway platform to change trains.

There the man finds a gum machine that accepts his coin but doesn't deliver; in frustration, he smacks it hard and is amazed and delighted when a stick of gum drops into his hand. He smiles then for the first time and unwraps the gum to pop it into his mouth. Looking at himself in the mirror of the machine, he notices the woman behind him, watching with a little smile. At that moment we feel, as we can see he feels, a lift of the heart: maybe—just maybe—his luck will change.

The remainder of the film shows us his funny, clumsy failed pursuit of the woman and his despairing arrival, at last, at the busy, factorylike office where he puts in his daily eight hours. The story of an ordinary workday has become a kind of archetypal journey.

Champion tells the story of a comical young man who falls in love with a pretty jogger at the reservoir in New York City's Central Park. In the beginning of the film, we watch him debate hurtling a wooden barrier at the entrance to the park, and decide to go around it instead. On an esplanade overlooking the reservoir—clearly his regular warm-up place—he finds a lithe young woman doing stretching exercises. Dazzled by her, he picks a spot close by to do the same, mirroring her every move. When she sets off around the reservoir at a leisurely jog, he follows at a discreet distance. Obstacles are everywhere—a nasty child on a tricycle, a group of junior high school students playing ferocious football, and so on. Eventually he falls through a gaping hole in a pedestrian bridge and loses sight of her, although he limps gallantly on, peering all around.

The next morning, the main character is at the warm-up place at (literally) cockcrow waiting for her. At last the young woman arrives, warms up, and once more sets off at an easy pace, with the shy hero lagging behind. Then, all unaware, she drops the scarf she is wearing; he picks it up, strokes it tenderly, and begins to run flat out after her. But as he overtakes her, he loses his nerve and continues on, scarf in hand, to become entangled with a ragged group of runners heading toward the finish line in a race. In the end, he finds a way to return the scarf without directly confronting her. When she looks around and smiles to herself, we feel, as he feels, that she knows who has put the scarf on her bike—and that there is always tomorrow. As the film ends, the main character approaches the barricade once again, boldly leaps over it, and jogs off to the sound of Irish martial music. The story of a couple of ordinary runs has become the archetypal journey of the smitten lover pursuing his or her beloved.

It is worth noting that *Champion*, while similar in structure to *Going to Work in the Morning from Brooklyn* and concerned with a similar theme, is completely different both in its main character and in what the philosopher Susanne Langer has called "feeling" and "feeling-tone."

Langer writes, "A work of art is an expressive form created for our perception through sense or imagination, and what it expresses is human feeling. The word feeling must be taken here in its broadest sense, meaning everything that can be felt . . . [including] the steady feeling-tones of human life."[4]

EXAMPLES OF THE RITUAL OCCASION STRUCTURE

Sleeping Beauties is the story of two sisters, aged fifteen and sixteen, who find that the imaginary male dream-figure they have created between them has come to life. The film opens with the sisters preparing for bed—the older sister, Iris, brushing out her younger sister Lucy's long hair. We witness the closeness of the two girls, almost as if they were twins.

Eventually Iris lights a cigarette, which they share, and announces that it's time to begin what is clearly a nightly ritual of imagining an ideal lover, step by step and in detail, disagreeing only about the color of his eyes. Then each climbs into her bed, and they fall asleep holding hands.

Time passes; the room is filled with moonlight as a pebble hits the window. The girls wake up and cross the room to look down on a biker gazing up at them from beside his Harley-Davidson on the lawn, three stories below. When he asks which of them wants a ride, they are dazed; Iris protests to Lucy that it's too soon, he's not yet "finished." Lucy says that one of them should go down, that Iris should choose. Iris tells her to go, that she will wait at the window; the dreamy younger sister climbs down the trellis to where he waits. Lucy describes him to her sister, and the two move off into the dark. Iris protests that it isn't fair, and there is a dissolve to Lucy and the biker embracing in the shadows.

Iris falls asleep, dreams of their caresses, and wakens, calling Lucy to come home. Lucy appears and climbs back up the trellis as the biker peels off on his motorcycle. When Iris asks her about what happened, she is evasive. The sisters go back to bed, Iris clearly estranged. After a little while, Lucy moves over to her sister's bed and lies down next to her, spoon-fashion. But when Lucy says her name, Iris doesn't answer, pretending to be asleep. In this film, the arrival of an archetypal stranger who conforms to the imaginary lover created by two sisters triggers the ritual occasion—in this case, a "coming of age"—around which the film revolves. Unlike many such stories, the main character in this one rejects the opportunity, suffering accordingly when the younger sister seizes it.

Another film, *Gare du Nord*, written and directed by noted ethnographic filmmaker Jean Rouch, uses the same archetype to explore very different territory. It is one of an anthology of six short films made by European directors, each set in a different section of Paris.

Gare du Nord opens with a young couple squabbling as they get dressed for work in a tiny apartment in a noisy high-rise. As they bicker their way through breakfast, we learn that the attractive wife is unhappy with the apartment, unhappy with her lumpish, complacent husband, and in despair about the dull routine of their life together. We realize that she is a romantic who dreams of adventure and luxury, while he is a dull, unimaginative man, content with his lot.

Descending alone through almost total darkness in an elevator very much like a coffin, the woman steps out onto the bright street below and is almost hit by a sleek-looking car. A gaunt, noticeably pale, elegant-looking man leaps from it, apologizing profusely. From this point on, the film—shot throughout in cinema-verité style—takes on the quality of a fairy tale. The stranger asks if he can drive her to wherever she is going. When she says no, she would rather walk, he asks if he can accompany her, and she indifferently agrees. As they walk along a bridge, high above a maze of railroad tracks, they talk. The man asks about her life, and she responds by telling him her dreams of a very different sort of life. He passionately offers her everything she wants and begs her to come away with him. The woman hesitates and then refuses, in a tragic gesture that cuts off all possibilities (not every fairy tale ends happily).

The ritual occasion, as in *Sleeping Beauties*, is the arrival of the archetypal stranger, here very probably representing the Angel of Death. The ending is somewhat confusing, but *Gare du Nord* would seem to offer its main character a choice between living in reality or dying with her dreams.

Because the ritual-occasion structure (where adventure finds the main character in his or her situation) is so much more widely used than the journey structure in short films, we will offer one more, very different example. *Grease Monkey*, written and directed by Laurie Craig, is set in a rural community in the United States right after the end of World War II. Soldiers are just coming home. The key characters are in their late teens or early twenties. The opening of the film, after a series of stationary shots of a small gas station on a country road, shows a grease-stained mechanic working under a car while listening to big-band swing. A loud-mouthed customer comes into the garage and begins to complain: why isn't his car ready? The mechanic wheels out from under the car, still on his back, and begins to defend himself vigorously. At this point, both the film audience and the stunned customer realize that he is a she. The grease monkey's father appears and tries to placate the outraged customer. After he goes, the father tells his daughter the good news: her brother is coming home any day now.

When next we see her, she is transformed into a stereotypical girl of the 1940s, vacuuming and baking with her mom as they prepare for the hero's return. She talks to her parents about going to a trade school, angering her mother and causing her father to turn away.

A pickup truck arrives loaded with her brother's friends, still in uniform. Dressed up, though not as much as the other girls in the back of the truck, she goes off with the gang to a picnic. From the start, she and one of the boys are clearly attracted to one another. At the lake, she tells him that she's been working as a mechanic in her brother's absence, and he responds that he won't hold it against her. After a heated exchange in which he grabs her and kisses her hard, she pushes him into the lake, and he pulls her in with him. When they are all ready to go home, the pickup won't start. After several boys fiddle around under the hood with no results, the main character adjusts a loose wire with the air of a crack surgeon, her would-be lover steps on the gas, the engine roars into life, and they all drive off. The grease monkey's brother gets home to find her working in the garage and assures her she won't have to do that kind of dirty work any longer. At the home-coming dinner, the family discusses the foolishness of her wanting to go to a school in "automotive engineering"; the girl looks more and more resentful and discouraged.

The climax of the film comes when she overhears her brother talking with a customer about his plans to expand the garage. "Atta boy! Once a fella knows what he wants to do . . . ," the customer enthuses. The girl takes this in, squares her shoulders, and goes off to fill out applications to the trade schools. The rest of the action briefly develops both the love story and the actions she takes toward her goal.

Because this film is close to thirty minutes in length, the writer was able to develop a secondary plot line—that of the love story. Because the main character's objective throughout is very clear—to get to trade school—the writer/director could have made a fifteen-minute film had she told only the primary story, simply curtailing or dropping the secondary one.

In his essay "Readers, Writers and Literary Machines," noted fiction writer and critic Italo Calvino says, "The storyteller of the tribe puts together phrases and images. The younger son gets lost in the forest, he sees a light in the distance. He walks and walks, and the fable unwinds from sentence to sentence and where is it leading? To the point at which something not yet said, something as yet only darkly felt, suddenly appears and seizes us and tears us to pieces like the fangs of a man-eating witch. Through the forest of fairy tale the vibrancy of myth passes like a shudder of wind."[5]

Male or female, we are all "younger sons" in one way or another, and what seizes us in its fangs as we read or listen to or watch a well-told story is that powerful intermingling of feeling and thought that Aristotle called recognition. If you substitute the word "image" for "sentence" in the quotation above, you will understand why it is that, as teachers, we have found myths and fairy tales so useful to the novice short-screenplay writer (who may well regard herself or himself as a filmmaker, and not a "real" writer at all).

A FIRST ASSIGNMENT

Write brief descriptions, using the present tense, of two quite different main characters as they go about their lives. Be sure to choose characters that engage you and situations you know something about. End each description with an encounter or incident that would make for a change in the character's situation. Set up one synopsis as if for a short script in which you employ the journey structure, and the other for a screenplay in which you use ritual occasion. At this point, don't concern yourself with plot, although if ideas occur to you, be sure to jot them down for possible later use. Here are a couple of examples to illustrate; we turned to the short films described above for inspiration:

1. A crack bicycle messenger travels about a large city at reckless speed, indifferent to pedestrians and unpleasant encounters with cab drivers as he makes his way, and impatient at his various delivery stops. Suddenly a car grazes him on a busy street and continues on without stopping as he and his bike go flying. Dazed and bleeding, he huddles on

the sidewalk as an indifferent crowd rushes by. Eventually a pedestrian stops, picks up his mangled bicycle, and sits down next to him on the curb.

2. A nine-year-old girl lives with her bossy older brother and quarrelsome parents in a small suburban house. She stubbornly refuses to be drawn into the family's mealtime squabbles, hurrying away from the table as soon as she can to gaze out the window at the house next door, where a lively, cheerful family is having its dinner. Although the house is some distance away and she can't follow much of what is going on, she watches happily. Then one day, hunting for something in a closet, she comes upon a pair of powerful field glasses and makes off with them.

This assignment may take several days and a number of drafts to complete. Because every assignment and exercise in this book is intended to lead to your writing an original screenplay, it will be worth your while to keep your notes, as well as any completed work, in a special folder.

NOTES

1. E. M. Forster, *Aspects of the Novel* (New York: Harcourt, Brace and World, 1927), 86.
2. Paul Zweig, *The Adventurer* (New York: Basic Books, 1974), 84, 85.
3. Aristotle, *Poetics*, ed. Francis Fergusson, trans. and introduction by S. H. Butcher (New York: Hill and Wang, 1961).
4. Susanne K. Langer, *Problems of Art* (New York: Charles Scribner's Sons, 1953), 15.
5. Italo Calvino and Patrick Creagh, trans., *The Uses of Literature* (New York: Harcourt, Brace, Jovanovich, 1986), 18.

FILMS DISCUSSED IN THIS CHAPTER

Annie Hall, directed by Woody Allen, 1977.
Champion, directed by Jeffrey D. Brown, 1978.
Chinatown, directed by Roman Polanski, 1974.
Gare du Nord, directed by Jean Rouch, from *Six in Paris*, 1965.
Going to Work in the Morning from Brooklyn, directed by Phillip Messina, 1967.
Grease Monkey, directed by Laurie Craig, 1982.
The Maltese Falcon, directed by John Huston, 1941.
Modern Times, directed by Charles Chaplin, 1936.
Sleeping Beauties, directed by Karyn Kusuma, 1991.
Unforgiven, directed by Clint Eastwood, 1993.

2

TELLING A STORY IN IMAGES

The cinema is still a form of graphic art. Through its mediation, I write in pictures. . . . I show what others tell. In Orphée, *for example, I do not narrate the passing through mirrors; I show it, and in some manner, I prove it.*

JEAN COCTEAU[1]

Perhaps no aspect of film and video is more powerful in terms of narrative than the appearance of reality. Images on the screen have a validity, a weight, of their own, in a way that words do not. What follows is an excerpt from the scene in *Orpheus* to which Cocteau refers. In the screenplay, based on the myth, the poet Orpheus has lost his wife to Death. Heurtebise is the chauffeur of the Princess of Death. The film takes place in 1950, the year in which it was made.

Note that the format is not proper screenplay format, which you will find in the Appendix, but a compressed version favored by book publishers.

The Princess' gloves are on Orpheus' bed.

HEURTEBISE

(removing the gloves)

Someone has left their gloves behind.

ORPHEUS

Gloves?

HEURTEBISE

Put them on . . . come on, come on. . . . Put them on.

He throws the gloves at Orpheus. Orpheus catches them, hesitates for a moment, and puts them on. (The action in the following scene is shown through reversed film.)

HEURTEBISE

(standing by the mirror)

With those gloves you'll go through the mirror as though it were water!

ORPHEUS

Prove it to me.

HEURTEBISE

Try it. I'll come with you. Look at the time.

The clock shows just a second before six o'clock. Orpheus prepares to go through the mirror. His hands are at his side.

HEURTEBISE

Your hands first!

(Orpheus walks forward, his gloved hands extended toward the mirror. His hands touch reflected hands in the mirror.)

Are you afraid?

ORPHEUS

No, but this mirror is just a mirror and I see an unhappy man in it.

HEURTEBISE

It's not a question of understanding; it's a question of believing.

Orpheus walks through the mirror with his hands in front of him. The mirror shows the beginning of the Zone. Then the mirror reflects the room once more.[2]

When Orpheus returns with his wife Eurydice, after a series of adventures in the Zone, the clock is just striking six. The scene is a brilliant example of how to write scripts that create magical effects by the simplest means. Cocteau the director had to shoot his films on extremely low budgets, so Cocteau the scriptwriter saw to it that his screenplays did not call for complicated special effects.

An image in Cocteau's *Beauty and the Beast,* as breathtaking today as in 1945 when the film was first released, is described in the screenplay very simply. The story is set in the seventeenth century; Beauty has just returned from the Beast's kingdom to visit her ailing father, a merchant. Her two wicked older sisters are hanging sheets in the yard, one of many household tasks that used to be left to poor Beauty.

> The merchant and Beauty walk across the yard. Beauty looks like a princess. . . . Her only piece of jewelry is a magnificent pearl necklace with a diamond clasp. The two sisters stare at her in disbelief.
>
> FELICIE
> (staring greedily at Beauty's necklace)
> What a magnificent necklace!
>
> BEAUTY
> (removing it and offering it to her)
> Take it, Felicie, it will look even better on you.
>
> Felicie grabs it eagerly. It turns into a bunch of dirty twisted rags.
>
> MERCHANT
> My God!
>
> ADELAIDE
> Put it down!
>
> FELICIE
> How disgusting!
>
> She drops it. As it touches the ground it turns back into pearls. The merchant picks up the necklace and puts it on Beauty.[3]

The metamorphosis of jewels into rags was accomplished by the very precise filming and splicing together of two different close shots. In the first shot, Beauty hands the pearl necklace to her eager sister. In the second, she hands Felicie the necklace of dried rags at the same pace, with an identical gesture. The transformation of one necklace into the other was effected by splicing the first half of the first shot onto the second half of the second one at the instant Felicie touches the jeweled necklace. Even today audiences, sophisticated in the ways of special effects, give a gasp of delighted surprise at the results: Cocteau indeed "proves" to us the reality of the world that his characters inhabit.

Writing a screenplay means writing for a medium that uses moving images to convey meaning. These images and the way in which they are put together are the "language" of film; to write an effective short script, you must understand that they can tell your story far more effectively than any dialogue or voice-over, however well written. So it makes good sense, when considering material for your short screenplay, to ask yourself early in the process the most important question of all: will this story lend itself to being told primarily in images?

THREE VISUAL OPENINGS

What follows are detailed accounts of the openings of three short films regarded as classics. Each uses little or no dialogue and no voice-over, although their sound tracks play important roles in establishing mood and tone. Note that these are not excerpts from the screenplays but simply descriptions of scenes from the finished films. In *Incident at Owl Creek* (Robert Enrico, 1962), the following sign is prominently placed on a burnt tree trunk:

ORDER
ANY CIVILIAN
CAUGHT INTERFERING WITH
THE RAILROAD BRIDGES
TUNNELS OR TRAINS WILL BE
SUMMARILY HANGED
THE 4TH OF APRIL, 1862

There is a long roll of drums, the hoot of an owl, a bugle call. Below, in the distance, we glimpse a wooden bridge, where a Union officer is bawling orders. We hear the sound of marching feet and get a look at a sentinel high above, a rifle at his side. A line of Union riflemen marches across the bridge and comes to attention before the officer. A brutal-looking sergeant carries a length of rope toward a man in civilian clothes who stands at the edge of the bridge, hands and feet bound. In his mid-thirties, he is dressed in the fine chambray shirt and brocaded vest of a Southern gentleman. His broad, pleasant face is beaded with sweat.

The sergeant painstakingly ties the rope into a noose, knots it securely, and tightens the knot.

The officer watches impassively as the prisoner is pushed onto a plank extending out over the wide river rushing below. The man gasps as the noose is dropped loosely over his head. He looks wildly about, sees the sentinel above and the riflemen all around him.

In less than five minutes, through a series of powerful visual and aural images, we have been enabled not only to grasp the main character's terrible predicament but to identify with him completely in the desperate struggle to escape that follows.

In *Two Men and a Wardrobe* (Roman Polanski, 1957), we see a wide expanse of sea and sky, from which two figures wade slowly toward us to the accompaniment of lively "silent-screen" music. Between them is what appears to be a large crate. As they draw closer, we can see that the crate is actually a large, old-fashioned wardrobe, and that the figures are two slight young men.

The youths come up onto the sand, gently set down the wardrobe, and begin to hop about in a comical fashion to shake the water out of their ears. Although they are dressed in identical cotton pants and tee shirts, one is dark haired and bareheaded, the other fair haired and wearing a workman's flat cap. He takes this off, wrings it out well, replaces it at a dashing angle, and checks his reflection in the mirror of the wardrobe.

The music shifts into a waltz. The two bow to one another and begin to waltz across the sand with exaggerated grace. After a few turns, they stop and begin to warm up as if preparing to exercise: the dark youth does a somersault or two and the fair one some sketchy calisthenics. Then, in perfect unison, they stop, lift up the wardrobe, and begin to stagger up the beach.

The music quickens and becomes discordant as the two men carry the wardrobe along a street, where cars and pedestrians rush by. When a crowded trolley appears, they try and fail to board it with the wardrobe, as passengers jeer and push at them.

Next we see a bird in a big cage set down on a quiet side street. A pretty young woman gazing down at it looks up to see the two youths approaching with their wardrobe. They all exchange smiles, and she sets off up the street, leaving the caged bird behind. The men put down the wardrobe, exchange a glance, and hurry after her. We watch at a distance as they bow, courteously shake hands with her, then turn back to retrieve the wardrobe. She looks after them a moment and continues walking away.

We see them at a distance, trudging by a bridge with their wardrobe. Two men on the bridge laugh at the sight; one keeps his arm about his companion's shoulder as he deftly lifts a wallet from his back pocket. The camera moves down to disclose a ravine below the bridge, where one man is battering another's head with a large rock.

Because the two protagonists treat the wardrobe so matter-of-factly throughout, we accept it as a given in this opening sequence of Roman Polanski's absurdist fable. Charmed by their liveliness and childlike ways, we quickly come to care about what happens to them in their quest for food and lodging in a savage and indifferent city. As in our previous example, our empathy with the protagonists has been accomplished in a remarkably short time through the use of images alone.

In *The Red Balloon* (Albert Lamorisse, 1956), we see a cobblestoned plaza surrounded by tall, gabled houses, in which a little boy of about five appears, carrying an adult-sized briefcase. He stops to pat a large cat, and something high on a lamppost catches his attention. He climbs up and untangles the long string of a red balloon caught at the top.

We follow as he runs down a stone stairway, walks through the town with briefcase and balloon, tries to board a bus, and is rejected. Finally he arrives at the big double doors of his school and gives the balloon to a passing streetcleaner to hold for him. We see a stern-looking man watching from an upstairs window as he goes inside the building.

A few seconds later (in what is called a "time lapse"), he tumbles outside along with a shouting mass of other boys and grabs his waiting balloon by its cord. It is raining, and he shelters the balloon under the umbrellas of various passersby. He runs up the stone steps, across the square and—still holding the balloon—into a house, where a woman stands waiting at an upstairs window. A moment later the window is opened, and the balloon is thrust outside, where it hovers uncertainly. In another moment the little boy reaches out to pull it back inside. One more moment goes by, and he puts it back outside.

There is a dissolve (indicating another time lapse), and the little boy emerges on the street, looking about for his friend. The balloon descends, keeping its string just out of reach like a playful dog. The boy tries to catch hold of it again and again, then finally gives up and moves off down the street as the balloon follows along behind.

Like the wardrobe in the Polanski film, the personified balloon in Lamorisse's contemporary fairy tale is presented in a logical and convincing manner. Unlike the wardrobe, however, the balloon is an object with the distinct attributes of a character, much like one of the magical animals who befriend the heroes of fairy tales. In a very short time, using visuals alone to establish the situation, this short film "proves" to us, in Cocteau's use of the word, how a spirited, lonely little boy and the playful balloon he rescues go about becoming friends in a provincial world that does not look with kindness on little boys or balloons.

WHAT THE IMAGES TELL US ABOUT CHARACTER

Analyze and imitate; no other school is necessary.

RAYMOND CHANDLER *on screenwriting*[4]

We learn from the cut and quality of his clothes that the condemned man in *Incident at Owl Creek* is not only a civilian but a Southern gentleman; we learn again from clothing that the two youths in *Two Men and a Wardrobe* are probably workmen; from the well-fitting dark suit he wears and the big leather briefcase he carries, we surmise that the child in *The Red Balloon* is from an upper-middle-class family and that he is expected to behave like a miniature adult.

In *Incident at Owl Creek*, the face of the main character is the only pleasant one in the sequence—the sergeant looks brutal, and the officer and soldiers are as impassive as puppets. We can see that the captive is desperate but brave: although there are beads of sweat on his face, he doesn't break down or plead with his captors. The involuntary gasp he gives when the noose is dropped over his head and his wild look around to see if there might be any way to escape serve to increase the audience's identification with him in his hopeless predicament.

In *Two Men and a Wardrobe,* both the look of the two main characters—amiable and slightly goofy—and their innocent exuberance on the beach quickly endear them to us. They treat one another and the young woman they meet with old-fashioned courtesy, and the wardrobe they have to lug about with respectful familiarity. In fact, their stylized behavior throughout brings to mind, as no doubt it was intended to, the kind of undersized underdog antiheroes portrayed in silent films by the great actor/writer/directors Charlie Chaplin and Buster Keaton.

In *The Red Balloon,* the young hero is slight but wiry, with an elfin, dreamer's face. We first see him as a very small figure in a very large square dominated by massive stone houses. His briefcase reminds us of the sort of small humiliations unfeeling adults can visit on children. In addition, it lends the boy a somewhat comical air. The balloon, of course, is red—the color of blood, the color of life, the color of trouble. In the context of the film, it is not only the main character's friend but his double, his secret self.

WHAT THE IMAGES TELL US ABOUT THE MAIN CHARACTER'S SITUATIONS

In *Incident at Owl Creek,* we read the sign and hear the roll of drums, the hoot of an owl, and a bugle call before we glimpse the main character. Each of these sounds acts as a powerful stimulus to the forming of mental images. Together, they provide us with important information and set a tone of foreboding that will quickly be justified. We hear the owl and realize that although there is faint light and it is growing brighter, it is still (technically) night—and executions traditionally take place at dawn. We hear a roll of drums and imagine soldiers marching; we hear a bugle call and realize that it must be reveille.

After this, we witness the grim realities of the main character's situation, including the carefully detailed looping, tying, and knotting of the rope in the hangman's hand. Time slows onscreen, as it is supposed to at such moments in life. Yet when the prisoner is pushed out onto the plank, we see the river rushing along below his feet. Although we do not realize it at that moment, what has been set up with this single image is a possible route of escape.

In *Two Men and a Wardrobe,* the main characters emerge from the sea with their wardrobe, like two children with an unwieldy suitcase, onto a wonderfully clean and empty beach. The scene is shot and cut in a leisurely way, and the young men behave as though they had all the time in the world. But as soon as they begin their journey through the streets and back alleys of the city beyond the beach, the rhythm and tempo of the film change. We are bombarded with visuals in the editing style of an old-fashioned documentary, and the villainous inhabitants grimace and use broad, threatening gestures, as if in a silent comedy.

The activity on and about the bridge further demonstrates the violent, hostile nature of the city by showing us separate events taking place simultaneously—a robbery, a murderous assault, and the two innocents trudging by with their wardrobe. In addition, by drastically varying locations early in the film (tranquil beach, bustling city boulevard, quiet side street, bridge, and dangerous ravine), the screenwriter establishes a powerful tension between the simple need of the protagonists and the unpredictable dangers of the environment in which they find themselves.

In *The Red Balloon*, our first glimpse of the little boy is of a small figure enclosed by towering houses. The images of a shadowy male figure watching him from an upstairs window of the school, and of the equally shadowy female figure watching him from an upstairs window of his house, serve to emphasize the lack of freedom in his life.

Although the balloon is eventually punctured by enemies, it is full and bouncy throughout much of the film, its long string as lively as a cat's tail. Its brilliant red, beside being emblematic of life and courage, serves to underline the dreariness of the stone-colored world through which the little boy ordinarily moves.

A FURTHER EXAMPLE OF SCREENWRITING IN IMAGES

The opening sequence of the script for the feature film *Dangerous Liaisons*, written by Christopher Hampton, provides a fine example of how a writer can delineate with images alone aspects of environment, character, and conflict.

The sequence that follows is written in what is known as "master format," the film script format most widely used in the United States at the present time. (Other examples, and a discussion of various kinds of formats, can be found in the Appendix. Thoughout, "INT." means interior, and "EXT.," exterior.)

2 INT. MADAME DE MERTEUIL'S DRESSING-ROOM DAY

The gilt frame around the mirror on the MARQUISE DE MERTEUIL's dressing table encloses the reflection of her beautiful face. For a moment she examines herself; critically, but not without satisfaction. Then she begins to apply her makeup.

ANOTHER ANGLE shows the whole large room, the early afternoon light filtering through gauze curtains. MERTEUIL's CHAMBERMAID stands behind her, polishing her shoulders with crushed mother-of-pearl. Three or four other female SERVANTS wait, disposed around the room. It's midsummer in Paris in 1788.

INT. VICOMTE DE VALMONT'S BEDROOM DAY

VALMONT is an indistinct shape in his vast bed. His valet-de-chambre, AZOLAN, leads a troupe of male SERVANTS into the room. One raises the blind and opens enough of a curtain to admit some afternoon light, another waits with a cup of chocolate steaming on a tray, a third carries a damp flannel in a bowl. As VALMONT stirs, his face still unseen, AZOLAN takes the flannel, leans over and begins a perfunctory dry wash.

INT. MERTEUIL'S DRESSING-ROOM DAY

A steel hook moves to and fro, deftly tightening MME DE MERTEUIL's corset.

This intercutting of the elaborate dressing rituals of De Merteuil and Valmont continues, without dialogue. Essentially, as the script makes clear in the last shot of the sequence that follows, we are watching as squires gird two seasoned warriors for battle. De Merteuil's stomacher is put in place by her maids, and the seamstress sews her into her dress. In the anteroom to Valmont's dressing room, a mask covers Valmont's face as a servant blows powder onto his wig. He lowers the mask, and we at last see his intelligent, malicious features.

> ANOTHER ANGLE SHOWS THE COMPLETE MAGNIFICENT ENSEMBLE: or not quite complete, for AZOLAN now reaches his arms round VALMONT's waist to strap on his sword.[5]

In the sequence that follows, battle of a sort is joined between these two characters in the grand salon of Mme de Merteuil's town house.

WHAT THE IMAGES IN THIS SEQUENCE TELL US

We learn immediately that Merteuil is beautiful and knows it, that both she and Valmont are enormously wealthy, and that they are being readied (and are quite accustomed to being readied) for some sort of formal occasion. The nature of the crosscutting indicates both that there is a parallel between the characters and that they are dressing to meet one another in a contest of some sort. We also realize that Valmont appears somewhat less eager—or perhaps just more indolent—than Merteuil. Brief references to clothing, accessories, furniture, and setting establish that the story takes place in the late eighteenth century—in fact, just before the French Revolution. And all of this has been told us in just two pages of film script!

A FEW WORDS ON THE WRITING EXERCISES IN THIS BOOK

They are intended (1) as aids to freeing perception and imagination, (2) as explorations to be embarked upon without thought of evaluating results in the ordinary way, and (3) as finger exercises, to be used as warm-up for future scriptwriting.

In doing them, don't concern yourself with grammar, spelling, or punctuation. To do so may inhibit the flow of images, associations, and vague, floating ideas that are the raw material from which good stories are made. If the work is being done in a classroom, students might read the exercises aloud if they choose, but in our experience, the exercises work best when there is no analysis or criticism afterward. Assignments, of course, are another matter. If you are doing the exercises on your own, you might want to read them aloud to a friend or friends—often reading work to an audience enables you to find things in it you might not otherwise be aware of. Just explain that it's better if there is no discussion of the material at the time.

A further note: in doing the exercises, it is helpful to use a timer of some sort so that you are free to focus completely on scribbling as fast as you can. Let your pen or pencil do the thinking.

EXERCISE 1: USING VISUAL IMAGES

X is your character, whoever he or she may turn out to be. Write down the following paragraph:

> Dusk. Sound of soft rain. Fully dressed, *X* lies on the bed, gazing up at the ceiling. After a moment, *X* gets up slowly and crosses to the dresser against the opposite wall.

Begin writing, stopping at the end of ten minutes. Put the page aside without reading it. Take a couple of deep breaths and have a good stretch before going on to the next exercise.

The writer/director Ingmar Bergman has said in a number of interviews that for him a screenplay begins with a single compelling image (in *Persona*, it was an image of two women; in *Cries and Whispers*, of a blood-red room). He then unravels that image, so to speak, and writes down what he discovers in doing so. If the results engage him, he continues; if not, he stops.

In the next exercise we will ask you to do something similar, working from your recollection of the previous exercise rather than what you have written down. Most of the questions you will ask your character are those actors often ask themselves (as the characters they are playing) before going onstage or in front of a camera. The responses to these questions are known as the "given circumstances" of a character's situation at any particular moment.

EXERCISE 2: USING VISUAL IMAGES

Quickly write down the following questions, leaving plenty of room for each answer:

- Who are you?
- Where are you?
- What are you wearing?
- Why are you here?
- What do you want at this moment?
- What time of day is it? What season? What year?
- What is the weather like?

You have only ten minutes in which to write down all the answers, so scribble whatever comes to mind, no matter how absurd it seems. You can always cross out later. Set your timer and GO!

SECOND ASSIGNMENT: REWRITING IN FORMAT

You should now have more than enough material for this assignment, which will require somewhat more time and thought than the previous exercises. It consists of two parts. The first is to rewrite your scene from Exercise 1, using whatever information you find useful or provocative from the answers in Exercise 2. (At this point, you don't have to justify anything in terms of story.)

Give your character at least a first name; if this threatens to hold things up, go to the phone book, open it, and choose a column at random. Pick a name from that column that seems right for your character.

The second part of the assignment is to revise the revision, keeping only those details that seem essential (again, no need as yet to figure out why), and to put the results into proper screenplay format. Follow the master-scene format of *Dangerous Liaisons*, but don't be daunted by Hampton's elegant style, as he is a professional writer, more gifted than most, with many plays and screenplays to his credit. Still, if you are going to learn by imitating and analyzing, as we suggest, then it makes sense to imitate and analyze the work of a master.

Aim at leaving yourself enough time before handing in the work to put it away for a day or two before doing the final revision—you will gain some detachment from the material and may see possibilities that you've previously overlooked.

The assignments, as opposed to the exercises, will benefit from reading and discussion in class or, again, if you are working on your own, with friends who have some idea of the writing process.

NOTES

1. Jean Cocteau, *Three Screenplays* (New York: Viking Press, 1972).
2. Ibid.
3. Ibid.
4. Frederick Luhr, *Raymond Chandler and Film* (New York: Ungar, 1982).
5. Christopher Hampton, "Dangerous Liaisons," unpublished screenplay, 1988.

FILMS DISCUSSED IN THIS CHAPTER

Beauty and the Beast, directed by Jean Cocteau, 1945.
Dangerous Liaisons, directed by Stephen Frears, 1989.
Incident at Owl Creek, directed by Robert Enrico, 1962.
Orpheus, directed by Jean Cocteau, 1950.
The Red Balloon, directed by Alfred Lamorisse, 1955.
Two Men and a Wardrobe, directed by Roman Polanski, 1957.

3

USING SOUND TO TELL THE STORY

Besides conveying what (as we have noted) philosopher Susanne Langer calls "the feeling-tone" of a film or tape, aural images can expand the frame in terms of offscreen space and extend the meaning of what is being shown, by using sound as metaphor.[1] When these images are an integral part of the story, they usually originate in the script.

The great French director Robert Bresson, whose films are known for the quality of their visual images, is a master at extending the frame through sound. In his chapbook, *Notes on the Cinematographer*, he states that sound always evokes an image, although an image does not always evoke a sound.[2] He applies this principle to great effect in a scene from his film *Pickpocket*, in which the impoverished hero stands behind a prosperous-looking couple at a racetrack, trying to get up the courage to make an attempt on the wallet in the woman's pocketbook. We hear the blaring announcement of the next race over a loudspeaker, a bell's loud clanging, the pounding of hooves, and cries of a crowd we can't see but that seems to be all around us. Meanwhile, the camera steadily regards the man and woman facing us and also the young man standing just behind and between them. Because of the background sound, as well as the reactions of the couple as they follow the race, we believe that it is going on somewhere "behind" us and so are able to focus our entire attention on the inner struggle of the main character.

Another example, which uses offscreen sound to create a rising sense of unease in both main character and audience, is from an independent feature called *The Passage*, which was written and directed by Pat Cooper, one of the authors of this book.

In the film, a ghost story, a writer called Michael Donovan has left his wife in New York and gone to a desolate part of Cape Cod to do research on nineteenth-century shipwrecks. He rents a handsome old cottage on a dune overlooking the sea at a spot where shipwrecks once were common, and he immerses himself in the history of the place. The sequence that follows describes his first encounter with the ghost.

(The abbreviation "POV" stands for point of view, and all descriptions of offscreen sounds are capitalized.)

38 INT. PARLOR DAY
In the morning, MICHAEL at the dining-table, typing from his notes.
SOUND OF FAINT RUSTLING ON THE STAIRS.
He looks around, then goes back to his work as THE SOUND DIES.
Again, SOUND OF RUSTLING.
THE RUSTLING FADES TO SILENCE as he gets up from the table and goes upstairs.

39 INT. FRONT BEDROOM DAY
MICHAEL glances about the untidy room, then crosses to the looking-glass and gazes into it. As in his dream of the previous night, the door under the eaves is open in the reflected image. He turns to stare at it.

DOOR, MICHAEL'S POV
It is closed.

He crosses to pry it open, and finds a long low dark space that runs the length of the room. He strikes a match, and in its flicker, we glimpse an old-fashioned seaman's trunk behind several ancient electric heaters. He hauls it out into the bedroom and lifts the heavy lid.

INSIDE THE TRUNK is a bundle wrapped in yellowed tissue paper; he takes this out and carefully unwraps it, revealing a folded paisley shawl in soft glowing colors.
FAINTEST SOUND OF RUSTLING, which he is too absorbed to hear.
He unfolds the shawl and finds inside it a black feather fan with a horn handle He strokes the fan softly with his fingertips, then moves it slowly down over his face.
AGAIN, THE RUSTLING.
Michael looks up, and around the room, but there is nothing. Shaken, he replaces the fan, folding the shawl carefully over it. He returns them both to the trunk and closes the lid, then straightens up to catch sight of himself in the looking-glass.

MICHAEL

(to his reflection)
Easy. Easy. . . .

He goes out of the room, closing the door after him.

PAN AROUND THE ROOM AS WE HEAR HIS FOOTSTEPS DESCENDING THE STAIRS. Behind us, THE RUSTLING—CONTINUOUS, as if someone were crossing the room—THEN FADING TO SILENCE.[3]

Long before we first glimpse the ghost, we are aware, with Michael Donovan, of her presence. While the objects Michael finds may give us the sense that she in some way continues to exist, it is the rustling of her silk dress that "proves" it to us.

A brilliant example of extending the frame can be found in Jacques Tourneur's low-budget horror classic *Cat People.* In it, the heroine has inherited a curse by which she is transformed, when agitated or jealous, into a panther. The scene we have chosen has her panther self stalking a young woman whom she sees as a threat to her own relationship with her fiancé.

It is night, and the young woman is walking down a deserted city street when she realizes that she is being followed. As her footsteps quicken, the branch of a nearby tree sways ominously under the weight of an invisibly moving something. The woman breaks into a run, sees an open door ahead, and dashes through it.

The building turns out to be an almost-empty YMCA. With the invisible panther padding along behind her, growling, she races to a large swimming pool in the basement and throws herself in. She quickly swims to the middle of the pool and begins to scream for help, as the echoing sound of the invisible cat's snarls ricochets off the tiled walls of the big room.

The entire sequence has the disturbing quality of a nightmare, and the images that we as the audience conjure up for ourselves are at least as terrifying as the actual visual of any live panther would be. Well-thought-out images and carefully orchestrated sound do it all.

USING SOUND AS METAPHOR

The sound of a ticking clock in a scene may be simply part of ambient sound, or, as in *High Noon*, serve as a metaphor for the passage of time, bringing the hero inexorably closer to a showdown he does not want. Sometimes the long wail of a locomotive reminds us that our character lives near railroad tracks; sometimes it serves as a metaphor for a character's yearnings to escape the confines of his or her life.

Sound used as metaphor can create a whole dimension of meaning not immediately apparent in the visual images of a scene. It is one of the more powerful tools available to us in writing the short screenplay.

The following example is a brief description of a short film made in 1970 by Ken Dancyger, coauthor of this book, as a graduate student at Boston

University. Titled *The Class of '75*, it is a futuristic story about the last five traditional students in a traditional university. Although the filmmaker used images of college uprisings at Columbia University and elsewhere at the start of the short, his primary objective was to create, without using much dialogue, a sense of his characters' day-to-day lives.

Within the university the five students lead monastic, bookish lives with their dean. Outside, a war rages for control of the university. When the dean dies, these last holdouts for tradition leave the building; the past that they and their dean had represented is over and done with.

The writer/director wanted to create a world that would appear, on one level, to be sheltered and monastic but on another level suffocating and jail-like. He was able to accomplish this by using sound to establish both images. The sounds of photocopying and microfiche machines, and so on, suggest that the university is essentially a library, but on another level, a synthesized music track provides a distancing, troubling effect—a sense that what goes on in that library is not entirely "bookish" but something patterned, repetitive, and destructive.

The clang of metal doors as the students are shut into their sleeping areas at night and the tone and pitch of the alarms that awaken them in the morning create a strong sense that the university/library in which they are living is in actuality a prison. The use of sound has altered the images pointing them away from their surface existence as a university and toward their true meaning, that the place is a prison.

The opening scene of Harold Pinter's screenplay for the feature film *Accident* offers a useful example of how sound can both extend the frame and create a metaphor at the same time. (Pinter's format here is one widely employed in Europe but not in the United States. Also, this version of the screenplay has been taken from a book; therefore the capitalization of certain descriptions, and so on, does not follow the format of an actual film script.)

Exterior. The house. Night. Summer.
Long shot.
The camera is still, looking at the house from outside the gate, up the short curved drive, across the circular gravel court.
In a meadow behind the house, dim shapes of animals.
The camera moves slowly forward to a position inside the gate. It comes to rest.
The house is silent, dark. One lower front window is curtained. Light filters through it on to the gravel.
Gradually, over picture, the hum of a car, in the distance.
The hum grows.
Closer but still distant, a sudden screech, grind, smash and splintering.

Silence.
Light goes on in the hall of the house.
The front door opens.
STEPHEN is silhouetted in the light.

Exterior. Lane. Night.
Camera jolting down the lane.
Sound of footsteps running.
Dark lane winding.
Tree shapes crossing, retreating, advancing.
Glimpsed fields through hedge. Shapes of cows.
A horse moving, head up.
Camera to sky. Stars.

Exterior. Foot of lane. Night.
Stephen halting.
Moonlight hits his face, sharply and briefly.

Exterior. The car.
Close shot from underside of car.
The smashed mass of the car, shooting at passenger seat front-section, lying on camera. Broken metalwork, jagged shapes of glass.
Two bodies heaped together, still, forming one shape.
Silence but for the ticking of the ignition.[4]

This is the story of a professor in early middle age whose pleasant, humdrum life is shattered when he becomes sexually obsessed with a young woman student who is the fiancé of another of his students. The juxtaposition of the serene and balanced image of the house at night in the opening shot with the progression of ominous sounds off screen establishes the theme of the screenplay immediately. In fact, both the visual and sound images of this first shot are repeated at the very end of the film, in a reprise that is both resonant and moving.

In a very different use of sound, the rhythmic ticking of the ignition in the last shot of the excerpt serves to give both Stephen and the audience important information: that the engine of the car is still on, so that there is an immediate danger of explosion, and, because the sound is reminiscent of dripping, that the lifeblood of one or both of the two people in the car may be draining away as the main character stares at their still bodies, "forming one shape."

When you come to write a screenplay yourself, it is useful to keep in mind that one can convey shifts in mood or tempo to readers by the brevity or length of the sentences used to describe a scene. Incomplete rather than full sentences can often give a more vivid sense of fractured images or heightened activity on screen.

MORE ON SCREENPLAY LANGUAGE

In an essay called "The Language of Screenwriting," the playwright and scriptwriter Ronald Harwood writes, "A screenplay cannot be judged by form and technique, or by the abandonment of either. In his attempt to realize in its initial form a story that is, in the end, to be told in pictures, the writer must discover or invent a language that is both personal and effective, and that, above all, stimulates the mind's eye."[5]

The following description by Harwood is the first sequence in the screenplay for the film *One Day in the Life of Ivan Denisovich.* It is somewhat more "literary" in its choice of words than many fine screenplays—perhaps because it is adapted from a famous novel—but it is wonderfully visual all the same. He evokes for us both the formidably grim *gulag,* which is itself a major character in the script, and the nature of Denisovich's own day-to-day situation. (The script uses the master-scene format referred to previously, although it would appear to have been somewhat compressed for publication.)

FADE IN:
1. EXT. THE CAMP—HIGH ANGLE (HELICOPTER SHOT)
BEFORE DAWN
From a distance the camp looks like a solitary star in the cosmos: it glows a sickly yellow; its circles of light are no more than a luminous blur. Beyond the star, as far as the eye can see, is snow. It seems like the middle of the night. It is intensely cold.

THE CAMERA MOVES IN VERY SLOWLY.
SUPERIMPOSE MAIN CREDITS AND TITLES.
Gradually it becomes possible to distinguish more of the area of the camp: two powerful searchlights sweeping from watchtowers on the perimeter; a circle of border lights marks the barbed wire fences; other lights are dotted about the camp. Now, slowly, the shapes of the huts and other buildings become discernible: the gates, the near watchtowers with their guards and machine guns, the prison block, the mess hall, the staff quarters.

END CREDITS AND TITLES.

A Russian SOLDIER, wearing the regulation long winter overcoat and fur cap, emerges from the staff quarters, pierced by the cold. He makes his way to where a length of frosted rail hangs.

THE SOLDIER takes up a hammer in his gloved hands and beats on the rail: a grating, clanging sound—

CUT TO:
2. INT. HUT 9 BEFORE DAWN
Under a blanket and coat lies IVAN DENISOVICH, bathed in sweat, etc.[6]

If the setting in which a hero finds him or herself is to serve as antagonist, it is essential that its features be described in a way that evokes it vividly. When the setting is not key to the story or would be familiar to us from life (or other movies), the architect Mies Van der Rohe's statement that "less is more" is the advice to follow. The following graduated series of exercises and assignments has been worked out with the idea of helping you to discover—or invent, if necessary—the screenwriting language that will best serve the kind of short script that you want to write. It is essential that the exercises be done in order, and with an open mind.

EXERCISE 3: LOCATION DESCRIPTION

Go for a long walk or ride in bus or car to find an unfamiliar location that interests you as a storyteller—one that appeals to you as a film location for any reason. (Keep in mind that just about any location can be shot in an arresting manner.) Study the scene carefully and list the details that you find compelling, or even just interesting. Before moving on, check to be sure you haven't missed anything you might want to use; if you have, add it.

As soon as possible, find a place where you can write undisturbed for fifteen minutes or so. Look over your notes and underline those bits of description that seem most likely to give the flavor or feeling-tone you would like to convey Then, in ten minutes or less, write a short descriptive paragraph, using the present tense of scriptwriting. When your ten minutes are up, check quickly to see if you have overlooked anything; if you have, quickly add it to your description.

Put away the exercise and notes for at least twenty-four hours of "seasoning."

THIRD ASSIGNMENT: LOCATION DESCRIPTION IN FORMAT

Take out your description, read it over carefully, and cross out whatever seems irrelevant or needlessly repetitive. In revising, you want to keep only those few details that are necessary to evoke the location—as you see it—in the mind's eye of a reader.

When you have done this, rewrite your final version in the master-scene format used in screenplay manuscripts. (Look at the examples in previous chapters or in the Appendix.) At this point, it would be wise to check grammar, spelling, and punctuation.

Again, put away the material for twenty-four hours before going on to the next exercise.

EXERCISE 4: USING SOUND IMAGES

Find a fairly quiet place and close your eyes. If indoors, sit by an open window. Take a few deep breaths, relax, and try to become aware of the layers of sound that surround you, night or day, city or country. As you begin to focus on these, you will be able to sort out those that are close by from those farther off, and background sounds that tend to be almost unnoticeable at first (the steady hum of machines or traffic) from those that declare themselves clearly. When you feel ready, list all the sounds that you can hear.

EXERCISE 5: USING SOUND IMAGES

Now think of ten sounds that are particularly evocative for you (and that may have unpleasant or ominous associations, as well as pleasant ones) and quickly list them on paper. When done, scan the list and add any additional sounds that occur to you.

FOURTH ASSIGNMENT: LOCATION DESCRIPTION USING SOUND

Take out your location description from the third assignment and reread it. One by one, imagine each of the sounds on your list, along with this image. Some of the results may be quite surreal, but they should all be interesting. When you have found the sound or combination of sounds that appeals to you most, add it to your location description. Annotate it at the beginning if it is to be heard throughout the scene or most of it (e.g., SOUND OF FOGHORN CONTINUING or SOUND OF FOGHORN THROUGHOUT), or at whatever point is appropriate (e.g., SOUND OF GLASS BREAKING).

Remember that offscreen sound is generally afforded a separate line in the script and printed in capital letters.

EXERCISE 6: INTRODUCING THE *X* FACTOR

If you feel inspired to go on, this writing exercise can be done as soon as you have added sound to your location description, or later the same day. It is best not to wait longer than a few hours before going on, because we are after what might be called a "unity of feeling-tone" in the piece you are writing.

Take out and reread the introductory scene you wrote as an exercise and then revised at length for the second assignment. In this revision, the character *X* was given a name, so use that name in this exercise.

Set your timer for ten minutes. Reread your location description, imagining the sounds. "Then *X* walks or runs, rides a skateboard, or drives a Model T Ford into the scene." No need to describe *X*—you've done that in the earlier assignment. *X* may remain alone or meet someone: let things happen as they will while you are writing, and allow yourself the great pleasure of being surprised. GO!

At the end of ten minutes, put the exercise in your folder and disregard it for twenty-four hours, at least.

FIFTH ASSIGNMENT: PUTTING IT ALL TOGETHER

Read and revise this last exercise, changing what happens and how it happens, if you want, and eliminating all unnecessary details. Use few adjectives and make those few count. (*Roget's Thesaurus* can often be more useful than a dictionary in finding the right word to make a scene or physical action come alive.) Now type out the whole scene in proper format, after which it would be helpful to have teacher, classmates, or friends knowledgeable about film read the work and respond to it.

NOTES

1. Susanne K. Langer, *Problems of Art* (New York: Charles Scribner's Sons, 1953).
2. Robert Bresson, *Notes on the Cinematographer* (England: Quartet Books Limited, 1986). trans. Jonathan Griffen.
3. Pat Cooper, "The Passage," unpublished screenplay, 1987.
4. Harold Pinter, *Accident, in Five Screenplays* (New York: Grove Press, 1973), 219–220.
5. Ronald Harwood, "The Language of Screenwriting," in *The State of the Language*, ed. Leonard Michaels and Christopher Ricks (Berkeley: University of California Press, 1980), 296.
6. Ronald Harwood, "One Day in the Life of Ivan Denisovich," in *The State of the Language*, ed. Michaels and Ricks, 292.

FILMS DISCUSSED IN THIS CHAPTER

Accident, directed by Joseph Losey, 1967.
Cat People, directed by Jacques Tourneur, 1942.
The Class of '75, directed by Ken Dancyger, 1970.
One Day in the Life of Ivan Denisovich, directed by Caspar Wrede, 1971.
Pickpocket, directed by Robert Bresson, 1959.

4

DISCOVERING AND EXPLORING A MAIN CHARACTER

The story for Thelma and Louise *discovered me. Two women go on a crime spree: the idea came with the velocity of a sixteen-ton weight hitting me. It hit me that hard. . . . It was then a question of discovering/exploring who these two women were and how they came to go on a crime binge.*

CALLIE KHOURI[1]

Callie Khouri chose the journey structure to tell her story, a particular variant of a structure combining two Hollywood genres, the road movie and the buddy movie. *Thelma and Louise* is a direct descendant of such films as *Butch Cassidy and the Sundance Kid* and *Bonnie and Clyde*, just as these are descendants of classics like *They Drive by Night*. The originality of the film and much of its energy stem from its humorous, sympathetic, and totally unsentimental portrayal of Khouri's protagonists, the two characters whom she discovered and explored, her "two women on a crime binge."

ON CHARACTER AS HABITUAL BEHAVIOR

In his work on psychology, Aristotle described character as "habitual behavior."[2] You are what you ordinarily do—that is, until some occurrence leads you to do something you would not ordinarily do. In general terms, this is what makes for a dramatic situation.

In the scene that follows, which is from the first pages of the second draft of *Thelma and Louise*, we are given in a few well-chosen lines a good deal of important information about each of the main characters.[3] (In this excerpt, "b.g." means "background," and "V.O." stands for "voice-over.")

INT. RESTAURANT—MORNING (PRESENT DAY)

Louise is a waitress in a coffee shop. She is in her early thirties, but too old to be doing this. She is very pretty and meticulously groomed, even at the end of her shift. She is slamming dirty coffee cups from the counter into a bus tray underneath the counter. It is making a lot of RACKET, which she is oblivious to. There is COUNTRY MUZAK in the b.g., which she hums along with.

INT. THELMA'S KITCHEN—MORNING

THELMA is a housewife. It's morning and she is slamming coffee cups from the breakfast table into the kitchen sink, which is full of dirty breakfast dishes and some stuff left from last night's dinner which had to "soak." The TV is ON in the b.g. From the kitchen, we can see an incomplete wallpapering project going on in the dining room, an obvious "do-it-yourself" attempt by Thelma.

Louise's well-groomed appearance as she slams dirty dishes around at the end of a heavy work day (ask anyone who's had a similar job) is more indicative of character than the fact that she is pretty, because it speaks of strength of will. That she hums along with the "country muzak" tells us that she is cheerful, at least at this moment, for whatever reason. The cut from her energetic activity to Thelma in a nightgown, dumping dishes into a sink full of dirty dishes, immediately establishes a link between the two women—they are both doing "women's work," though under very different circumstances.

We go back to Louise, who goes to the restaurant's pay phone and dials a number she knows by heart, then again to Thelma's kitchen, where the telephone rings. Thelma answers, "hollering" to someone offscreen that she's got it. The dialogue that follows gives us more information about each character in an exchange indicative of their relationship through most of the screenplay. It also sets up what is supposed to happen next, and with great economy—always a virtue in screenwriting. In the lines that follow, note that just as a character's dress, gestures, and surroundings can indicate what kind of person that character is, so too can his or her manner of speaking. The script cuts back to Louise at the pay phone:

LOUISE

I hope you're packed, little sister, 'cause we are outta here tonight.

INT. THELMA'S KITCHEN—MORNING

THELMA
(whispering guiltily)
Well, wait now. I still have to ask Darryl if I can go.

LOUISE (V.O.)
You mean you haven't asked him yet? For Christ's sake, Thelma, is he your husband or your father? It's just two days. For God's sake, Thelma. Don't be a child. Just tell him you're goin' with me, for cryin' out loud. Tell him I'm having a nervous breakdown.

Meanwhile, Thelma is cutting out coupons from a newspaper, pinning them onto a bulletin board covered with recipes and more cuttings. Here we get a first glimpse of Thelma's characteristic mode of passive resistance: she may feel a little guilty about procrastinating, but she'll still do things her own way. At this point, and for most of the script, the two women's relationship is that of irresponsible little sister and responsible big sister. The tension between them ebbs and flows, and the balance of power shifts with changing circumstances. It is one of the more suspenseful and engaging aspects of a very action-oriented script.

As for Louise, the tone of her speech makes it clear that she has more at stake in their going on this trip than her friend does. Her clipped sentences, used here to get the lackadaisical Thelma moving, are used elsewhere, and characteristically, to guard against giving anything away about her private life.

MORE ON BEHAVIOR DEFINING CHARACTER

In his treatise known as the *Poetics*, Aristotle defines dramatic action as "the movement of spirit or psyche that produces a character's behavior." Film and theatre director Elia Kazan, in his notebook for *A Streetcar Named Desire*, remarks that "finally directing consists of turning psychology into behavior." Substitute the word "screenwriting" for the word "directing," and Kazan's statement would still hold true. A character's desires or needs, that movement of the psyche to which both Aristotle and Kazan refer, can be expressed only by his or her behavior. The accomplished screenwriter selects those few details, out of all that come to mind, that will best describe the essence of the character to the director and actors, as well as to the producer, the director of photography, the costume designer, and the set designer—to name a few of the creative people involved in bringing any script to life on the screen.

ANOTHER EXAMPLE OF SCREENPLAY SHORTHAND

Screenwriter Robert Towne has a distinctive, ironic, and rather leisurely descriptive style. Nonetheless, he condenses a great deal of information into a few lines on this first page of a late draft of *Chinatown.* The script opens with close-ups of a series of snapshots of a man and woman making love. These visuals are accompanied by the sound of anguished moans and a male voice crying out, "Oh, no!" At this point, we cut to:

INT. GITTES' OFFICE

CURLY drops the photos on Gittes' desk. Curly towers over GITTES and sweats heavily through his workmen's clothes, his breathing progressively more labored. A drop plunks on Gittes' shiny desk top.

Gittes notes it. A fan whirrs overhead. Gittes glances up at it. He looks cool and brisk in a white linen suit despite the heat. Never taking his eyes off Curly, he lights a cigarette using a lighter with a "nail" on his desk.[4]

This first glimpse of Gittes is of a private eye who is also very much the successful small businessman, as evidenced by the shiny desk, the white linen suit, and his special lighter. He is alert to his distraught client's every move, because Curly is very large and very upset, a dangerous combination in a nicely furnished new office.

The next lines describe the sobbing Curly, who rams his fist into the wall and kicks a wastebasket. The scene goes on:

Curly slides on into the blinds and sinks to his knees. He is weeping heavily now, and is in such pain that he actually bites into the blinds.
Gittes doesn't move from his chair.

GITTES

All right, enough is enough—you can't eat the Venetian blinds, Curly. I just had 'em installed on Wednesday.
Curly responds slowly, rising to his feet, crying. Gittes reaches into his desk and pulls out a shot glass, quickly selects a cheaper bottle of bourbon from several fifths of more expensive whiskeys.

Gittes pours a large shot. He shoves the glass across the desk toward Curly.

Curly is not just comic relief in the film but a secondary character who plays an important role in the last third of *Chinatown*. The emotionalism and lack of guile we see here and in the rest of this first scene make him an ideal target for Gittes' manipulation later, when the detective desperately needs help in arranging a getaway.

Most fiction films, comedy as well as drama, tend to portray a particular character (or characters) in a challenging situation: something unexpected happens to someone—how does that person react? Does he or she struggle to change, or instead try to turn away from what has happened, to find a way back to things as they were? If the main character engages us, that struggle—which is, in essence, the story of the film—will most likely engage us too. Even in slapstick shorts, whose heroes remain unchanged as one wildly improbable situation follows another, character is paramount. As an audience, if we don't care, why should we watch?

Jake Gittes is not an immediately attractive character, nor is he meant to be. He is a cynical private eye who has seen it all—or thinks he has. His client's real pain moves him only to a wisecrack; the glass of cheap whiskey he shoves at Curly is simply an efficient way to help the big guy to collect himself. (Note that there is a variety of whiskies in the cabinet to serve to a variety of clients.)

Chinatown was released in 1974. While seventies audiences might well anticipate Gittes' jaundiced viewpoint, because of its familiarity with such forties and fifties private-eye classics as *The Maltese Falcon* and *The Big Sleep*, none of these would have prepared them for Gittes' elegant white suit (I'm a prosperous businessman who doesn't have to dirty his hands. . . .) or the fancy, bourgeois office.

Yet Gittes engages our interest from the very first page of the screenplay. How?—by his nonchalance, his mocking humor, and an air of easy authority that speaks of the consummate professional.

EXAMPLES FROM STUDENT SCRIPTS

Here is a description of the protagonist of Christian Taylor's *Lady in Waiting*, the first time we see her:

> INT. A sticker is placed on the box which reads AUCTION. There is a sigh from the owner of the hands, MISS PEACH. Miss Peach is a grey-haired, formal-looking woman in her late fifties. She sits awkwardly on a suitcase in the middle of the dining room, which is bare of furniture. . . . Miss Peach is conservatively dressed in a drab woolen coat and unassuming hat.[5]

Beyond the somewhat detached description of Miss Peach and the sigh, the box marked "auction" and the bare dining room set a feeling-tone that expresses in visual terms something about her inner state. In a metaphorical sense, the screenplay is about how that empty inner space becomes furnished. Note the different style of the language Taylor uses to describe his antagonist on her first appearance. Miss Peach is alone in the elevator of a Manhattan high-rise:

> INT. The elevator continues to rise, 25 . . . 26 . . . 27 . . . 28, and PING, it comes to a stop. Miss Peach is jolted from her daydream as the doors open, and there stands SCARLET, a stunning and heavily made-up black woman. She boasts a pair of sunglasses, a large wig, a fancy theatrical dress, and a large leather zipper bag. She rushes in, ignoring Miss Peach, and presses the lobby button.

Very shortly, battle is joined between these two unlikely combatants. It is important that we have been given Miss Peach isolated in the elevator before Scarlet bursts in, because we then identify with her in her shock, rather than with the newcomer. Also, a small but telling word in the description of Scarlet's big bag is "leather"—she may be dressed flamboyantly, but not cheaply.

Another example comes from the opening of Lisa Wood Shapiro's *Another Story*. Two little girls, perhaps the protagonists, are at the window of a country cottage, gazing out at the rain:

> INT. Through the doorway into the small kitchen is NIVY. She is a handsome woman in her late sixties/early seventies. She is stylishly dressed, with intricate silver earrings. WE CAN HEAR THE CRACKLE OF THE FIRE IN THE FIREPLACE. The fireplace casts a warm glow over the living room, which is oak paneled with an Oriental rug tossed on its hardwood floor. NIVY is making hot chocolate.[6]

This is another case in which a character is described not just by how she is dressed, though that is nicely done in very few words, but by the feeling-tone of her surroundings. The cottage is hers; its furnishings—including the fire—are used to express her character. That she is dressed in fashionable clothes and wears "intricate earrings" while making hot chocolate for two granddaughters tells us immediately that this is not "good old Granny" as usually depicted.

SIXTH ASSIGNMENT: MORE ON DESCRIBING A CHARACTER

Read in their entirety the first four student scripts in the Appendix: *Another Story, Lady In Waiting, Sleeping Beauties,* and *The Wounding*.[7] Pay special attention to the way in which characters are described the first time you meet them. After you have read each script, go back to evaluate these descriptions. How well do they function, in light of what you now know of the character's behavior? Is there particular information you weren't given about a character that would have been helpful? If there is change or growth in a character, how does the writer show this? (Try to be specific.)

These are the kinds of questions that screenwriters ask themselves on rereading a first draft, preparatory to going on to the next. (Screenwriting, for the most part, is about rewriting.) As you read these scripts, note that script format is not a straitjacket but is flexible enough in its outlines to accommodate the very different writing styles of Towne, Khouri, Shapiro, Taylor, Kusama, and Emerling.

WHEN APPEARANCES ARE DECEPTIVE

In one of his aphorisms, Oscar Wilde, the Irish playwright and dandy, turned a general belief upside down by suggesting, "It is only shallow people who do not judge by appearances." We laugh at this deft reversal of what is commonly held to be true, and we may even agree that it makes a kind of topsy-turvy sense. However, if you reflect upon it, the witticism also makes straight forward sense: in life, people unconsciously give themselves away all the time. What is revealed to the acute observer may seem very much at odds with what one first notices, with what the sociologist Ervin Goffman has called their "presentation of self." That brings us full circle, back to the Wilde quotation.

You can understand, therefore, that the first step in learning to develop characters for a screenplay, long or short, is focused observation of the ways in which particular human beings behave in particular situations. The great Russian teacher/director Konstantin Stanislavski has said that art is never general, it is always specific. Although he was addressing actors, he might as well have been speaking to directors and scriptwriters.

As you go about your day, try to take note of any incongruous details of people's clothing: the handsome silk blouse with a button missing, the well-tailored business suit worn with scuffed shoes, the street person with a jaunty hat, the workman in ironed blue jeans. (Remember the man-sized briefcase toted by the small boy in *The Red Balloon:* while it doesn't tell us about his character, it certainly informs us about his situation.) On the other hand, if the character's appearance is "perfect," as is Louise's in the excerpt above from *Thelma and Louise,* that too is useful information.

Notice the many different ways in which human beings express weariness, uneasiness, impatience, or contentment when they are unaware of being observed. Notice also the way this can change when they become aware of the presence of a stranger who interests them, or of an acquaintance, or a friend. Reflect on your own behavior, private or public, if you can do so without becoming self-conscious or uncomfortable.

EXERCISE 7: FINDING CHARACTERS

Go to a public place—café, park, train station, supermarket—wherever you can watch someone who might engage you as a possible character without being noticed doing so. (Don't choose anyone you know.) Try to memorize quickly the person's appearance and general style; then find a place where you can scribble down a list of items that seem characteristic or revealing about this person. Be as specific as you can where it seems important—for instance, not "glasses" but "big tortoise-shell glasses"; not "knapsack" but "battered plastic knapsack." Give us some idea of your subject's age. Now, underline the items that seem essential to giving a sense of your character *as you see him or her at this point.*

Find another subject, not necessarily in the same location, who intrigues you, and follow the same procedure. Put both lists aside to mellow: unless you feel inspired, wait a day to go on to the next, related exercise.

ABOUT THE CATALYST

Catalyst is a term borrowed from chemistry, where it refers to any substance that precipitates a chemical reaction. In dramatic narrative, the catalyst (or *agent for change,* or *inciting incident*) is the occasion or character that sets events in motion, precipitating the dramatic action of the protagonist. Let's say that the main character learns that a former gunslinger has just ridden into town, or unexpectedly glimpses a former lover at a train station, or suddenly loses a job—any of these events could be a powerful catalyst moving the protagonist into action, into change. In a short film, we are usually introduced to the protagonist before the catalytic event occurs, so that we will have a chance to identify with him or her. Such an introduction is often, though not always, quite brief. (The first assignment at the end of Chapter 1 gave two examples of brief "treatments," up to and including possible catalysts.)

Something unexpected happens to someone—how does that person react? Does he struggle to change the way he does things, or does he instead turn away from what has happened, trying to get back to the way things had been? Does she do first one and then the other? How does any or all of this psychological activity manifest itself in the character's behavior, so that the audience has some idea of what is going on?

SEVENTH ASSIGNMENT

Read *Dead Letters Don't Lie,* in the Appendix.[8] Then look over all four scripts again; in each of them, try to locate the catalyst that sets things moving in a new direction for the main character or characters. In order to do this, you must first try to determine which of the characters is the protagonist. (Short films often begin and end with a focus on the protagonist.)

EXERCISE 8: A SIMPLE INTERACTION

Take out your lists from Exercise 7. Without too much thought, choose one of your locations and visualize both characters in it. Begin to write, starting with brief character descriptions culled from the underlined items on your lists, using simple declarative sentences. This should not take more than several minutes. Then give us the setting, in a few words (a Greenwich Village café, a thruway McDonald's, the Chicago Amtrak station, etc.).

Although triggered by your observations of real people in a real setting, what you are going to write will be fictional. You will be transforming the people you observed into characters, *your* characters, so feel free to adjust the descriptions as you go. Set your timer for two minutes and close your eyes, so that you can imagine both characters in the setting you have chosen, placing them in relation to one another in that space. Are they side by side, or facing one another? Are they close to one another, or at a distance? Are they in line, one behind the other?

Once your characters are in place, your objective will be to write at least a couple of short paragraphs describing a silent interaction between them. Remember that this is only an exercise; there is nothing to be lost, and much to be gained, by letting your characters do the work.

Now set your timer for ten minutes and begin to write. Don't reread, just keep going. If you lose the thread, close your eyes again to visualize your characters. When the timer goes off, finish the sentence you're writing and jot down the answers to the following questions from Exercise 2, first for one character, then for the other:

Who are you?
Why are you here?
What do you want at this moment?

Put this away with Exercise 7 and leave both in your portfolio for another twenty-four hours. At that time, go through both exercises, underlining the phrases or sentences that best describe your characters and their interaction, especially in light of your answers to the questions above.

If you already have a catalyst, make note of it. If not, find one before going on to the next assignment.

EIGHTH ASSIGNMENT: WRITING A CHARACTER-BASED OPENING

You are now going to revise Exercise 8, with the result put in proper screenplay format. Use your thesaurus, if necessary, to find words that convey what you see in your imagination, words that will make your characters come alive for the reader. Once again, it would be helpful to have your teacher, classmates or knowledgeable friends respond to what you have written—essentially the first draft of an opening for a possible short script.

NOTES

1. Callie Khouri, symposium on *Thelma and Louise*, Writers Guild of America West, November 1991, unpublished.
2. Aristotle, *Poetics*, ed. Francis Fergusson, trans. and introduction by S. H. Butcher (New York: Hill and Wang, 1961).
3. Callie Khouri, "Thelma and Louise," unpublished screenplay.
4. Robert Towne, "Chinatown," unpublished screenplay.
5. Christian Taylor, "Lady in Waiting," unpublished screenplay.
6. Lisa Wood Shapiro, "Another Story," unpublished screenplay.
7. Karyn Kusuma, "Sleeping Beauties," unpublished screenplay; and Susan Emerling, "The Wounding," unpublished screenplay.
8. Anais Granofsky and Michael Swanhaus, "Dead Letters Don't Lie," unpublished screenplay.

FILM DISCUSSED IN THIS CHAPTER

The Red Balloon, directed by Albert Lamorrisse, 1955.

5

TELLING THE DRAMATIC STORY

You judge films in the first place by their visual impact instead of looking for content. This is a great disservice to the cinema. It is like judging a novel only by the quality of its prose.

ORSON WELLES

Orson Welles undoubtedly would have agreed that the images of a narrative film, whether visual or aural, should, like the language of a novel or short story, serve to illuminate the tale. Rust Hills, in his excellent book on writing the short story, elaborates on a similar point: "A successful short story will thus necessarily show a more harmonious relationship of part to whole, and part to part, than it is usual to find in a novel. Everything must work with everything else. Everything enhances everything else, interrelates with everything else, is inseparable from everything else—and all this is done with a necessary and perfect harmony."[1]

What he writes is as true for the short film in relation to the feature film as it is for the short story in relation to the novel. But unlike novels and short stories, which are meant to be read, narrative film and television are forms of drama; if a story is to work as drama, its content needs to be organized in terms of dramatic structure.

The word "drama" derives from the Greek word *dran*, which means to do or to act. A drama, whether presented on a stage or on a screen, is the story of an action intended for presentation before an audience. In previous chapters, we have been exploring storytelling in images; in this one, we will discuss storytelling in terms of drama.

SOME BASIC DEFINITIONS

What follow are some of the important and widely used terms that we will be using throughout this book:

Protagonist, meaning main character, is a word that comes from the Greek words for "first" (*protos*) and "struggler" or "combatant" (*agonistes*). So the protagonist is the main struggler in the story.

The word *antagonist* comes from the Greek words for "against" (*anti*) and, once more, "struggler" or "combatant" (*agonistes*). The antagonist, whether human, manmade, or a force of nature such as a mountain, desert, or raging storm, is the force or obstacle with which the protagonist must contend. It is the story of that struggle that provides the plot. In some stories, the main characteristics of the antagonist are virtually the direct opposites of those of the protagonist; in others, the antagonist can seem almost a twin or second self of the protagonist. That is not to say that the most engaging antagonist of all can't be the protagonist's own nature, his or her own arrogance, fear, or unadmitted needs.

It is also important to note that the stronger the antagonist, the stronger the conflict, and the harder the protagonist must struggle to achieve his or her goal. The decision as to who or what should be the antagonist in a film script is always a crucial one; the designation sometimes shifts from one character to another as a writer goes through revisions.

In any drama, the *main conflict* is the struggle between protagonist and antagonist—again, whether the antagonist is another character, a manmade disaster, a force of nature, or simply an aspect of the protagonist's own character. The more there is at stake, the more dramatic—in every sense of the word—the conflict.

Dramatic action, or "movement of spirit," as Aristotle defines it in the *Poetics*, is the life force, the heartbeat, of any screenplay.[2] *Psyche*, the word he uses for spirit, meant both "mind" and "soul" to the ancient Greeks—the inner energy that fuels human thoughts and feelings, the underlying force that motivates us.

The *climax* is generally the moment of greatest intensity for the protagonist and a major turning point in his or her dramatic action. Even in a fairly short script, the climax is often the culmination of a series of lesser crises.

Recognition—according to Aristotle, "a change from ignorance to knowledge"—usually, though not always, closely precedes or follows the climax;[3] it is the point at which the protagonist realizes where the dramatic action has taken him or her through the course of the events that have made up the story. In some forms of comedy, where the protagonist does not experience any kind of illumination, recognition is often reserved for a character who is an interested onlooker, or for the audience itself.

Scene is a word with many definitions. We will be using it primarily in the sense of an episode that presents the working out of a single dramatic situation. The scene is the basic building block of any narrative screenplay. Every scene in a short script should serve to forward the action.

ADAPTING A MYTH OR FAIRY TALE: A FIRST EXAMPLE

One of the interesting things that becomes apparent on reading a number of myths—whatever tribe or culture they come from—is how soon after relating the birth of the cosmos storytellers found it necessary to introduce conflict. And no wonder! Generation after generation, people looked about them and tried to make sense of what they had observed, what they knew from their own experience: that human beings have needs and that these needs bring them into conflict with one another, as well as with the gods.

In the Book of Genesis, we are told in a beautifully worded, carefully detailed listing how God created all things, animate and inanimate, in six days and rested on the seventh. We are told that He formed the first man out of dust, breathed life into him, and planted a marvelous garden for him to live in. Then God gave Adam a single prohibition: he could eat the fruit of every tree in that garden except one—the Tree of the Knowledge of Good and Evil. Also, most important for any kind of dramatic story, He left Adam and Eve the freedom to choose: eat or don't eat, obey or disobey—it is up to you. Familiar as we are with our own curiosity, our own desire to get to the bottom of things, as well as our own need to resist authority, we recognize that the seed of conflict has been sown in Paradise. In that seed lies the beginning of a dramatic situation, for Eve (and then Adam as well) wants one thing, while God wants another. The serpent is God's antagonist in all things; the serpent's initial approach to Eve serves as catalyst in this story of the Fall.

Two questions often prove major stumbling blocks for film and video students, as well as for filmmakers who have never written a narrative script. What, specifically, do I write about? How, specifically, do I write about it? In screenwriting, general ideas are of little or no use when you sit down at a desk to write, and it is often difficult for those who are not "natural" writers (in the way one may be a "natural" cinematographer or director) to come up with fruitful story ideas. Yet, as anyone experienced in the arts knows, learning a skill is a process, and that process has to start somewhere.

Where?—In the case of a short script, with a simple adaptation.

From the very beginning of the film industry, fiction and drama have proved unending sources of film stories, and it has been our experience in many years of teaching that adapting a myth or fairy tale offers the novice screenwriter an immediate way to learn how to structure a short script.

Stories that began as oral narratives almost always are dramatic in structure and lend themselves easily to visualization. For these reasons, and because such material is both readily available and in the public domain (that is, not under copyright), we will be using examples of such adaptations throughout the rest of this chapter. If you have a short story already in hand that you would like to adapt, the working techniques we describe are much the same.

STRUCTURING A FIRST ADAPTATION

What follows is an example of the process by which a myth can provide source material for very different narratives, any one of which an audience might enjoy without being familiar with the original story—which is not to say that a viewer's experience of the film wouldn't gain in depth and resonance if he or she were familiar with it.

The myth we have chosen to adapt is the fall of Icarus. Briefly, the story material we are working from is this: Daedalus (which means "cunning artificer") was both a renowned artist and a brilliant architect and inventor. Jealous because his nephew and favorite pupil Perdix seemed likely to surpass him in every way, he took the boy to the top of the Acropolis and hurled him off. For this he was condemned by the authorities, but he managed to flee to the island of Crete with his young son Icarus.

There the tyrant Minos gave him sanctuary and an almost impossible assignment—to design and oversee the construction of a prison for the Minotaur, a sacred monster with the head of a bull, the body of a man, and an appetite for human flesh. Because the Cretans had to feed the Minotaur youths and maidens allotted to him, the prison would have to be designed so that the victims could be forced to enter but would not be able to find a way out. Daedalus solved this problem by designing, and overseeing the building of, the first labyrinth. Instead of rewarding him, however, the tyrant Minos imprisoned both Daedalus and his son in a high tower overlooking the sea. Determined to escape, Daedalus painstakingly fashioned two pairs of wings from feathers dropped by seabirds, binding them together with melted candle wax. When the wings were completed, father and son each strapped on a pair. Daedalus warned Icarus not to fly too high or Apollo, the sun god, would melt the wax of his wings. The boy promised to be careful, and the two set off from the tower over the water. Everything went well until Icarus, intoxicated by the glories of flight, began to climb higher and higher toward the blazing sun. Daedalus cried out to him in warning, but the boy ignored him until at last the wax holding the feathers of his wings together melted, and he plunged headlong into the sea—which is how that particular body of water came to be known as the Icarian Sea (in the Aegean).

Here then is our basic material, culled from a number of versions of the Daedalus/Icarus myth. There is more material than we could possibly use for a short screenplay, but we won't know which details will be important until we have answered some key questions. These are questions you may find it helpful to ask yourself each time you begin writing (or, for that matter, critiquing) a short screenplay.

FINDING A STRUCTURE: EIGHT PRELIMINARY QUESTIONS

1. Who is the protagonist?
2. What is the protagonist's situation at the beginning of the script?
3. Who or what is the antagonist?
4. What event or occasion serves as catalyst?
5. What is the protagonist's dramatic action?
6. What is the antagonist's dramatic action?
7. How is the protagonist's action resolved?
8. Do you have any images or ideas, however unformed, as to the climax? the ending?

What follows are the answers we came up with for a short project we imagined as an animated film or video of three or four minutes' length. (The approach would be basically the same whether for animation or live action.) To give you an idea of the process, we have included something of the reasoning we employed in responding to each of the questions.

1. Who Is the Protagonist?

Before considering this question, it is important to note once more that most short films or tapes work best with a single protagonist; there simply is not enough time for an audience to identify with more than one. The exception is with certain kinds of comedy—slapstick, parody or satire, for example—where a writer may not want the audience to identify with the main character but to maintain a psychological distance from all the characters. (Think of how one views W. C. Fields, the Marx Brothers, or the main characters in most cartoons.) Thus, short comedies often have two or even more main characters.

As the project we are considering is a drama, however, we will want to have a single protagonist. What we must ask ourselves right off is, do we want our script be about what happens to Daedalus, or about what happens to Icarus? Either one would be intriguing. Do we want to tell the story of a bold and willful exile, a brilliant inventor, who works out an ingenious way to escape from prison with his son and, in so doing, loses that son? Or do we want to tell the story of a boy in exile, almost as bold and willful as his father, who escapes from prison only to destroy himself by flying too close to the sun?

These are two very different main characters, whose actions would lead to very different plots.

For this project, we have decided to choose Icarus as our protagonist; however, to demonstrate how profoundly different the plot could be were we to choose Daedalus, we will give, after the story outline about Icarus, a synopsis for a longer, live-action project about Daedalus.

2. What Is Icarus's Situation at the Beginning of the Script?

The shorter the film or video is to be, the more license is given the scriptwriter to plunge right into the middle of things. In this case, because the film is to be so short, it makes sense to open with a scene showing the boy and his father in the tower as if they'd been there for some time. In order to give viewers the opportunity to discover for themselves what kind of youth Icarus is and how he feels about being imprisoned, we need to show the dailiness of his life in prison. However powerful the images onscreen, viewers won't be able to identify fully with the boy's intoxication at flying if they haven't first observed the soul-destroying nature of his captivity.

So, the answer to Question 2 is that Icarus has been imprisoned for some time, along with his father, in a tower by the sea. Visualizing the scene, we came up with the idea that Daedalus has been supplied with parchment and stylus to pass the time, but that Icarus has been given nothing. Perhaps he's gathered up gull feathers from the parapets around their chamber and amused himself as best he can with them.

3. Who or What Is the Antagonist?

In every version of the myth that we looked at, Icarus was warned by Daedalus not to fly up toward the sun, and in every version he ignored the warning. Because of this, and because we do not want to complicate the story by introducing another character, Daedalus is the logical choice.

4. What Occasion or Event Serves as the Catalyst?

There will be times you would like to skip this question, leaving it until the last, and there will be times you'll be able to answer it immediately—only to find that the catalyst changes with each draft of the script. Either way, you are engaged in discovering what it is that you want to say, rather than what you *think* it is you want to say. Still, it is important to realize that a screenplay should not be considered complete until the catalyst is in place.

Calling up our image of Icarus trying to occupy himself with the gull feathers, in the answer to Question 2, and knowing that the climax must take place during his flight, it seemed to us that the catalyst, or agent for change, in the script must be the moment when Daedalus first conceives of escaping on wings made of feathers and wax. The difficulty was that Daedalus was not our protagonist. Therefore the question became: How could we involve Icarus in this pivotal event?

We turned to Aristotle, who had some very practical advice for dramatists in his *Poetics*: "In constructing the plot and working it out . . . the playwright should place the scene, as far as possible, before his eyes. In this way, seeing everything with the utmost vividness, as if he were a spectator of the action, he will discover what is in keeping with it, and be most unlikely to overlook inconsistencies."[4]

Close your eyes with us, then, and imagine a stone chamber at the top of the tower. Imagine Daedalus busy at the only table with his parchment and stylus. Imagine young Icarus, restless and bored, with little to do and nothing to look at but his father, the sea, the sky, the sun, and the gulls that perch on the open parapets. Imagine a pile of the feathers he's gathered and the ways he invents to play with them—trying to make them float, keeping them up with his breath, pasting them onto his skin with water or spit so that he can spread his arms wide and pretend to be a seagull. . . .

Ask yourself what this particular father would do if he were disturbed while working. Probably he would rebuke his son sharply; only then, because he is by nature a "cunning artificer," would he realize that there might be a way to construct real wings of feathers and . . . yes, candle wax.

In answer to Question 4, then, the catalyst will be Daedalus's realization, at the sight of Icarus imitating a bird in flight, that he might be able to design wings on which he and Icarus could escape.

5. What Is the Protagonist's Dramatic Action?

We arrived at an answer by a roundabout way. Because Daedalus is a doer, not a dreamer, a desire to escape prison with his son would serve him as a strong dramatic action. We could simply have made Icarus's dramatic action complementary—to escape prison with his father—but it might be more dramatic to follow through on our perception of him as a dreamer, very different from his father. This difference would exacerbate the natural tension between father and adolescent son.

For when we go back to the original material, hunting clues to the father's character, we are reminded that Daedalus killed his nephew—and favorite pupil!—out of fear that the boy might surpass him as an architect. Such a man would probably be an irascible, competitive parent.

In which case, it makes sense that, in answer to Question 5, Icarus's dramatic action is to escape his father any way he can.

6. What Is the Antagonist's Dramatic Action?

As discussed above, Daedalus's dramatic action is to escape prison with his son.

7. How Is the Protagonist's Dramatic Action Resolved?

Daedalus escapes, but without his son.

8. Do You Have Any Images Or Ideas, However Unformed, as to What the Climax Might Be? the Ending?

Keeping in mind that the climax, by definition, ought to be the most intense moment in the film or video—both for the audience and for the protagonist—we should be searching for a powerful image, or series of images, that will express not just what Icarus is doing at that moment but what he is feeling.

Sometimes a writer is in possession of such an image from early on and needs only to articulate it; sometimes he or she finds ideas by going back to the original material, or by doing further research. Sometimes an image of the climax does not appear until the writer is actually working on an outline, or even the first draft, of a screenplay. As professionals know well, each project can prove quite different in the writing from every other; the imagination works in mysterious ways.

This myth is a tragic one, but it doesn't at all follow that the script should be unrelentingly grim. On the contrary, if viewers are to identify with a doomed character such as Icarus, it's essential that they empathize with the passion that drives him to destruction, that they be able to feel compassion for his belief in the possibility of achieving his heart's desire. In our project, where the climax will be the moment in which Icarus ignores his father's shouts of warning and continues soaring up toward the sun, we need images that convey the wonders of such flight, the glory of wheeling and swooping and gliding like a seagull. In answer to the first part of Question 7, then, the climax is to be a series of images in which a joyful Icarus swoops, glides, and wheels up and up through the dazzling sunlight.

What about an ending? Because death is the ultimate escape from any situation in life, we can say that Icarus has achieved his dramatic action—to escape his father any way that he can. But at what a cost!

It seemed to us that in order to explore the irony of this, we would need two different sorts of images for the ending—those showing the boy's terror as he falls, and those showing the indifferent world through which he falls: blazing sun, tranquil sea, cloudless sky, and fields where peasants labor. (This last is suggested by a renowned painting by Pieter Breughel the Elder, "The Fall of Icarus.")

At this point, we imagine the very last image of the film to be that of Icarus plunging into the sea and descending underwater in slow motion past the camera.

WRITING A STORY OUTLINE

Discussing in an interview the architecture of the screenplay, screenwriter William Goldman, author of the film scripts for *Butch Cassidy and the Sundance Kid*, *Marathon Man*, and *All the President's Men*, says, "I've done a lot of thinking myself about what a screenplay is, and I've come up with nothing except that it's carpentry. It's basically putting down some kind of structure form that they [the actors and director] can then mess around with. And as long as they keep the structure form, whatever I have written is relatively valid; a scene will hold, regardless of the dialogue. It's the thrust of a scene that's kept pure."[5]

One of the most valuable tools we have for structure is the *story outline*, wherein each step briefly describes a full scene—ideally a scene that furthers the action.

The writing of a story outline often begins with collecting notes or making observations on character, location, events, bits of dialogue, or images that you have about the project. When these notes take on some sort of coherence, you can start asking yourself the questions we've listed. Keep in mind, though, that for most people the best way to work on ideas for writing anything is with pen in hand or fingers on keyboard.

In the short script, where dialogue is best kept to a minimum, a detailed story outline can occasionally serve the purposes of a first-draft screenplay. There are students who prefer to answer the questions and move directly to a rough draft. If this second method is your choice, you will probably find that writing a bare-bones outline of this draft can help you spot problems in motivation and structure before the next draft. It is much easier to see such difficulties when the scenes are laid out in sequence on a single sheet of paper.

There are those who find that using index cards, or photocopied cutouts from the draft of the outline, for each step and moving them around helps in finding the sequence that works best. (Most people who have done any film editing at all discover, sooner or later, that casual or even accidental juxtapositions can yield extraordinary results.)

When you arrive at the assignment, keep an open mind and be prepared to experiment with these strategies to find out what works for you. Because our first example of such an outline is intended for a very short animated film or video, and story-boarding is all-important in animation, it will be somewhat more detailed than it would be for most live-action films. Essentially, what we are aiming at is an outline that could serve as a first draft of the screenplay.

STORY OUTLINE FOR "ICARUS'S FLIGHT"

1. Day. Icarus and Daedalus imprisoned in a room at the top of a tall tower. Icarus stands at one of the parapets, gazing out at sea and sky; Daedalus sits at a crude table, working on a plan of escape. He looks up, sees Icarus dreaming, and orders him to sweep the room. Icarus takes his time about obeying.
2. Night. Daedalus asleep on a cot, Icarus gazing out, as before. Daedalus stirs, sees the boy at the parapet, and orders him back to bed. When he closes his eyes, Icarus makes a face at him.

3. Day. Daedalus at the table, Icarus at the parapet. From his point of view, we watch seagulls ride the wind. Quietly, he spreads arms wide and dips and turns in place, imitating them.
4. Day. Icarus collects discarded feathers from the sills of the parapets and adds them to a pile by his cot. Icarus at work, trying ways to paste feathers onto his arm.
5. Night. Daedalus at the table, working by candlelight. Behind him, Icarus swoops about on feathered arms. He knocks against a stool and Daedalus looks up. "Stop that!" Then he really sees what is going on, jumps up, and crosses the room to touch the feathers on his son's arm. Icarus pulls away. We watch from his point of view as Daedalus goes back to the table and scrapes up a bit of melted candle wax, rolling it around between his fingers.
6. Montage of Icarus and Daedalus crafting the wings: gathering wax and feathers, stripping a cot of its straps to make an armature, and so on. As they work together, side by side, Daedalus impatiently corrects everything the boy does.
7. Night. Sound of a key in the lock. Quickly, they hide their work underneath one of the cots, and Icarus sits down on it, dangling his legs to hide what's underneath. The door opens and the jailer comes in with supper tray and fresh candle. He leaves these and goes. Icarus runs to light the candle.
8. Day. Icarus and Daedalus gaze down at the completed pairs of wings, which are huge and very beautiful. Now Daedalus warns the boy to stay close behind him when they set out and—above all!—to be sure not to fly up toward the sun. Its rays would surely melt the wax that holds their wings together. They help one another tie on the wings. A winged Icarus stands out on the sill of one of the parapets. He gazes after his father, already in flight toward the distant shore. He takes a deep breath and launches himself into the air.
9. In the distance, we see the two figures flying, Daedalus in the lead. Intoxicated by his new freedom, Icarus begins to swoop and glide, flying up toward the sun. Daedalus turns, sees what is happening, and calls out to Icarus to come back. But at the sound of his father's voice, the boy soars even farther. As Daedalus's cries grow faint in the distance, he begins to find it hard to move his wings and looks back over his shoulder in terror to see that they are losing their shape. Icarus cries out to his father to save him as he begins to fall.
10. A wide shot of sea and sky as Daedalus, wings beating furiously, races to catch the boy. A shot of Icarus, plummeting down. The camera follows as he plunges into the sea and the water closes over his head. He descends slowly underwater, twisting and turning.

As often happens, another image presented itself as a possible final one after we had finished the outline:

> 10a. A wide shot, with Daedalus circling above the place where his son vanished, calling Icarus's name over and over.

This last shot may not work in the film, because it leaves us contemplating Daedalus's suffering rather than that of our protagonist, Icarus. But it is worth thinking about, possibly even shooting, with the final decision left for the editing room.

REFLECTIONS AND COMMENTS

If you look over the outline, you will see that each step represents a scene that forwards the action, whether the scene is more or less continuous or takes place at different times.

For instance, the first step essentially sets up the main character's situation and shows tension between Icarus and his father, even hinting at the struggle that will develop between them. Step 2 is a variation on this and could easily be considered a part of 1. Step 3 shows us Icarus as a dreamer, imagining himself a seagull. Step 4 shows us Icarus carrying the fantasy a degree farther, and Step 5, even farther—to the point where he forgets himself enough to disturb Daedalus as he works.

Then we have the reprimand, the boy's display of anger at his father, and Daedalus's realization that he might be able to craft wings for them of feathers and wax. From this point until step 9, each scene moves the two toward escape from the tower—and Icarus's escape from his father.

Looking over the outline, you can see that there is nothing extraneous—everything counts. A writer has more freedom in writing a longer script; digressions that are pleasurable in a feature are apt to lose the audience in a short one. Still, there are aspects of the story that have not yet been explored. In writing the actual screenplay, we would want to be sure to develop the suspense latent in Step 7, when the jailer comes into the chamber, as well as that in Icarus's struggle to stay aloft as his father tries desperately to reach him.

A screenplay is a narrative, and one of the tasks of any narrative, whatever the medium, is to engage the curiosity of its audience. How?—by the time-honored method of "raising questions in their minds, and delaying the answers," as novelist and critic David Lodge writes in *The Art of Fiction*. Lodge believes that the questions raised in narrative "are broadly of two kinds, having to do with causality (e.g., whodunit?) and temporality (e.g., what will happen next?) each exhibited in a very pure form by the classic detective story and the adventure story, respectively."[6]

The particular challenge for writers of short scripts is that there usually isn't time to establish the protagonist's character and plight in a leisurely way and also tell the story. There are exceptions to this "rule," of course—many of them comedies, or experimental films, or videos.

All the same, if you are interested in making narrative films, it's useful to learn the ground rules before you take to the air.

ON CHARACTER AS HABITUAL BEHAVIOR

As we have noted, Aristotle referred to character as habitual action. You are what you ordinarily do—that is, until you do something you don't ordinarily do, which is what makes for drama. To be believable, the character's capacity for out-of-the-ordinary behavior needs to have been glimpsed by the audience—even if not recognized for what it is—at some point in the story before it appears full blown. (If your aim is to create cartoon characters in a live-action world, none of this matters much.) For example, in the outline above, Icarus ordinarily obeys his father without question, if sullenly, until the moment in the flight when he realizes that Daedalus is no longer in command, that he can do as he chooses. His out-of-the-ordinary behavior in disregarding Daedalus's warnings would make sense to us as an audience, because we have witnessed for ourselves earlier signs of possible rebelliousness. In Cocteau's sense, the logic of it has been "proven" to us.

It is the "movement of spirit or psyche," as Aristotle calls dramatic action, that produces a character's behavior. In any of the dramatic forms, the inner life of a character has to be expressed in what that character does, as well as in the way he or she does it. In a good screenplay, both dialogue and physical action flow from a character's dramatic action (or want or need).

ANOTHER ADAPTATION, WITH DAEDALUS AS HERO

Now we are working from the same source material as before (the myth) but in a very different way, using Daedalus as our main character. We will answer the seven questions briefly as a step toward writing a bare-bones synopsis of the projected script, which is for a live-action, realistic film of fifteen to eighteen minutes, set during the time of the American Civil War. The *synopsis* is a useful tool, one required by many teachers as a first step in writing any screenplay—a kind of trial balloon. It is also useful for an initial class discussion of a student's work. Widely used in the industry, it is often required in applications for foundation grants.

Here are the questions and our answers:

Who is the protagonist? Mark Dedalus, a captain in the Union army, in civilian life an architect. (We have changed the spelling of his family name to reflect the fact that in our story he is an American.)

Who or what is the antagonist? Dedalus has been captured by Confederate troops and is being held prisoner under close guard. Therefore, the prison and his captors are the antagonists.

What is the protagonist's situation at the beginning of the script? The time is 1862, early in the Civil War. Dedalus believes that his captors won't hold him much longer in the great, old house that serves as makeshift military headquarters for the area, but that they will send him on to a prisoner-of-war camp. Meanwhile, he gathers whatever information he can on their movements in long hours spent at the window and by the door.

He shares a small room at the top of the house with a boy who is awaiting court-martial—and most likely death by firing squad—for having fallen asleep while on sentry duty.

What event or occasion serves as catalyst? Dedalus accidentally cuts his hand on the sharp edge of his cot's metal bedspring and finds that one of the coils has pulled away a little from the frame. He succeeds in working it free and begins to fashion himself a tool.

What is the protagonist's dramatic action? To escape to the Union lines, at any cost, with the information he has gathered.

What is the antagonist's dramatic action? To prevent any prisoner's escape, by death if necessary.

Do you have any images or ideas, however unformed, as to the climax? The ending? During the two men's descent down the high outside wall of the mansion, footsteps can be heard approaching in the yard below. The youth loses his nerve and freezes. The climax comes as Dedalus has to decide whether to waste precious minutes trying to talk him down or to leave him and go on. The ending could be Dedalus running toward the woods beyond the house; he slows and looks back to see his cell mate still frozen on the wall. He hesitates (a close shot here), then heads off into the darkness of the woods.

How is the protagonist's action resolved? He succeeds in escaping prison with the information. We assume he will get to Union lines.

The synopsis that follows is a distillation of this information into a couple of paragraphs.

> *Just south of the Mason-Dixon Line, 1862. Union Captain Mark Dedalus is being held prisoner in an old mansion used as a military headquarters by the Confederate Army. He is determined to escape back to Union lines with valuable information he has gathered. A skilled craftsman, he fashions a tool from a bedspring coil and sets to work on the frame of the barred window.*
>
> *But the major obstacle to a successful escape turns out to be not the guards or their prison but his cell mate, a terrified Southern youth who is awaiting court-martial, and probably death, for falling asleep on sentry duty. His only chance to live is to escape*

with Dedalus—who reluctantly agrees to take him along. At night, Dedalus and the boy remove the barred frame from the window and drop a rope made of twisted sheets down the side of the house. Dedalus quickly descends and waits for the boy, who starts down but freezes when he hears footsteps somewhere in the yard below. Dedalus gestures him on, but the boy can't move. The footsteps fade, and Dedalus sets off at a run for the deep woods beyond, turning at one point to look back at the boy on the wall. In a moment, and with a curse, he continues on.

This story outline and synopsis bear a strong family resemblance to a number of feature films in the escape genre, particularly Robert Bresson's *A Man Escapes* and Don Siegel's *Escape from Alcatraz* (said by Siegel, in fact, to have been heavily influenced by *A Man Escapes*). However, this story is set apart by its setting, the specific moral dilemma faced by the protagonist during the escape, and the ambivalence of the outcome.

The main challenges in writing the script would be twofold: developing each character fully enough in a short time and exploring the relationship of Dedalus and the Icarus-figure.

ADAPTATIONS OF MYTHS AND FAIRY TALES

Some contemporary adaptations of myths and fairy tales done by students working collaboratively in workshops given by coauthor Pat Cooper include the following:

1. A teenager in a bright red jacket wends her way with a bagful of groceries to her grandmother's apartment through a shadowy labyrinth of burnt-out inner-city streets. The wolf is a drug dealer hanging out on a corner, but this Red Riding Hood turns out to be wily and fierce and gets the better of him with a few well-placed kicks.
2. Goldilocks is a talented unknown singer, the three bears a group of up-and-coming pop musicians.
3. Icarus is an arrogant, adept, but reckless hang-glider, and Daedalus is his instructor.
4. In an adaptation of "Bluebeard," the heroine is a young schoolteacher who makes the mistake of marrying a smooth but dangerous wheeler-dealer in slum properties.

Adaptations of fairy tales, particularly, tend toward the melodramatic, and that can be a good part of the fun of doing one.

NINTH ASSIGNMENT: FINDING A MYTH OR FAIRY TALE TO ADAPT

Find yourself at least two good collections of myths or fairy tales, and pick a tale you'd like to work on. After you've located it, photocopy at least two copies of several versions of the story—one to keep as a clean copy, the other to mark up as you work on your outline. In addition, photocopy any other material that interests you, such as illustrations or observations by the book's editor. At this point it is better to have too much material rather than too little, for you can't tell which bits and pieces of information may prove useful in writing your outline.

While collections of myths or fairy tales intended for children can be good sources, depending on the audience you want to reach, they are often heavily expurgated or simplified. Adults, not children, were the original audience for most folktales; for earlier versions, it would make sense to consult more scholarly collections, like LaRousse's *Mythology*, or a good encyclopedia such as the *Encyclopedia Britannica*.

Researching and locating the right myth or fairy tale can take a good deal of time, but it is important to choose a story that is personally meaningful, one that you will enjoy working on. It is also important that this assignment not be rushed.

TENTH ASSIGNMENT: GETTING STARTED

Consider the character in the story who appeals to you, the one with whom you can most readily identify. In writing narrative of any kind—except farce or parody, where one doesn't necessarily have to identify with the main character or characters—identification is really more important than whether you approve of the character. One often identifies with characters or finds them appealing even if one doesn't approve of them (Richard III, for example). When you have decided, take that character as your protagonist. Now think about whether you would like the script to take place in the present, at some period in history that particularly interests you, or in the mythical time in which it was originally set. If you can't decide at the moment, choose the last option, at least for your first rough draft.

For this next part of the assignment you will need two or three different-colored pens. Mark on one of your photocopies the events, images, and remarks on characters or setting that seem essential to the story you want to tell. Then, using a different color, mark material you think you will probably want. Last of all, in a third color, mark anything that seems problematic but intrigues you.

At this point, it makes sense to look back over the seven questions listed earlier in this chapter, as well as the answers we gave to them. By now, you should be ready to try answering these questions for your own project. Write as clearly and simply as you can, unless you are planning to do a detailed story outline in place of a first draft script, as discussed earlier; in that case, you can overwrite and revise, as we did with the outline for "Icarus's Flight." Either way, the question-and-answer process may take you as much time to complete as the actual writing of your story outline, but it will be time well spent. When you've completed the answers, some sort of feedback—from a class session, your teacher, or informed friends—would be helpful before continuing. It is especially important that the dramatic action of your main character be clear and make sense to your audience as well as to you.

ELEVENTH ASSIGNMENT: WRITING THE STORY OUTLINE

Now take up pencil and paper, or lay hands on a typewriter or word processor, and write down the steps of your outline, the spine of your story. Revise at least twice before handing it in or showing it to anyone, giving yourself enough time between each revision to develop some sort of detachment about the writing. As for criticism, listen and take note but use only what works for you.

NOTES

1. Rust Hills, *Writing in General and the Short Story in Particular* (New York: Houghton Mifflin, 1977), 4.
2. Aristotle, *Poetics*, ed. Francis Fergusson, trans. and introduction by S. H. Butcher (New York: Hill and Wang, 1961), 62.
3. Ibid., 72.
4. Ibid., 87.
5. Quoted in John Brady, *The Craft of the Screenwriter* (New York: Simon & Schuster, 1981), 115, 116.
6. David Lodge, *The Art of Fiction* (New York: Viking, 1993).

6

WRITING AN ORIGINAL SHORT SCREENPLAY

Narrative is the art closest to the ordinary daily operation of the human mind. People find the meaning of their lives in the idea of sequence, in conflict, in metaphor and in moral. People think and make judgments from the confidence of narrative; anyone, at any age, is able to tell the story of his or her life with authority.

E. L. DOCTOROW

At this point, if you have faithfully done the exercises and assignments laid out in previous chapters, you will have learned, among other things, how to write and revise both character description and location description in format; how to use offscreen sound to create mood and evoke offscreen events; how to begin to develop a character; how to gather and transform material for an adaptation; and how to do a story outline for a short screenplay to be written using that material.

What follows is a discussion of ways in which character can be revealed in speech, and ways in which speech can be used to further a character's dramatic action. In good screenplay writing, dialogue is as much a form of behavior as any physical action; it is also a form of dramatic action.

FINDING A CHARACTER'S VOICE

Here is part of another scene from *Chinatown*. Two characters talk in the scene, each with a very different way of speaking. If you haven't seen the film or read any of the drafts of the script, you won't know the context—but you should be able to hear two very individual voices and to follow what is going on in a general way. (Note that Evelyn is called YOUNG WOMAN until she identifies herself; this is a subterfuge used to make sure that the reader, like Gittes himself, doesn't anticipate the surprise that is about to be sprung.)

The scene takes place in the outer office of Jake Gittes' suite. He has just burst in on his associates, told them an off-color joke before they can stop him, and is "laughing his ass off." He looks up and sees a stunning young woman watching him. She asks Gittes if they've met and, ever the wise guy, he says no, they haven't—he would have remembered. . . .

YOUNG WOMAN
That's what I thought. You see, I'm Mrs. Evelyn Mulwray—you know, Mr. Mulwray's wife?

Gittes is staggered. He glances down at the newspaper.

GITTES
Not that Mulwray?

EVELYN
Yes, that Mulwray, Mr. Gittes. And since you agree with me we've never met, you must also agree that I haven't hired you to do anything—certainly not spy on my husband. I see you like publicity, Mr. Gittes. Well, you're going to get it—

GITTES
Now wait a minute, Mrs. Mulwray—

She's walked past him toward the door. He stops her.

GITTES
(continuing)
—there's some misunderstanding here. It's not going to do any good to get tough with me—

Evelyn flashes a cold smile.

EVELYN
I don't get tough with anybody, Mr. Gittes. My lawyer does.

Evelyn starts out the door and Gittes starts after her. This time he's stopped by the gray-haired man who has also come out of his office and up behind him.

At this point, Gittes is handed a summons and complaint by the gray-haired man, who remarks that he supposes

> they'll be hearing from Gittes' attorney. He speaks pleasantly—just a lawyer doing his job. Then Evelyn walks out the door, and the scene ends with Gittes staring down at the thick sheaf of papers.

Gittes quickly modifies his usual rowdy voice to the more genteel one he uses with female clients as soon as he speaks to the young woman. When she threatens him with publicity, he reverts somewhat to his usual way of speaking, and that only because he is in shock. (It's not going to do any good to get tough with me—) Evelyn Mulwray's voice is that of a well-educated, wealthy, quite imperious young woman, one who appears to be accustomed to getting her own way. These two are worlds apart.

When you are not familiar with the way a character would speak, it is often necessary to do research the way that actors and professional scriptwriters do: take yourself off to the kind of place in which such a person might spend time and listen carefully to conversation around you. In the short script *The Lady in Waiting*, the authentic-sounding and very different voices of Scarlet and Miss Peach are the result of considerable research on the writer's part.

However, we all have many voices available to us—the voices of family members, of friends, of the people with whom we've gone to school, or played, or worked. Accessing this material is often a first step in discovering how to write dialogue that works.

EXERCISE 9: AN INTERVIEW

You are going to conduct a friendly interview with someone whom you know, or have known, well enough to have a good idea of how they usually spend a day off. For obvious reasons, don't choose anyone you live with or are involved with, or anyone who would be uncomfortable at being interviewed by you. Close your eyes and imagine this person in the room in which he or she would be most at ease talking to you. Explain that the interview is just a writing exercise in which they will be (as they should be) anonymous.

You will be given a single (apparently) innocuous question to start off your interview, with a second question as backup in case the person falls silent for longer than, say, ten seconds. Anything less than that qualifies as a pause, or long pause. Pauses, as well as any ahs, hmms, ums, smiles, laughter, or physical actions, should always be noted: these can often be more revealing than speech.

Remember that your purpose in doing this exercise is to hear the interviewee out, not to control the way in which the interview shapes itself. Try to avoid interrupting by responding to what is being said; respond only with encouraging murmurs rather than talk—uh-huh, mmm, right, etc. If things falter, ask the backup question, which may well lead to a sudden flow of speech. If you are skeptical, think of all the voices running through your head in any given day; think of the way in which actors work to create a character; think of the way you talked to yourself as a child. Then put aside your skepticism and go to work.

Here, then, is the first question: *How do you spend your day off?* (Or, *how do you spend your Sunday?*)

The backup question: *If you could do anything you wanted on that day, what would it be?*

Set your timer and GO! At the end of ten minutes, stop writing and read the exercise. Did you capture the sound of the person's voice, the way that person would react to talking to you about him or herself? If not, it is worth choosing someone else and trying again. When you move on, as you shortly will, to writing an original short screenplay, this exercise can prove a useful tool for exploring your characters' backgrounds: what it is they want out of life, and whether they are getting it.

DIALOGUE AS EXPOSITION

In the fourth chapter, we discussed just how much exposition was buried in the first page or so of *Thelma and Louise*. Reading the script or viewing the film for the first time, we are enough engaged by the two women—what they are doing and what they are saying—to be unaware of the fact that we are also being fed essential information about each of them in a masterful way.

Beginning screenwriters often tend to pack their characters' speeches with information, necessary and unnecessary. What is necessary—and, in the short film, it shouldn't be much—can often be given through behavior, or through dialogue whose primary purpose is to forward the dramatic action, as in the excerpt given from *Thelma and Louise*.

In the following scene from the comic script *Dead Letters Don't Die*, we learn about the main character in a completely "natural" way—no forced feeding. We are shown, rather than told about, his innocence, his passivity (the man's been in love for two years!), and a basic tenacity that helps him resist the fellow-worker who is aggressively handing out unwanted advice. Chuck shows Thomas the tacky negligee he has bought for his girlfriend and asks what Thomas got for his "ole lady." Thomas stammers that she deserves more than he could give her. . . .

```
                    CHUCK
      Still haven't talked to her, huh?

                    THOMAS
      Oh, not yet.

   Chuck faces Thomas.
```

CHUCK
Fupper, you've got to take the bull by the balls.

He crumples the letter he is holding into a ball.

CHUCK
This Stevie Wonder, secret lover crap has gone on for much too long.

THOMAS
It's still too early.

CHUCK
It's been two years! She writes to her dead husband for God sakes; you can't tell me she doesn't need a friend.

THOMAS
I don't want to rush it.

DIALOGUE AS DRAMATIC ACTION: TEXT, SUBTEXT, AND CONTEXT

In art, as in life, gesture and speech have to be seen or heard in context in order to be fully understood. Someone may say, "Come in, and close the door after you," in a manner that implies a request for privacy, suggests wonderful things to follow, or threatens your physical well-being. In order to grasp the subtext of a particular line or gesture in any script (the text)—that is, in order to grasp its underlying or implicit meaning—we need to place it in proper context, to examine that line or gesture in relation to the events or circumstances that surround it.

Again, in art as in life, people often don't mean what they say or say what they mean. For a variety of reasons, some of which appear to make sense and some of which do not, we frequently choose to express ourselves obliquely rather than directly, using tone of voice and physical emphasis to convey our real meaning. For instance, in the example just given, you might respond to the line of dialogue by coming in and closing the door after you with a bang, or very slowly, or with exaggerated care, each choice denoting a different subtext.

Among the pleasures afforded us in viewing a first-rate narrative film or video are a kind of automatic deciphering of possible subtext along with an appreciation (the more conscious, the more pleasurable) of the tension that exists between text and subtext.

EXERCISE 10: DIALOGUE AS ACTION

Write down the following dialogue, in format or not, as you choose. As soon as you have the lines on paper, begin writing further lines, or even physical actions of the characteristics, as fast as you can, without worrying about exposition or concerning yourself as to whether or not any of it makes sense. Write for ten minutes and stop.

A:

What are we going to do about this?

B:

I dunno.

A:

Well, we've got to do something.

A pause.

B:

Why?

Immediately afterwards, ask your characters the questions from Exercise 2 (see page 29) and write down the answers. The answers will establish the context for your scene. When you have answered them, put everything away for the usual twenty-four-hour period. The novelist and scriptwriter Raymond Chandler wrote in an article on writers in Hollywood that "the challenge of screenwriting is to say much in little and then take half of that little out and still preserve an effect of leisure and natural movement. Such a technique requires experiment and elimination."[1]

If this is true for screenwriting in general, it is particularly so for the short screenplay and for dialogue in the short screenplay. To illustrate the process of "saying much in little," here is the opening scene of a short script by one of the coauthors of this book, in first-draft and then in rewrite form. The script is called "Annie's Flight," and its protagonist is a seven-year-old girl whose parents are about to get a divorce.[2] Through much of the title sequence before the scene, we have heard muffled sounds of a man and woman quarreling.

FADE IN:

INT. DININGROOM DAY
A pleasant room in an old house: bright reproductions of paintings, hanging plants, a large round table with a lace tablecloth. KIRSTIN and DAVID, a couple in their late thirties, sit facing one another at the table.

KIRSTIN

So . . . when do we tell her?

DAVID

You decide.

KIRSTIN

I don't know. . . . I don't know. . . .

DAVID

But soon, it should be soon.

KIRSTIN

Well, you say, then.

A slight pause.

DAVID

I've got meetings all week. . . .

Silence.

Listen, Kirstin—I honestly think it would be better if you told her.

KIRSTIN

We agreed to tell her together.

CAMERA MOVES DOWN PAST THE TABLE to a place where the cloth is rucked up eighteen inches or so. In this space, we see a little girl peering out. This is ANNIE. As we watch, she disappears into the darkness underneath the table. Again, KIRSTIN AND DAVID.

DAVID

Then it has to wait.

A pause.

KIRSTIN

You don't really give a damn about her, do you.

DAVID

That's not true! (pause) You know that's not true. (pause) We'll tell her on the weekend.

KIRSTIN

Fine.

DAVID pushes his chair back and gets up from the table.

KIRSTIN

It's not her fault, after all.

HOLD ON KIRSTIN, watching him go. After a moment, she gets up herself, and goes out.

CUT TO ANNIE, UNDER THE TABLE.

When the time came to revise, the writer was aware of two significant factors before starting: (1) this was too lengthy an opening for a film of seven or eight minutes in length and (2) the tension between the parents could be increased if certain lines were used as subtext rather than text (that is, implied rather than spoken). Here, then, is the revision, with her rationale for the changes:

THE IDENTICAL SCENE REVISED

(Description of room and characters remains the same.)

KIRSTIN

So, when do we tell her?

DAVID

You decide.

KIRSTIN

I don't know. . . . I don't know. . . .

DAVID

But soon, it ought to be soon.

KIRSTIN

Well, you say.

DAVID

The thing is, I've got meetings all week.

A pause.

KIRSTIN

Cancel them.

DAVID

O, come on, Kirstin. . . .

KIRSTIN

We agreed to tell her together.

A pause.

DAVID

Friday morning, then.

KIRSTIN

Friday morning's fine, David.

He gets up and abruptly goes out of the room as KIRSTIN sits gazing after him. After a moment, she gives a sigh and crosses past the CAMERA to go off as well. The CAMERA MOVES DOWN THE TABLECLOTH to a place where it is rucked up about eighteen inches or so. In that space, we see a little girl of seven peering out from under the table. This is ANNIE. She looks after her mother a moment, then pulls back into the darkness.

THE RATIONALE BEHIND THE CHANGES

The father's inner action is to get the mother to tell the child about the divorce without his having to be present, while the mother's is to ensure that they tell her together. His line "I honestly think it would be better if you told her" is too supplicating and is in any case implied by "I've got meetings all week." Her response, "Cancel them," is far stronger than her accusation of not giving a damn about his daughter—the implication is that if he cared about her at all, he would do what was necessary to take part in telling her. Other lines have been dropped for similar reasons—to make the conflict between them stronger and more indicative of what is wrong with the marriage.

The writer's goal throughout the revision was to emphasize the struggle between the couple by compressing their language, increasing the tension by bringing their anger "under," as the expression goes. She also wanted to imply that this kind of conflict is not at all unusual for them—just the particular subject on this occasion. (All of this would set up the conditions for Annie's flight.)

You should note that a pause before a response usually denotes some kind of struggle or debate on the part of the responding character; a pause within a speech indicates some kind of struggle or debate on the part of the character who is speaking.

In rethinking the structure of the scene, it seemed better to avoid breaking up their exchange, because removing the interruption increased the tension between them, while holding off on the discovery of Annie under the table until the very last moment made it more effective.

TWELFTH ASSIGNMENT: REVISING YOUR DIALOGUE

Read your answers to the seven questions from Exercise 2 about your dialogue sequence and then the scene itself. Try to figure out what is going on between the characters and what each of their inner (or dramatic) actions is, or seems to be. If this is unclear, come to a determination of what actions would make the scene work as you would like it to. (The initial four lines given were intended to suggest conflict.) If you want to extend the scene, do so now.

Think about any other changes you want to make, and rewrite the scene in screenplay format.

STEPPING BACK TO MOVE FORWARD

Assignments and exercises in the first part of this book have been set up to encourage the kind of messages from the unconscious that produce specific and authentic story material, rather than the lifeless copies of copies that make for hackwork. To write an original short screenplay, you will be utilizing all the skills you've learned so far, so it makes good sense at this point to take a quiet half-hour to look over your completed assignments in the order in which they were written. Note the kind of material that you choose to write about and the mood or tone in which you most often write. Do you tend to go for the drama in things? the melodrama? the humor? Do you like to deal with your characters subtly? with bold strokes? and so on.

This is information about the way you see the world and about your writing style, information that should be of great help as you move on to doing a short screenplay.

EXERCISE 11: WRITING A LETTER

First, letting your mind run free, try to call up two or three painful incidents from your past, incidents in which you were essentially the protagonist. Take a few moments to reflect on each of these, dismissing any memories that still seem "in process"—occasions that you can't recall without feelings of discomfort. Then choose a recollection to write about, even if you have to do so arbitrarily.

Second, imagine that you are about to write a letter describing, and perhaps explaining, the incident in detail (or in as much detail as you can recall—the act of writing about the past in an uncensored way usually stimulates memory to a surprising degree). Choose a person to confide in—friend, relative, or imaginary confidant—who would hear you out with sympathy and without judgment of any kind, the kind of ally who might even defend you to yourself.

Third, set your timer for fifteen minutes. If you finish writing sooner, go back over your letter to see if you have left anything out; if you are not yet finished with describing the incident when the timer goes off, continue until you are done. Then fold the letter and put it away in a safe place for at least several days. As this is raw material of a very special kind, it should not be shown to anyone else.

THIRTEENTH ASSIGNMENT: GETTING STARTED (AGAIN)

In this assignment you will be following procedures outlined earlier for adapting material gathered about a folktale or myth into the dramatic structure of a script outline: making several photocopies of your letter, then marking off in different colors on one of these (1) the events, images, and remarks on characters or settings that seem essential, including descriptions of the main character's thoughts or feelings, where important; (2) any other material that you are likely to use; and, finally, (3) whatever seems problematic but intriguing. Look this over and revise, if necessary, on your second copy.

Now ask yourself the questions that we asked of the Icarus/Daedalus myth, getting two very different sets of answers—one in which Icarus was the protagonist, set in "mythical time," and one in which Daedalus was the protagonist, set in the time of the Civil War. Who is the protagonist? (Choose fictional names throughout.) Who or what is the antagonist? What is the protagonist's situation at the beginning of the script? (This should be written in as objective a manner as possible.) What event or occasion could serve as catalyst? What is the protagonist's dramatic action? Do you have any images or ideas as to the climax? the ending?

Remember that this is an autobiographical fragment on its way to becoming fiction; change what you want, as long as the changes don't undermine the credibility of your story (sometimes changing the gender of a main character makes the scriptwriting easier). At this point, it would be a good idea to employ some or all of the exercises presented in earlier chapters. What you will be writing is fiction based on autobiography: the people in your letter are to be thought of as characters, the rooms and landscapes as settings and locations.

If, after doing the next several exercises, you find this to be in any way anxiety producing, you should accept the fact that the material has not yet been fully processed by your unconscious and is still too "live," so to speak, to be used as the basis for a screenplay. In our experience, trying to exert willpower or to "tough it out" in these cases simply doesn't work; in fact, it is more likely than not to lead to writer's block. You are better off putting away the material, choosing another incident, and beginning again. All that matters is that you end up working on (or playing about with) material in which you can take pleasure.

EXERCISES 12 AND 13: USING VISUAL IMAGES (AGAIN)

Exercise 12 takes ten minutes. Imagine an indoor hobby or activity of choice that your main character might pursue any time he or she has a chance. Close your eyes and visualize the setting. Then write down the following, substituting the name of your character for *X*: *Night. Gusts of wind outside. X sits (or stands) at a table (or bench or whatever) working on things, completely absorbed in what he or she is doing. A long moment, and Y opens the door without knocking to come into the room.*

You have ten minutes in which to describe for the camera what *X* is doing, how *X* is doing it, and what happens when *Y* comes into the room. If the characters go to dialogue, fine—just be sure that the emphasis remains on the visual.

If, at the end of ten minutes, you are still writing, and particularly if the description should turn into a full scene, continue on until you finish or run out of steam.

Now, for Exercise 13, quickly write down the answers to the by now familiar questions: Who are you? Where are you? What are you wearing? Why are you here? What do you want at this moment? What time is it? What season? What year? Besides being windy, what is the weather like? Take a break, short or long, and go on to the next two exercises.

EXERCISES 14 AND 15: FURTHER EXPLORATIONS

For Exercise 14, think of a suitable location in which to place your main character, whom I'll call *X* but you call by name, and write a brief paragraph describing it. When you have done this, let *X* walk, run, or leap into the frame and see what happens. At any point after that, let another character—possibly, but not necessarily, *Y*—come onscreen, and see what happens then. Stop at ten minutes, unless you find yourself writing a scene that you might be able to use in your screenplay.

For Exercise 15, consult your list of favored offscreen sounds and try to find one or more that might add mood or even significant content to either the interior or exterior scene.

FOURTEENTH ASSIGNMENT: WRITING A STORY OUTLINE FOR YOUR SCRIPT

First, reread the suggestions for writing story outlines in the previous chapter. Then, using both the results of the last few exercises and your marked-up copy of the original letter, make a bare-bones outline for the screenplay, no more than a page long. Put this away for a day or two, while you reflect on the tone you want to adopt toward the material. When you are ready, look over the outline to see if you've taken a step toward introducing the character in his or her situation (perhaps by way of one of the exercises), included a catalyst, and offered some sort of ending, even if it is not yet one you consider the right one. Most importantly, change the order of the scenes if necessary. Second, write a more detailed story outline, in which most of the "steps," or numbered descriptions of the action, indicate a full dramatic scene. Remember to use the present tense of screenwriting, and—most important—try to give us access to your characters' thoughts and feelings through their actions and reactions.

At this point, a reading and discussion of the outline, either in class or to knowledgeable friends, should prove invaluable to you before you move on to writing your script. Take notes of any ideas or criticism that might be useful, as it is easy to forget such suggestions. We suggest that you don't rewrite the outline unless it seems absolutely necessary, but instead go on to a first draft of your screenplay.

FIFTEENTH ASSIGNMENT: WRITING A FIRST DRAFT

Consult our examples or the short screenplays in the Appendix for the appropriate format. Then, keeping your portfolio of exercises and assignments nearby and your outline at your elbow, begin writing. Remember that the first draft of any screenplay is an exploration: the main thing is to get the story on paper so that you have something to revise. If you find it difficult to work at home, go to a café; if you find the word processor wearying, go to pen or pencil; if you find any or all of the process daunting, break the actual writing into ten-minute segments.

BEFORE GOING ON TO PART II

After the usual discussion of the script in class or with informed friends, and before moving on to the next part of this book, you might want to take stock. Do you want to continue with this screenplay? Would you rather work from a myth or fairy tale? Or would you prefer to find an altogether different kind of project? In the following chapters of Parts II and III, we will suggest, among other things, routes to other kinds of source material, as well as how to revise what you've written.

NOTES

1. Raymond Chandler, foreword to *Raymond Chandler Speaking*, ed. Dorothy Gardner (Boston: Houghton Mifflin, 1962).
2. Pat Cooper "Annie's Flight," unpublished ms., 1993.

PART II

MOVING FORWARD: WRITING STRATEGIES

7
STORYTELLING STRATEGIES

Although screen stories have unique qualities particular to film, screen stories for short and long films more often than not share characteristics with other kinds of storytelling. In this chapter we will discuss those general qualities and suggest links to other forms of storytelling, forms that provide the first and best source of material for short films.

STORY QUALITIES

All stories must engage the curiosity of an audience, whether that audience be one or a thousand. The storyteller must build on that curiosity to engage the viewer in the life of a character; that engagement must grow to identification; and so on. The storyteller must engage our curiosity, invite our involvement in a character's situation, and finally allow the viewer to identify with the character and the situation.

To hold the audience and move it through the story, a variety of devices are used. Some are operating principles, others are artificial techniques, but in each case the goal is the same—to move the audience from curiosity to a more emotional state. If the story works, the results can range from amusement to tragedy. But in each case, it is the storytelling qualities that transcend medium and that engage audiences.

These story qualities can be broken down into two groups: *character qualities*, and *plot qualities*. The primary character quality of a story is that we have to identify with the main character. We have to become concerned with his or her dilemma, and we have to care about the outcome.

In order to identify with the characters, we have to know who they are and how they've arrived at the point where we join the story. A main character may be active or passive, young or old, male or female. These qualities should be specific and appropriate to the story; it is no use to tell a story about a passive Olympic athlete, because the drive to become an Olympic athlete requires, by definition, a forceful rather than passive character. Specificity about culture, family, and career is also helpful in creating a person we recognize.

What are the person's goals? What are his or her hopes, dreams, fears? Any or all of these details can also help create a recognizable character. That recognition is the first step toward identification—if we recognize the character and his or her situation, we will begin to connect with the character.

As much as our identification with the main character relies on recognizing and caring about the character, that identification can be equally influenced by the role of the antagonist. The antagonist can be a mountain, a desert, or a raging storm, as well as an angry father, an overprotective mother, an unjust boss. Often the most interesting antagonist of all can be one's self: our own flaws (fear greed, anger, passivity) can play the role of the enemy.

As we have observed, the more forceful the antagonist in a story, the greater the struggle of the protagonist. If the goal of the story is to portray heroic behavior, the role of the antagonist can be crucial. If the goal is more to portray realism and complexity in the protagonist's actions, here too the character of the antagonist is critical.

It is notable that the character of the protagonist and antagonist are very often opposites. This may be in appearance as well as behavior. This *polarity* is the most overt use of opposites in storytelling. Polarized characteristics are also used with characters other than protagonists or antagonists, and to good effect. The greater the number of polarities in the story, the greater the conflict and the resulting interest to the reader, listener, or viewer. Polarity is an extremely useful storytelling device.

Plot qualities are closely related to character, but because they involve events outside of character, they can be considered separately. A good example of this notion is the role of conflict in storytelling: the more powerful the barriers that stand in the way of the character achieving his or her goal, the more compelling the plot. If the character faces no barriers in achieving his or her goal, there is no story. This is the nature and the role of conflict in storytelling—to provide barriers to the characters and their goals.

What if the character does not have a goal? This will pose a problem for developing a conflict. What if the character's goal is unrealistic? The storyteller may focus on the conflict inherent in discovering that the goal is unattainable. In both examples, the linkage of conflict to character is intentional. Plot cannot stand alone, outside of character, without the story being penalized. Character, plot, and conflict are intricately related to one another. One dimension of conflict is how much a character wants to achieve his or her goal. Do they want, do they desire, do they need to achieve this goal? The greater the desire of the character, the greater the potential for conflict. The parallel with regard to the plot is also true: the more powerful the resistance, whether through the antagonist or other forces, the greater the conflict potential. It is useful to restate that barriers to the character's goal may be external (a place, another person) or internal. What is most important to the story is that the viewers or readers understand that the barriers are the source of conflict for the character. In the most simple fable, such as "The Tortoise and the Hare," or a more complex short story, such as Hemingway's "The Snows of Kilimanjaro," the sources of conflict are clear to the readers, and through the story they become clear to the protagonist.

Whether the character succeeds, as in "The Tortoise and the Hare," or fails, as in "The Snows of Kilimanjaro," it is the struggle to overcome the barriers that is the fabric of the story. In each case the motivation of the protagonist seems primal, and that desire fuels our identification and understanding. Good stories tend to have a powerful conflict associated with a character we understand and whose desire fuels the story.

PLOT STRUCTURE

The first notable characteristic of a good story is that it presents an interesting interpretation of a situation that, on one level, we have seen before. A specific example will illustrate this. We are all familiar with the experience of the first day of school; the situation conjures up all kinds of associations for each person. Building on our familiarity with this situation, we can make it more interesting and arouse curiosity by introducing a new factor—the age of the new student. What if the new student in the local high school is forty years old, and he is joining a class full of fourteen-year-olds? The key here is that there is comfort for the viewer or reader in known situations—birthdays, weddings, funerals, and first days in school. The good storyteller uses our knowledge of the situation and whets our appetite for the story by introducing a new element.

Another factor in the plot is that point at which the storyteller chooses to join the story. It is crucial that we join the story at a point where the dramatic possibilities of the story can be maximized. The goal of the storyteller is to energize the tale, and the point of entry is critical in accomplishing this goal. A few examples are instructive. We join Ambrose Bierce's short story "An Occurrence at Owl Creek Bridge" at the point when a civilian has been caught trespassing on a bridge held by Union soldiers during the Civil War.[1] Will the unfortunate Southerner live or die for his transgression? This question forms the substance of the story that unfolds.

At the beginning of Raymond Carver's short story "Cathedral," a blind man, who has recently lost his wife, plans to visit an old friend and her husband.[2] The issue is whether the friend's rocky marriage can bear a visitation from a sightless rival. The main character is the husband in the problematic relationship. The announcement of the visit is the point at which we join the story.

Good storytellers will find a point to join a story that will serve to generate tension and attract attention. If we do not join the story at such a point, not only is dramatic opportunity lost, but the chance to harness our curiosity will be lost. We will, in effect, be waiting for the story to begin. To summarize: an interesting situation, a strong entry point, and enough conflict are necessary to start the story.

PLOT STRATEGIES

In order to carry us through the story, the storyteller will rely on two plot strategies—*surprise* (or *reversal*), and a *rising level of action* in the course of the plot. Surprise is critical, because if we are maintained on a steady diet of what we expect, we become bored and leave the story. Part of the storyteller's task is to keep us from getting bored: to maintain, use, and stimulate our curiosity about the story.

Surprise may be found in an unexpected plot twist or an unexpected behavior on the part of the character. In either case, the reversal or surprise upsets our expectations; it maintains and builds upon our curiosity. Think about your favorite film or fairy tale. How often in the course of the film or the fairy tale are you surprised by the course of events? Just as we both suffer through and enjoy a roller coaster ride, we need the same pattern of plot movement in a story.

A notable difference between a roller coaster ride and a story, however, is that although there are pauses in a story, there tends to be a pattern of *rising action* rather than the peaks and valleys of a ride. That rising action means that the surprises in the plot become more intense as we move through the story. Only through this progression of greater surprises can the story move toward a climax.

Just as every joke has a punch line, every story has a climax. The climax is the payoff, the point at which the character's efforts against all odds are successful. The climax is the high point of the story, and for many storytellers the very reason for their writing, telling, or filming a story. Without a rising level of action, this culmination would not be a climax but merely another event in the story. Consequently, the action in the climactic scene tends to have an all-or-nothing quality. It is the scene in which the stakes are highest for the main character.

Every good story also has a sense of resolution. Too often the climax is mistaken for the resolution: the resolution is the aftermath of the climax. The resolution brings us back to an even state after having experienced a growing feeling of intensity. The resolution in terms of the plot is the very end of the plot.

REALISM VERSUS FANTASY

There is a general decision to be made by every storyteller, a decision that will affect how powerfully the audience engages the story. That decision is the choice of realism or fantasy as the storytelling mode. Good stories can be realistic or the opposite, fantastic, but the choice will affect how the storyteller deploys character and plot, among other things. If a story is realistic, the detailing of the plot and of character has to be convincing and recognizable. If, on the other hand, the choice is fantasy, the characterizations will be more representational or metaphorical. Realistic characterization is complex, believable, recognizable; in a fantasy, characters may represent a class, gender, or race. In other words, a character may be used as a metaphor for a purpose that serves the story, in this case a fantasy. Consequently, the level of detail will tend to be less. Plot, on the other hand, will become that much more important—because the character in a fantasy is not as easy to identify with as a realistic character would be. Consequently, the plot needs to involve the viewer more actively than the character alone can. The choice between realism or fantasy will help the storyteller determine how to deploy the other storytelling elements; devices, surprise, twists, and turns of plot are more important in the fantasy. The narrative devices are the writer's tools. In choosing a realist approach, the author opts for character devices; in fantasy, he or she opts for plot-oriented devices.

THE NEED FOR STORYTELLING

We need look no farther than the number of television channels—to say nothing of the number of hours that television broadcasts news stories, sports stories, nonfiction stories, and fiction stories, stories of all lengths—to realize the number of stories available to the public every day. Add the number of films, the number of newspapers and magazines, the number of oral stories (from jokes to anecdotes to elaborate tales, from gossip to reportage, from free association to analytic interpretation), and it is evident we are all telling stories. There are stories on every level, from casual to the most meaningful. It's not so much that we hunger for any one kind of story but rather that we need a full range of stories. Human experience functions on a wide band, from superficial to highly meaningful, and storytelling reflects human experience.

Why do we need stories? We need stories to help us make sense of our world. We need to make sense of the past and of the present, so that we can make our way to a future.

But there are other reasons stories have been important, beyond the need to understand, and one is the need of the teller to communicate. Whether in pantomime or Elizabethan tragedy, storytellers want to communicate with others. The cave painter and the short-film director may have different means, but both want to use their medium to bind artist and audience together for that instant or that half-hour of the storytelling experience. For that time, storyteller and audience become a community, with all the historical implications of the relationship between artist and audience. Another goal of storytelling is the education of the community. Many cultures have used storytelling to educate, particularly about the ethics of living in the society. The passing on of tradition and ethics has been a central focus of storytelling, from the fairy tale to the fable to the documentary film. Finally, storytelling provides a legitimate access route to the world of our dreams and our fears; it provides an outlet for both of these types of psychic experiences. The goal of the story is to incorporate these dimensions of life into consciousness. Dreams and fears are important elements of storytelling.

SOURCES FOR STORYTELLING

Whether your goal is a contemporary story, a story specific to a culture, or a more universal story, there are many sources of inspiration, information, or insight.

Many writers and teachers of writing believe that the best source is your own experience. Our feeling is that your experience is only one of many sources. Should you choose your own experience for a story, the detailing of the story is clearly less problematic. The problem writers face with their own experience is their loyalty to the memory of that experience.

For example, John Updike uses personal experience and observations in the "Rabbit" series to tell a story about a man trying to understand his life as events and other people take control of it. He uses real concerns and real observations and applies them to a fictional character, in writing that shows this technique at its finest. This is how many writers proceed. Their loyalty is to the veracity of observation rather than to a detailed and literal reliving, in writing, of their experience. Writers like Updike use observation to comment on themselves and their readers rather than to indulge in, relive, or purge themselves of a memory or experience. This is the creative response to experience and observation.

Writers can be more personal than Updike (like Clark Blaise), or they can be less personal, as Frederick Forsythe tends to be. Our advice is that personal experience is an excellent source of material but that considerations of narrative and audience should mediate between the totally personal and the opposite—the accessible, engaging story. The personal can often be self-indulgent and sophomoric, whereas the opposite tries to engage the audience more fully. The former leaves the audience as witnesses instead of participants.

There are many other sources of stories beyond personal recollection, the most obvious being the daily newspapers. What we would like to do in this chapter is to illustrate how periodical accounts and other sources can be used as the basis for excellent stories for short films. We begin with a magazine, because it is one of the most readily available materials.

The Periodical Article as a Source

In February 1992, two years after reunification, the following story was reported from the former East Germany.[3] The recently opened Stasi (secret police) files had revealed that a thirty-year-old woman who had been involved in a human rights demonstration in the mid-1980s had for the next six years been under observation—and that the spy who had reported her activities throughout this time was her husband. She filed for divorce. Her husband stated in an interview that if the Communists had remained in control he would have continued to spy on her.

Here is a marital relationship—which, in an ideal world, we might expect to function to protect husband and wife from the problems and challenges of society, in this case a Communist regime in East Germany. This expectation proves to be wrong, since the husband represented the intrusive government and spied on his wife, whose activities defied the government's philosophy and policy. What we might expect to be the most cherished haven from Communism and government, the family unit, was therefore no protection for the individual. The implication is that there *is* no protection for the individual.

Although there is sufficient story potential here for a longer film, there are also a number of ways the story can be developed for a short one. The following is one suggestion for a short film script.

There are many points where it would be effective to join this story. We suggest that the drama is least interesting after the public discovery of the husband as a spy. What remains at that point is only resolution—what will happen to the marriage and to the husband and the wife (does he get his comeuppance?). We suggest that the presence of the state is important but needn't be elaborated. We also suggest that the story concentrate on the two characters in the marriage. A critical choice will be which character should be the main character. If it is to be the wife, the story should focus on the danger of her activities and her expectation that the haven from the danger is her marriage. In this version she needn't find out that he is a spy, but we in the audience have gradually to discover that and realize that she will suffer, without understanding why, for her activities.

On the other hand, if he is the main character, we want the story to focus on why a man has to betray his family for the state. Here he may be his own antagonist. The story line should focus not only on his betrayal but also on an understanding about his character—as the story in Bertolucci's *The Conformist* does. In *The Conformist*, set in Fascist Italy of the '30s, an upper-middle-class intellectual will do anything to belong; in this case, belonging means joining the Fascists. The rite of passage is a betrayal of his former professor.

We should confine the story to a very simple situation—let us say, the day of a human rights march. Let's assume that the woman is our main character. We needn't see the march itself but can confine the film to the preparations for the march and the aftermath. The scenes should clarify the relationship by highlighting the sense of trust on the part of the wife, and the planning and preparation of a report on the part of the husband. The government-controlled media—state radio, television, and newspapers—should be omnipresent. It may be necessary to embody the state in another character—a neighbor, for example. If the person who represents the state is too far from home—at work, say—we would dilute the emphasis in the story on the immediate threat of spies at and near home. The closer the spies, the more intense the story will be.

We can distract the audience from the true nature of the neighbor by making the neighbor an attractive woman. The initial impression should be that the husband is having an affair, rather than reporting to another spy. This way, when we do discover that they are both spies, the surprise and shock will be that much greater. In this state spying, not sex, is the highest form of leisure and pleasure!

It would be useful to the story if the wife suspects the husband of an affair and if the climax of the film involves her accusation and his admission of an affair with the neighbor. But we will know that the truth is more sinister. She accepts the affair, and the marriage—and the spying—go on. The story can grow only more suspenseful because of her husband's activities.

This short film will have much in the way of conflict between wife and husband/neighbor/state, but the situation will be simple, no more than "a day in the life of." When the wife chooses to accept her husband's story of infidelity, we begin to understand that the real danger to the individual is not infidelity but rather the state. Her choice implies much about priorities and life in 1985 East Germany.

The approach we have taken in developing a magazine article into a short-film outline can be applied to any other source. We move now to a simple source, a joke.

The Joke

Jokes or anecdotes can readily be the source of a short film, since they have a character, a narrative, and a climax. The writer need only add another character or two and provide a resolution, so that the audience will not be left in an unresolved state regarding the fate of the main character. The following joke will provide a constructive example.

Mark Twain tells the story of trying to get rid of the wreck of an old umbrella. First, he threw it in the ash can, but someone recognized it as his and returned it. Then he dropped it down a deep well, but someone repairing the well saw the umbrella and returned it. He tried several other methods, but always the umbrella came back., "Finally," says Mark Twain, "I lent it to a friend, and I never saw it again."[4]

Not only does this particular joke have a simple narrative, a conflict, and a main character, but it also has interesting opportunities for sound—not dialogue, but rather the use of creative sound effects and music. Indeed it is possible to envision this script entirely without dialogue. It also has the virtues of visual action and of personal interaction that can be easily understood visually. A short script version should include some action that illustrates why the character needed the umbrella in the first place.

We recommend a time frame of a few hours, beginning with the character preparing to leave the house. His wife reminds him to take the umbrella, because rain is forecast. The character is already resentful. Of course his wife is right, but he doesn't like to be wrong.

He leaves home with a specific errand—to purchase particular foods for dinner. His wife provides him with a list. He proceeds to the food store but is caught in a terrible downpour. A gust of wind ruins his umbrella just before he reaches the food store. He carries in the ruined umbrella and proceeds to shop. When he's finished the clouds haven't quite blown over, so he keeps the umbrella. After he has walked about a block, the sun bursts out, and he makes his first attempt to discard the umbrella.

What follows are his three attempts to get rid of the umbrella. Twice he leaves the umbrella in an ash can, and twice a good citizen runs after him with it, once an adult and then a young boy.

Carrying the groceries and now the broken umbrella, he carries on. He drops the umbrella down a well near his home and goes home thinking no more of it. No sooner has he unpacked the groceries than a workman who had been in the well knocks on his door and returns the umbrella. Now he is more than irked. He wants to destroy this ruined umbrella. He can't put it in the garbage; the garbage man will no doubt return the precious object. He can't share the problem with his wife; she will not understand. Then it comes to him. He puts the umbrella back in the closet.

The next day it is raining heavily. He takes the broken umbrella and an unspoiled one and goes out for a walk. He sees his friend Don. Don is getting wet rushing to the grocery store, list in hand. Our main character displays the spare umbrella under his arm, basking in his dryness from the working umbrella. Naturally, Don asks if he can borrow an umbrella from him. The main character agrees and saunters back home. Don struggles with the broken umbrella. A subtitle tells us that the main character never sees the broken umbrella again.

Although the use of the subtitle at the end is the "easy way out," it quickly makes the point or moral about lending things to friends.

The Idiom

An idiom can provide an excellent starting point for a short story, since the idiom provides a character and an editorial position on that character. It also implies a narrative.

For our example let's use the idiom "fall guy." According to a recent guide, the etymology of "fall guy" is as follows: "By one account, the original fall guy was a wrestler who deliberately 'took a fall'—as commercial ('exhibition') wrestlers are still doing. Well, maybe. In British criminal slang 'fall' has meant 'be arrested' since the 1880s (it derives from a much earlier figurative sense, a descent from moral elevation, as in Adam's fall)." A fall guy, then, is someone paid or framed to "fall" for a crime; as Sam Spade explains it to the Fat Man at the end of *The Maltese Falcon*, "He's not a fall guy unless he's a cinch to take the fall."[5] The modern fall guy takes the blame, or "carries the can," for some kind of misconduct or blunder.

The premise here is that our main character is going to be a scapegoat. Why he will be a scapegoat and how he becomes one is the thrust of the narrative of this particular short film. We have to choose a person and a situation. We do not necessarily have to choose a situation that will predestine the outcome or telegraph the fate of the main character to the audience. Perhaps the most critical task here is to create a situation that will make the outcome (that the character will become the fall guy) logical and that will create a character with whom we can empathize in spite of his or her plight.

Our story will be about an IRS bureaucrat who decides that he has had enough of saying no, that from now on he will say yes. He is the man in charge of income tax refunds. When the IRS communicates to the Treasury Department that it needs more money for refunds, the Treasury official replies that the Treasury had been about to ask the IRS for money (of course, the Internal Revenue Service essentially collects money for the Treasury). The official at the Treasury, also a bureaucrat, will not be able to report to his superior that he has the necessary money; the Treasury's mission is not accomplished. Will he be the fall guy for the IRS? The story can unfold in a few ways, but in any case the bureaucrat at the Treasury should be the fall guy. Clearly, the bureaucrat at the IRS is someone we all want to succeed.

This bureaucratic fantasy should focus on the fall guy at the Treasury, and we should on one level feel satisfaction at the fact: we can identify with and appreciate the prospect of greater refunds. In this story the fall guy's fate fulfills the audience's fantasy—to get a refund—and, consequently, the audience will accept not only the premise but also the fate of the fall guy.

The Anecdote

An anecdote, whether told by a friend or picked up in a newspaper, can be an excellent starting point for a screen story. The following is an example of such an anecdote.

> Desmond Tutu is the Anglican bishop of Johannesburg, South Africa. With a smile and some sly wit, he is able to make important points with a minimum of bitterness, which is perhaps why he was awarded the 1984 Nobel Peace Prize. He demonstrated this skill in a recent speech in New York City, where he stated, "When the missionaries first came to Africa they had the Bible and we had the land. They said

> 'Let us pray!' We closed our eyes. When we opened them, the tables had been turned: we had the Bible and they had the land!"[6]

This particular anecdote does not have much narrative or a main character, as did our earlier source material. It does, however contain a powerful irony: the subjugation, under the name of religion, of indigenous people. This is not a unique story, since it could easily be used to describe the early incursions of Western European powers into North and South America. In a sense, it is one of the major patterns of colonialism.

Our problem as writers is to use this powerful fact and metaphor and make it the spine of a short film story. Our approach can be realistic, dramatized, or animated. For the sake of providing an example of a different type from those used earlier, we will approach this anecdote with the goal of creating a story suitable for animation.

In order to focus on the concept of a moment of prayer turning into subjugation, we need to decide on a narrative and a character. We also need to make the point that at a certain time, blacks owned the land and were the power in South Africa. If possible, we should avoid the horrible cliché of traders giving gifts to the natives in exchange for property; to evoke Manhattan being purchased for a handful of trinkets can undermine the originality of our approach.

We suggest a story focusing on the meaning of prayer, in particular a specific prayer with meaning across different cultural groups and various historical periods. We can choose from prayers thanking the deity for the harvest, for the birth of a child, or for a death, or prayers asking or inviting the deity to provide. In our story approach, we will focus on prayers for a bountiful harvest. This will unify the story around prayer. It will also allow us to spotlight the land, the need to feed the local population, and the power structure in the area.

We will focus on a tribe, with a king and a shaman. The characters are black. In our story a king shows his son how to lead his people to a bountiful harvest. The king will speak of the need for rain, for peace with one's neighbors, and for sons and daughters to reap the harvest. Each scene focuses on an aspect of this prayer—for rain, for peace, for sons and daughters. Each scene ends with success, and in each scene the point should be made that the son in each scene is the king in the next. In this way, continuity over time suggests success and, implicitly, ownership. In the last three scenes white men are present, first as observers, then as traders. In the final scene there is a priest who leads the prayer for the harvest. The king closes his eyes as instructed, and when he opens his eyes, the men and women in the field are white; he and his children stand by and watch in wonder. Then a white man offers the king a tool. He does not accept it. The man offers it again. The priest sternly looks on. The king accepts the tool and is told where to work, and as he moves into the background, the foreground fills with white priests and soldiers and their sons and daughters. The king and his people recede into the background, and our screen story ends.

The Fairy Tale

Fairy tales are often used to instill in children life lessons, particularly about codes of behavior. Every country has its fairy tales, generated throughout its history. Good collections of fairy tales include *Best Loved Folktales of the World*, *Spells of Enchantment*, and *Jewish Folk Tales*.[7]

For our example of a fairy tale we will use "The Pied Piper."[8] The elements of the story are these. A town has a problem with rats. It has tried to rid itself of the pests but has been unsuccessful. The Pied Piper suggests that for a price he will rid the town of its rats. Skeptically, the town elders agree. Playing his instrument, he leads the rats into deep water, where they all drown. He has succeeded where all others have failed.

He asks the town elders for payment, but they renege on their agreement and offer less. The Pied Piper refuses the reduced payment and warns that they will be sorry. He is dismissed.

The Piper begins to play, and all the children in the town follow him into the woods. The townspeople look on. He leads the children away from their families. The magic of his playing is successful, and the town never sees the children again.

The moral of this story is that we should honor our obligations. Subtextually, the story is also about a spellbinder, in this case a piper, whose power is so great that he can lead innocents to any fate. Parents who warn their children of strangers bearing gifts are often, at the back of their minds, thinking of the power of the Pied Piper and his hold over the imagination of children.

There are numerous strengths here—a narrative, a main character, and a purpose. Rather than create a literal treatment of the fairy tale, we can modernize the story. We can also tell it from a variety of points of view: the Pied Piper's, a child's, the parents', or the point of view of the official who reneges on his agreement. We can also alter the genders of the participants to give the story a stronger male-female dimension; if we wish, we can choose a time and a place for the story that would speak more strongly to a contemporary audience. The strength of the fairy tale, the reason that it has lasted over time, is the power of the moral of the tale. As long as it is the moral that centers the story, we will not lose the narrative power of the fairy tale.

EXERCISE 16

Anecdotes, fairy tales, jokes, newspapers, real-life experiences, all provide starting points for storytelling. The writer must use narrative tools to shape the story and make it suitable for the medium he or she has chosen. In order to give you practice at culling a story from a source and using narrative tools to shape it for the short film, we suggest the following exercise using the fairy tale:

1. Find a fairy tale or myth you like or identify with. Be sure to choose a true folk tale—not one by an author, such as Hans Christian Anderson or Oscar Wilde, but one that is credited to Anonymous. (The Grimm's collections and stories assembled by Andrew Lang are good. There are also many ethnic collections in bookstores and libraries.) Make several photocopies.
2. Read over your story carefully. Answer the following questions.
   a. Who is the main character of the story?
   b. What are the person's goals?
   c. Who is the antagonist of the story?
   d. Outline all the opposites you recognize in the story. This can include people, settings, actions, reactions.
   e. What is the plot of the story?
   f. How is the plot structured around the main character?
   g. How does the plot begin?
   h. Name the barriers to the character's achieving his or her goal.
   i. How does the plot end?
   j. What are the surprises in the plot of the story?
3. In order to gain preliminary experience with plot and structure, we suggest breaking down your story into three major sections (I, II, and III) and marking off each. Sections I, II, and III may each be as long as several paragraphs or as short as a sentence. Each section represents a change in the character's situation.

AN EXAMPLE: PERRAULT'S "LITTLE RED RIDING HOOD"[9]

Once upon a time there was a little village girl, the prettiest that had ever been seen. Her mother doted on her. Her grandmother was even fonder of her and made her a little red hood, which became her so well that she went by the name of Little Red Riding Hood.

One day her mother, who had just made and baked some cakes, said to her: "Go and see how your grandmother is, for I have been told that she is ill. Take her a cake and this little pot of butter."

Little Red Riding Hood set off at once for the house of her grandmother, who lived in another village.

On her way through a wood she met old Father Wolf. He would have very much liked to eat her but dared not do so on account of some woodcutters who were in the forest. He asked her where she was going.

The poor child, not knowing that it was dangerous to stop and listen to a wolf, said: "I am going to see my grandmother and am taking her a cake and a pot of butter my mother has sent to her."

"Does she live far away?" asked the Wolf.

"Oh yes," replied Little Red Riding Hood; "it is yonder by the mill, which you can see right below there, and it is the first house in the village."

"Well now," said the Wolf, "I think I shall go and see her too. I will, go by this path, and you by that path, and we will see who gets there first."

The Wolf set off running with all his might by the shorter road, and the little girl continued on her way by the longer road. As she went she amused herself by gathering nuts, running after butterflies, and making nosegays of the wild flowers she found.

The Wolf was not long in reaching the grandmother's house. He knocked.

Toc Toc.

"Who is there?"

"It is your little granddaughter Red Riding Hood," said the Wolf, disguising his voice, "and I bring you cake and a little pot of butter as a present from my mother."

The worthy grandmother was in bed, not being very well, and cried out to him: "Pull out the peg, and the latch will fall."

The Wolf drew out the peg, and the door flew open. Then he sprang upon the poor old lady and ate her up in less than no time, for he had been more than three days without food.

After that he shut the door lay down in the grandmother's bed, and waited for Little Red Riding Hood.

Presently she came and knocked.

Toc Toc.

"Who is there?"

Now Little Red Riding Hood on hearing the Wolf's gruff voice was at first frightened, but thinking that her grandmother had a bad cold, she replied: "It is your little granddaughter Red Riding Hood, and I bring you a cake and a little pot of butter from my mother."

Softening his voice, the Wolf called out to her: "Pull out the peg, and the latch will fall!"

Little Red Riding Hood drew out the peg, and the door flew open.

When he saw her enter the Wolf hid himself in the bed beneath the counterpane.

"Put the cake and the little pot of butter on the bin," he said, "and come up on the bed with me."

Little Red Riding Hood took off her clothes, but when she climbed up on the bed she was astonished to see how her grandmother looked in her nightgown.

"Grandmother dear!" she exclaimed, "What big arms you have!"

"The better to embrace you, my child!"

"Grandmother dear, what big legs you have!"

"The better to run with, my child!"

"Grandmother dear, what big ears you have!"

"The better to see with, my child!"

"Grandmother dear, what big teeth you have!"

"The better to eat you with!"

With those words the wicked Wolf leaped upon Little Red Riding Hood and gobbled her up.

DIVIDING THE STORY INTO SECTIONS

Section I would cover the first four paragraphs. Section II would begin with her meeting the Wolf and end with her arrival at her grandmother's cottage. Section III would include the action in the cottage: her undressing and climbing into bed with the Wolf. The section ends with her being eaten by the Wolf.

When we develop the outline and treatment of the proposed script, we will have to make decisions about what to include and what to exclude, but at this stage it will be more important for you to think about how to grip the contemporary audience. A literal treatment of the fairy tale won't speak to an audience your own age. It is important to understand what has gripped you so powerfully about the fairy tale. What about this story has a hold on you? The answer may have something to do with listening to your elders, or it may have something to do with the fear of the forest—fear of the unknown, fear of animals. Whatever it is, it is important for you to get in touch with that core idea.

A creative way to articulate that core drive is to begin to collect images of forests, children, animals, that may give you a clue. What you are simultaneously looking for is the tone of the story. For this story you might also look in children's books, where illustrations are often a supplement to the written story. Once you have found the images that contribute to your core notion about the fairy tale, you will be ready to proceed more deeply into writing a short screenplay based on the fairy tale.

For now the structure you've outlined and the tone you have decided on will help you use the answers to the questions about character and plot.

NOTES

1. Ambrose Bierce, "An Occurrence at Owl Creek Bridge," in Ernest J. Hopkins, ed., *The Complete Short Stories of Ambrose Bierce* (Lincoln: University of Nebraska Press, 1984).
2. Raymond Carver "Cathedral," in Shannon Ravennel, ed., *The Best Short Stories of the Eighties* (New York: Houghton Mifflin, 1990).
3. "Stasi Files Now Open," *Time*, 3 February 1992, 33.
4. Quoted in E. W. Johnson, ed., *A Treasury of Humor* (New York: Ivy Books, 1989), 202.
5. Quoted in R. Clairborne, *Loose Cannons and Red Herrings* (New York: Ballantine, 1988).
6. Quoted in Johnson, *A Treasury of Humor*, 144.
7. Joanna Cole, ed., *Best Loved Folktales of the World* (New York: Doubleday, 1982); Jake Zipes, ed., *Spells of Enchantment* (New York: Penguin Books, 1991); and Pinhas Sadeh, *Jewish Folktales* (New York: Bantam Doubleday, 1989).
8. "The Pied Piper," in Cole, *Best Loved Folktales of the World*, 228–231.
9. Charles Perrault, *Perrault's Fairy Tales* (New York: Dover Publications, 1988).

8

VISUALIZATION STRATEGIES

In the preceding chapter, we highlighted the storytelling characteristics that transcend particular media, including film. In this chapter, we want to highlight the principal difference between film and other forms of storytelling—that film is a visual medium, and consequently, that stories told in film form must take advantage of the visual or the story may disappoint, or fail to reach, its intended audience.

This does not, however, mean that film has more in common with painting or photography. As a narrative form it has more in common with theater and the novel than it does with a single photograph or painting. But when directly compared with these narrative forms, it quite quickly reaches the limits of that comparison.

The best way to understand film and film writing is to consider film writing to be a narrative storytelling form that shares common narrative qualities with other narrative forms, such as the play or the novel. Film, however, is also a visual medium that must conform in its narrative to the qualities unique to film, qualities that will differ considerably from other narrative forms. In this chapter we will clarify the similarities and highlight the differences.

STORYTELLING IN THE CONTEXT OF FILM

As we have established, film stories come from many sources. Looking at a number of recent films, we find stories, such as Miller's *Lorenzo's Oil*, based on newspaper accounts of real-life events (in that particular case, a parent's search for a scientific cure for her child's illness in spite of the medical establishment's pronouncement that her son is incurable). Other films are based on national figures such as James Hoffa (David Mamet's screenplay *Hoffa*) and Malcolm X (Spike Lee's film *Malcolm X*). In both cases, published biographies were a major source of the material for the films. Robert Redford turned to the Norman McLean novella *A River Runs Through It* to make his film of the same name. Rob Reiner turned to the Aaron Sorkin play *A Few Good Men* for his film of that name. Francis Ford Coppola went back to the Bram Stoker original to make his own version of Dracula (*Bram Stoker's Dracula*), and James Ivory and Ismail Merchant turned to the E. M. Forster classic *Howard's End* to produce the film of the same name.

Whatever the source, all of these films have strong visual qualities, and each has transcended the form, and in some cases the quality, of the original. Another storytelling quality of the film story is the importance of genre films. Audiences know what to expect in terms of visual qualities from a western, a science fiction film, a horror film, or a musical. The result is the creation of a visual shorthand for the writer of these genre films. We bring a set of expectations to a western, such as Clint Eastwood's *Unforgiven* (script by David Webb Peoples). Also, we know what to expect when we see the horror/science fiction film *Alien 3* (written by David Giler, Walter Hill, and Larry Ferguson), at least in terms of visualized action.

But audiences also want to be surprised. While the writer has to adhere to particular narrative conventions to facilitate audience recognition, he or she has to throw a curve that surprises or shocks. The risk is that the writer will lose the audience if the story veers too far away from convention; the gain can be a unique insight into an experience. This is precisely what happened in Neil Jordan's mixed-genre thriller/melodrama *The Crying Game*, and in Agnieszka Holland's satiric war story *Europa Europa*. However, although the narrative strategy may shift, the corresponding need for visual action does not. Both films remain powerfully visual.

FILMIC QUALITIES

In terms of visual characteristics, film stories can take advantage of both the physical and dramatic properties of film. Perhaps no quality is more apparent or more underutilized in screen stories than the appearance of reality. Because it looks real, the viewer will enter into a film experience more readily and in a more unconscious manner than, for example, when watching a play in a theater.

The appearance of reality also offers the writer the opportunity to develop complexity of character or situation in a more believable manner. The benefit here for the writer and the audience can also be considerable. Film can also offer the writer the power of movement. Not only does the camera record the motions of people, but editing offers the viewer a range of time and place limited only by the imagination of the writer and the budget of the producer. The resulting dynamism means that the writer doesn't have to be confined to one geographical place or to one time. You are free, and if you tell your story well, we in the audience will follow.

But time and space are not the only variables the writer can introduce. Sound design can help create alternate places and spaces without actually going there. For example, Alfred Hitchcock in his first sound film, *Blackmail* (1929), wanted to allude to the sense of guilt the main character feels. The setting is the breakfast table, in a dining room behind the parent's store. A customer speaks to the main character about a murder that happened the night before. What the customer doesn't realize is that the main character was the accidental perpetrator of the murder. She is overwhelmed by guilt while the customer gossips about ways of killing people. The visual we see is the bread knife in the hand of the main character. On the sound track we lose the gossip and hear only the word "knife." Here sound and image together create the subjective emotional state of the main character—guilt!

Sound juxtaposition is one option. Visual juxtaposition is another. That can mean juxtaposition of two disparate shots to introduce a new meaning beyond the meaning of each visual separately, or it can be juxtaposition within a single shot. An image is contextual: it has a right side, a left side, a middle, a foreground, and a background. If you wish, you can present a particular visual juxtaposition that highlights a power relationship, the shifting importance of two elements, or a developing relationship. All are visual interpretations of what the audience will see.

Although writers do not write camera shots in their scripts, they are constantly dealing with relationships and shifts in relationships. Our point here is that visual detailing by the writer can articulate those juxtapositions and shifts.

Finally, in terms of physical properties, the level of visual detail will create as much complexity as you need. An example will clarify our meaning. In a theatrical stage scene where the goal is to suggest the character's obsession with appearance, we see only one set of clothes; few in the audience can see the makeup or the clothing changes made earlier. Consequently, if we want to make the point about the character's obsession, we have to have a full closet on stage or have the character or another character comment on this particular obsession.

In film, on the other hand, we have the option of showing characters trying on one set of clothing after another. We can see characters change their makeup, we can follow them to shops, and of course, we can see them add to their closet of clothing. The level of physical detail can suggest that a character is a kleptomaniac, or simply insecure about his or her appearance. In other words, we can make the point about the obsession, and if we wish, we can begin to explore the psychology of the obsession. How complex we want to be depends totally on our writerly wish. We can have complexity or simplicity; it's strictly a matter of visual detail.

In terms of dramatic properties, the principal quality of film is that visual action is crucial to the establishment of motivation, to the characterization of both the main and secondary characters, and to advancement of the plot. The story spins out through visual action. If the story was spun out through dialogue, there would be very little to differentiate a film from a play. In the theater, dialogue is everything; in film, visual action is everything. A more subtle, but no less important, characteristic of film is that the point of view of the narrative is underscored visually. The narrative may point out that X is the main character, but it is the fact that events happen to X, events in which he is not an observer but something between victor and victim, that will underscore the point. These visual articulations will also facilitate identification with X, and they will if necessary give us insights into his subjective world. It is the struggle of his subjective world with the objective real world that is at the heart of the drama of the film. Only by understanding his world can we appreciate the deepest dimensions of his struggle in the larger world. All this must be accomplished visually if the film writer is to work with this medium.

CALLING THE SHOTS

The two most familiar types of shots in film are *close-ups* or *long shots*. Films are made up of disparate fragments of film, of which close-ups and long shots are but two types. Another would be the extreme long shot (dolly, tracking, trucking, stedicam, tilt, pan).

Having mentioned the visual variety of images in film, we must also state that determining shots is the prerogative of the film's director. What creative decisions, then, does this leave the writer? Should the writer think in terms of shots (single images) or in larger dramatic units?

The answers to these questions are both simple and complex. The writer should be thinking in terms of images as he or she writes the script, but it is not necessary for him or her actually to detail those shots in the script. Indeed it will probably be counterproductive to do so.

How then can you tell your story in images, if you can't list those images in detail? In order to answer this question, we turn to the terms used in writing film scripts.

FILM-WRITING DEFINITIONS REVIEWED

The dramatic terms introduced earlier can be divided into two groups: those that are character related and those that are plot related.

There are two groups of character types: *main characters*, and *secondary characters*.

The Main Character

The main character, the subject of your story, often called the protagonist, is the reason for your film story and should be situated in the middle of the action. The story, or plot, gives the main character the opportunity to overcome his or her dilemma.

The main character should have the energy or drive to carry us through the story and should also appeal to us in some way. Some writers use a charismatic main character; others will place a goal-directed character in a situation that creates an identification or empathy with that character. In both cases the main character should be visually and behaviorally defined in such a way as to help the story.

The more visual consideration given to who the character is and what he or she looks like, the more likely the character's look can help the story. Whether the main character is heroic or tragic, the writer should be very clear about the goals of the character.

A word about goals. In a sense, a character has a goal in every scene. That goal may be simple. What the writer also needs to keep in mind is the character's overriding goal, sometimes called the *supergoal*. The supergoal forms the larger issue that drives the character throughout the story. Many writers now talk of their screen story as a journey for the character (after the writings of Joseph Campbell on the importance of myth). The supergoal is what prompts the main character to undertake his or her journey,

Secondary Characters

Secondary characters have much simpler roles in the screen story. Often they are almost stereotypic. They have a purpose, and they live out that purpose in the course of the story. They too have goals, but their goals are more or less related to that of the main character. They are in the story either to help the main character or as a barrier to the main character's goal. Secondary characters should also have visual and behavioral characteristics that help the story.

The most important of the secondary characters is the antagonist, whose goal is diametrically opposed to the goal of the main character. Often the antagonist is the most complex of the secondary characters.

The Plot

The plot is the series of scenes that leads the character from dilemma to confrontation to resolution, following a line of rising action. In the course of the plot the writer should never forget where the main character is. Plot cannot exist without character. If it does, we lose our involvement and as an audience become voyeurs rather than participants in the film story.

The Catalytic Event

The catalytic event is that critical event that precipitates the main character's action. It is the trigger for energized action to achieve his or her goal. In the short film, the catalytic event is central, because it precipitates the story.

The Climax

The climax is that point when the character is faced with making his or her choice. It is the ultimate scene, in which the main character will finally achieve, or fail to achieve, his or her goal.

The Subtext

Every story has a surface meaning and a secondary, often more important, meaning. If the surface meaning in "Little Red Riding Hood" is "beware of wolves in grandmothers' clothing," the subtext is that children should listen carefully to their parents.

Plot Twists, Surprises, and Reversals

Plot twists, surprises, and reversals all refer to the same device. The writer employs twists and turns in the plot in order to create tension and maintain viewer interest. Plot twists and turns, whether they are called twists and turns, plot points, surprises, or reversals, are necessary mechanically to the film story. They keep us guessing and involved with the story.

The Structure

The dramatic organization of the film story is referred to as the *structure*. The structure is chosen as a mode of organization that best suits the narrative goals of the story, and it often revolves around a number of acts.[1] Writers will emphasize plot over subtext in particular film genres. Some genres, such as adventure films, are all plot and virtually no subtext; others, such as film noir and the horror films, have much more subtext than, for example, situation comedies. The genre the writer is working within will determine the balance of plot to subtext. The best structural choices are made when the writer is thoroughly familiar with the narrative characteristics of the genre. Structure is the shape of the plot.

The Scene

The scene is the basic building block of the structure. One act will comprise a number of scenes. Scenes are sometimes clustered, in a sequence of two to four scenes that share a narrative purpose.

Each scene should advance the plot. Within each scene, characters have specific goals. The scene is visually constructed around a narrative purpose but worked out in terms of character goals. If Character 1 has one goal and

Character 2 has an opposing goal, the scene will proceed until Character 1 or 2 has achieved his or her goal. When that has happened, the scene is over. In the course of the scene, the other character does not achieve his or her goal. The success of one character or the failure of the other links directly to the advancement of the plot.

Scenes tend to be relatively short and specific; transition scenes are less common than they used to be. Consequently, the best test for the validity of a scene is the question, does this scene advance the plot? If it does, how? If it does not, the scene should not be included in the screenplay.

The Outline

The first step in the film writing process, after conceiving an idea, is forming an outline. The outline is actually a brief summary of the idea. The focal point of the outline is the character. After identifying the character, the writer should define the premise in terms of a conflict for the main character. It would also be useful to identify the catalytic event.

The outline should not be a plot summary; consequently, it should fit easily on a single page.

The Treatment

After the development of the idea, the character, and the premise of the outline, the writer next faces the task of creating a plot line, which, when completed and broken down into a series of scenes, is called the *treatment*. For a short film, a treatment should be two to four pages long, and it should summarize the scenes in single paragraphs or numbered paragraphs. Treatments are sometimes called *step outlines*.

The Script

The script is essentially the elaboration of the treatment, including visual description and dialogue. The script should always be presented in *master scene format* (an example of master scene format is given later in this chapter). The key controversy about script format is whether to include short descriptions in the scenes. We recommend omitting them.

The master scene format allows readers of the script to visualize the story more readily than if they were stopping for technical descriptions, such as of a close-up or long shot, in the body of the script.

These are the primary film script terms you will encounter. We turn now to the principle of visualization, in order to assist you in telling stories in images.

THE PRINCIPLE OF VISUALIZATION

Whether the writer imagines the film, conjures up a dream, or simply draws an image, the operating principle is that the writer should visualize rather than verbalize. The key to the success of that visualization is the meaning it gives to the story. Images can be neutral, moving, or overwhelming. The creativity of the writer and later of the director makes the difference between functional and fantastic. We propose to take you through a process of visualization that will help you aspire to the latter.

THE PROCESS OF VISUALIZATION

The first step in visualization is to consider the way you tell your story. We suggest that a retrospective approach to telling a story is less effective than telling the story in the present. Presenting a story so that it seems to be occurring as we are watching it gives the story immediacy and energy and puts the writer in the strongest position to direct the story.

To tell the story retrospectively is to tell it in the past tense, therefore making it more distant. To tell the story in the present is to use the active, action-oriented grammatical option.

The second step in the process of visualization is deciding how to present your main character. A character who is lost, confused, or passive is more likely to talk than to do. A character with a goal is likely to act in order to achieve that goal. Consequently, presenting your character as goal directed will help you visualize his moving toward that goal.

The third step is to set the action of the story in settings where there are visual opportunities and where the setting helps your story. The young girl in "Little Red Riding Hood" is in a forest. Forests can suggest tranquillity or danger; in either case, the setting of the forest adds visual opportunity to the story.

The fourth step for the writer is to apply the magnifying lenses of "watching, waiting, wanting" to the story. By this we mean that the idea of *watching* should permeate your story. The audience should be watching events unfold for the main character.

Waiting involves a second layer of interaction with the story. What visual events can we inject into the story to help propel the character into a setting that also, in a sense, contributes to the story?

Finally, the tool of *wanting* needs to be developed. What is the character willing to do to achieve his or her goal? The writer needs to provide steps to allow the character to climb toward the goal. As the character strains to reach the height of the goal, the viewer should also experience the shortness of breath due to that climb. Only by taking this upward journey with the character can we in the audience join the character in wanting to reach the summit.

The fifth step is to provide visual surprises along the way. Those visual surprises may be exciting, expressions of the character's anticipation. The visual surprises may be character related or plot related; in either case, they help flesh out the visualization of the story.

By this time it should be clear that the writer's goal is to move the viewer from the position of voyeur of the story to the position of participant in the story. This happens through identification with the main character and through the main character's struggle to attain his goal.

The question of whether you are keeping viewers outside the story as voyeurs or bringing them into the story as participants is one you should return to on a continuing basis throughout the writing process. In order to reinforce the sense of being inside the story with the character, the writer should rely on visual detail to cement the believability of the character, place, time, and plot. Visual details can range from the time of day to the climate particular to a place, clothing, gait, mode of interaction, and so on. The greater the visual detail in the script, the greater the believability in the story.

One more step remains to exploit fully the visualization process. Look over your story, rethink it, and rewrite it as a silent film. Distancing yourself from language will help you think and make writing decisions visually. Now that you have thought about your script in visual terms, we recommend that you add sound in order to add another level of credibility. Sound can also help you introduce a level of metaphor to the story. We will discuss this point in the following section.

SOUND DESIGN AS COMPLEMENTARY TO VISUAL DESIGN

Whether the sound is synchronized (directly related to the visuals—hearing the sound of a door opening when we see the door open) or is used asynchronously (in contrast to the visual), the overall pattern of the sound adds another dimension. In this way, the sound can be used to support an aura of realism arising out of the visuals, or it can be used to create an alternate or multilayered view, as described in Chapter 3.

The key is to use sound purposefully. Having used the visual dimension to tell your story, to characterize, and to create a sense of place, you should view sound as yet another opportunity to tell your story even more powerfully.

SOUND AS THE INTERPRETER OF VISUAL IDEAS

Sound can alter visual meaning; it can complement visual meaning. In Ken Webb's *The Waiters*, sound does both.

This film, about the process of waiting, moves through a variety of characters and settings—a suburban commuter waiting for a train, a woman waiting for a sign from above, an actor waiting to be discovered, a young man waiting to fly, a young boy waiting for Santa Claus. The narrator explains in an amusing way why each is waiting. The reasons given range from the rational to the irrational. Nevertheless, the visuals suggest that most of the characters get what they want, particularly when their wish was irrational or supernatural. Consequently, the surprise of seeing them get what they want, no matter how preposterous, is extremely funny. Webb ends the film with a low-angle single visual of a waiter reciting the items on a menu in an Italian restaurant. The shot makes up a quarter of the entire film. The result is to shift our attention away from people waiting and wanting, to people waiting *on* and offering. The result is to bring us back to earth.

In *The Waiters* it is the sound track that explains the diversity of visuals, linking them to one another. The narrator also tells us why the people are waiting. When each person's situation resolves, it is the narrator who explains how that resolution has been achieved. That is not to say that the visuals are unnatural at this point, but rather to underscore that the diversity of people and visuals means that the visuals cannot do the entire narrative job on their own. They need sound and narration to tie them together and to help us understand the solution and lead us to a response to the diverse expectations. The subtext of the story—that all of us wait for something out of our control to resolve dilemmas—is quite touching, and Ken Webb's ability to make us laugh about the issue reflects how effectively sound and visual have worked together in this short film.

FORMAT

The format that you use can emphasize the importance of the visual in your script. The format we suggest, as discussed earlier, is the widely used master scene format, an example of which follows:

Title
By
For__________
(TV program or production company)

1. It is raining, a thunderstorm. A young man, Brad, walks to his mailbox. He opens the box with much anticipation. He opens it. The rain is falling like a sheet. He can barely read, but he notices the words "pleased to offer you." He stuffs the letter into his pocket and begins to run.

BRAD

Mom! Dad! I'm in! I'm in!

He runs and is lost in the hail that begins, but we can hear his voice. Brad is a happy man.

Cut To:

2. Int. Kitchen. Day.

Brad's Mother is stirring the soup. He is soaked to the skin.

MOTHER

You'd better get out of those clothes or you won't live long enough to go to that fancy school.

BRAD

It's not fancy. It's just good.

MOTHER

Good and fancy.

BRAD

Good.

MOTHER

They won't make you soup like this.

BRAD

You can mail me some every week.

MOTHER

Now you're making fun of me.
Wait till you're up there. You'll probably think of me and your dad as sources for your humor. I hope you won't forget us, Brad.

BRAD

I haven't left yet, Mom.

MOTHER

And don't forget where you came from, son, don't forget.

End of Scene 2

What is notable about the master scene format is that it is organized so that the reader can visualize the story as easily as possible. There are no camera angles, no detailed technical instructions, only description and dialogue. You should acquaint yourself with the format and use it to develop your own short screenplay.

EXERCISE 17

In a ten-minute writing exercise, write as fast as you can without stopping to think or worry about logic, spelling, or punctuation. Use a timer and try not to look at the timer.

1. Place a picture in front of you. Imagine the picture as a freeze-frame. Imagine that the character of the picture begins an action. Write for ten minutes. Put aside your work without reading it.
2. Do the same with a second picture.
3. Now list ten sounds that are particularly evocative for you.
4. Make a list of five sounds that could establish the feeling-tone of the first picture.
5. Make a list of five sounds that could establish the feeling-tone of the second picture. Note that silence is also "a sound."

9

DRAMATIC STRATEGIES

You have an idea for your story, and the problem before you is to find the drama in your idea and shape it into a story.

Something about the idea, which may have come from any one of the sources mentioned in Chapter 6, has captured your imagination and unlocked an emotional reaction. Whether it touches your unconscious or conscious synapses, the deed is done, and the idea seems to haunt you. It won't go away until you convert it into a script, and from a script into a film that you can share with others. The film gives others an insight into you: it's a gift to them and an invitation to join with you for the length of the film experience. These are the motivations for converting an idea into a dramatic story. We turn now to the means to achieve that transformation.

THE IDEA

At the beginning of the process of developing an idea into a dramatic story, it's important to consider a number of questions whose answers will direct you.

First, does the idea have only the shape of a photograph, or does it have an implied narrative? The observation or photograph of a young girl rushing down the wintry street carrying her winter coat and a knapsack implies that she is going to school. Will the story be shaped around the events of this day at school? Is there something special about this day? Or is it simply an ode to the freedom of being sixteen and having no greater obligation than to join your friends at school?

If the idea or observation does not suggest a direction, it is important to decide what it is about the image that stays with you. Let's decide that it is the latter feeling—that it's great to be young—that appeals so much to you about this image. The basic idea, then, revolved around the joy (and other qualities) of being young. What other notions or events might support that feeling of being young and enjoying it?

The key at this stage is to let the idea breathe. Respond to it, and *roam* around it. You are looking for a direction. Young girls like to window-shop, and they stop to buy if they have money. They like to meet their friends en route to school and travel together. They like to exchange clothing, as a bonding device that makes them feel closer to each another. They like to assess males they observe and comment about them if with friends. They like to eat muffins and orange juice. Some like to smoke.

At school they might assess their status based on the number of members of the opposite sex who greet them or attend to them. They like to talk in class. They make dates to talk more. They make plans for the weekend. They discuss potential companions and destinations for the weekend. They talk about college. They talk about their siblings and sometimes their parents. When desperate for something to do they will exchange views on their teachers. They do schoolwork. They exercise, eat lunch, and eventually go home.

Narrative design options here include the following: "a day in the life of," life at sixteen, girls and boys, contemporary style, herding, high school style. If the emphasis is on the joy of being sixteen, any of these shaping devices can work. Joy is the overarching attitude you want to be evident in the narrative. You will want to avoid the pain of being sixteen and emphasize the pleasure. In order to dramatize the story, however, you must find a framing device that will tell the story from your chosen point of view.

FRAMING THE STORY

The writer has a number of shapes or forms available to him or her to frame the story. Since this is the first important decision you make in directing the presentation of your idea, you should deliberate carefully about the *frame*. In the longer film, these shapes are referred to as *genres*. This device isn't as useful in the short film: the framing devices of the gangster film, melodrama, film noir, or the horror film are not as helpful in the writing of the short film (although they can be critical in writing a long one). The story forms that are available and useful to the writer of the short film include the docudrama, the "mockumentary," the comedy, the satire, the fable, the morality tale, the journey, and the event.

The Docudrama

If your idea is generated out of the daily news, is about a famous person, or should be related as closely as possible to real life, the *docudrama* could be an important framing device for you.

The docudrama requires a level of veracity that suggests detailed research of your idea. You need recognizable people and events to reinforce and place your story in a category of believability far beyond that of the conventional drama.

In a docudrama the writer often refers to the media—at least television, possibly radio. Just as Orson Welles used radio news techniques to create a panic reaction to his "War of the Worlds" broadcast in 1938, so too will the docudrama writer employ a television news style that should be convincing. You have to observe qualities of the news, reporters, and the types of observations they make on the news, and avoid kinds of observations you don't see on the news. You are trying to use the patina of the evening television news to enhance the believability of your story. It's a good idea to study very good docudramas such as *The War Game*, *All the President's Men*, and David Holzman's *Diary*. Learn from the masters. What you are trying to do is to frame your story as if it really happened, or just as it did happen. In either case, the credibility of your dramatic story will depend on successfully using the frame of the docudrama.

The Mockumentary

Ever since *This Is Spinal Tap*, student films about performance, filmmaking, writing, and music have relied on the hybrid form loosely called the *mockumentary*. This is a form that both evokes realism and pokes fun at it. Not quite as intense as the satire, the mockumentary criticizes gently the subject of the film, which is often the media as it interacts with, and often creates, a star. In this sense, the mockumentary is a self-reflexive and self-critical form, as the "mock" in the word suggests. If your idea centers on the relationship between the public and a character, and if the media can play a role in the story, the mockumentary is an amusing and often insightful form.

In order to use this particular framing device, detailed research into the creation of a music video, a political advertisement, a television show, a rock concert, and so on, is critical. References to production will help create a level of believability.

Beyond the research, the mockumentary also implies a particular structure for the story—the rise and fall of a film or television show, a weekly episode of television, even the day-long production of a soap opera. The pattern of the structure must be quickly understood and accepted by the viewer. One final comment about the mockumentary: this frame affords many opportunities for humor. The more outrageous the humor, the more likely the story will succeed. If your goal is to make a humorous film, the mockumentary is a natural story frame.

The Comedy

The mockumentary is a particular comedic story frame; the writer has other options to choose from. *Comedy* runs the gamut from farce, which is principally visual, to more sophisticated forms, where character and dialogue are more important. If the idea is character oriented, what are the characteristics that lend themselves to comic opportunity? If they are physical, the comedy is aimed at the character; to put it another way, we laugh at the character. If the characteristics are more behavioral, we have a broader band of comic opportunity. We needn't laugh at the character, but we may laugh *with* the character. How does the source of humor blend with your attitude about the idea? If we laugh at your character, in other words, does it undermine or support your idea?

Similarly, if your idea is situation driven, do you want us to see your character victimized by the situation or victorious over it? In each case, does the approach support or undermine your idea?

Another approach is to examine what humor, rather than a more straightforward approach, will add to the story. The humor, aside from its understandable appeal, should bring other narrative dividends. For example, the fact that the balloon in *The Red Balloon* does the unexpected (it follows the boy and later displays a mind of its own) is humorous, but it also humanizes the balloon. Through humor, the balloon becomes the boy's friend rather than remaining an inanimate object.

Using comedy should help your story. It should make your story seem fresh, and it can, if deployed well, energize your story. Comedy, whether farcical or cerebral, visual or verbal, can help you frame your story in such a way that your idea is strengthened.

The Satire

Satire is a very particular form of comedy. It is more savage than other forms, because the object of the satire, in the mind of the writer, deserves to be ridiculed.

There is a long tradition of satire, from the Greeks through Kurt Vonnegut, Terry Southern, Luis Buñuel, Salvador Dalí, Eric Rohmer, Michael Verhoeven, Earl Morris, and Lizzie Borden. The key decision for the writer considering satire is whether the target of derision merits the treatment. The form works best when the target is important or well known, because the bigger the target, the more likely the target is a candidate for satire. Modest subjects will appear ineffective when presented in a satire.

Satire is a genre of excess—excessive humor and exaggerated character, story, and language. The rules of realism are readily bent in this genre. Examples of subject matter successfully treated in film satires include middle-class values (by Buñuel in *L'Age d'Or* and Lizzie Borden in *Working Girls*), a shameful history and a community's attempt to hide it (Michael Verhoeven's *The Nasty Girl*), and the excessive power of television (Paddy Chayevsky's great script *Network*). Other notable targets are the health care system in the United States (Paddy Chayevsky's script "The Hospital") and in Great Britain (David Mercer's *Britannia Hospital*), and, in one of the greatest film satires, nuclear war (Stanley Kubrick and Terry Southern's *Dr. Strangelove*).

Satire is a very free writing form, but it does involve the constraints of the scale of the subject and of the attendant idea. The larger the subject, the more likely that the frame of satire will be effective.

The Fable

> *Fable,* a term most used in the sense of a short story devised to convey some useful moral lesson, but often carrying with it associations of the marvelous or the mythical, and frequently employing animals as characters. Famous examples include Jonathan Swift's *Gulliver's Travels* and George Orwell's *Animal Farm.*[1]

If your idea is best presented with the elements of moral lessons, the mythical, and animal characters, the fable can transport your idea from the realistic to the fantastic. Although the fable may pose particular filmmaking challenges, it can be done. Jean-Jacques Annaud's *The Bear* is a recent example.

Fables require a powerful moral at their center; without it they can seem preachy. If you are going to use the fable to frame your story, consider whether the idea can carry its moral freight. Keeping this requisite in mind may help you freshen up the other narrative properties so that you avoid the pitfalls. If you can avoid them, you may well have a charming and fresh story.

The Morality Tale

The *morality tale* is an allegorical story whose intention, like that of the fable, is to take a position on an issue. The goal of the morality tale is to offer a life lesson to those who would veer in another direction. The key difference between the morality tale and the fable is the use of human beings rather than animals in the story.

If your idea lends itself to allegory and seems to serve as a life lesson for a particular group—adolescents, young women, elderly men—the morality tale could be a very useful device.

As a form, the morality tale seems fresher, more creative, than a more realistic approach. The danger, however, is that your audience may not be receptive to the treatment if it is too simple and is interpreted as being aimed at young children rather than adults. This is the most subtle problem associated with using the morality tale as a framing device.

The morality tale offers the widest possibilities for stories. Your story can be as simple as the tale of a property-tax collector and a property owner, or a script about the origins of war, such as Norman McLaren's great short film *Neighbours*. There are numerous collections of such tales that can illustrate the form for you. Reading such tales will help you appreciate the shape of this particular form.[2] Elizabethan drama, such as the plays *Macbeth* and *Julius Caesar*, is also a good source for morality tales.

The Journey

The *journey* has a broader shape than the morality tale or the fable, but because it is so often used, we include it as a shaping option.

> The journey is the oldest, truest, most inescapable shape for a story. From the nursery story to biblical narrative to contemporary novel, someone is always setting out from home.[3]

Whether the idea revolves around life as a journey, or a specific journey, the form offers a wide range of opportunities. Also, as a form it is more open ended regarding interpretation than the morality tale, fable, or satire. If you are not entirely sure how you feel about a subject, the journey is a safer form to undertake.

The Event

The *event* is another general shaping form, but it is less open ended than the journey. Using this shape emphasizes a particular happening. It also has implications, particularly for the character: either the character will achieve greatly or fail greatly in the course of the event.

One of the benefits of using the event as a shaping device is that it concentrates the drama of the story, creating a useful intensity and a natural rise to the story. Once you determine how you want the audience to feel after the event, you will have a strong sense about whether the event is the best shaping device for your idea.

VOICE

Once you decide upon the shape that will frame your story, you need to bring to bear the operating principles that will help us move through your story. How we feel about the events of a story and a character is colored by the voice of the writer. If no *voice* is present, the script seems shapeless. The first operating principle to decide on is voice, your attitude toward the idea. How do you want us to feel at the end of your story?

In order to articulate a tone, you need to make a number of choices. How close do you want us to get to the events of your story? If you want to get us deeply involved, choose events that place the character in intense situations, close to the dramatic core of the story. If, on the other hand, you want us to have a more distant relationship with the events, position the character farther from the dramatic core. In fact, if you want to create a sense of detachment, you should employ irony, to distance us from the story. That distance will allow us to reflect upon the character and what is happening to the character. This sense of detachment or irony is particularly useful in the morality tale, in the mockumentary, and in the satire. An ironic tone will give you a more deeply intense approach. Is it useful to you to interpose yourself so definitely into the story?

TONE

The second operating principle, *tone*, is an offshoot of voice. An ironic tone is most related to voice. Irony gives guidance about how we should feel about plot and people. If you are telling a love story from a cynical point of view, your tone will be cynical. On the other hand, if your goal is to describe a positive relationship, a romantic tone may be more appropriate.

The writer creates tone by the type of observation incorporated into the story. If romance is your goal, the beauty of the day can be as useful as the beauty of the date.

Beyond the issue of visual detail, a second element of the tone is the relationship of your main character to the screen story.[4] Is the character in the middle of the story, or positioned as more of an observer? Every decision you make about dialogue, visual detail, and narrative structure will support a particular choice of tone.

CONFLICT AND POLARITIES

The central role of conflict in the development of your story cannot be overemphasized. Throughout your story, the struggle of character against character, character against setting, character against community, and character against society mines the dramatic possibilities. You should maximize those dramatic possibilities in order to tell your story.

This may seem synthetic, mechanical, and forced, but it must be that way. Unlike real life, dramatic life relies on coincidence, intensification, and artifice in order to fulfill the dramatic intentions of the writer. Real life too has its conflicts, but they are not quite as accelerated as dramatic life. A writer must use conflict to advantage in the story.

You should make the most of all the opportunities in terms of conflict the frame you've chosen yields. You should also highlight the opportunities that voice and tone choices offer, as well. Clearly, a more distant voice neutralizes some of the opportunities for conflict. Nevertheless, you should make the most of those that remain.

Use polarities to facilitate conflict. Conflict is amplified by polarities of character, behavior, goals, and situations. It is crucial for you to use as many polarities as possible; they will make your job as a writer easier. Here are some illustrations of useful polarities.

A *physical* polarity is readily apparent in the blind detective. How is he going to discover the solution to the crime if he can't see? A detective investigates a crime. How can he investigate (see) and solve the crime (interpret) if he is blind? Here the opposites pose more conflicts within the character.

A *behavioral* polarity would be represented by the sadistic minister in Ingmar Bergman's autobiographical screenplay *The Best of Intentions*. The minister is expected to be loving and filled with charitable feeling; instead, he is demanding and cruel when it comes to his own family. We expect a minister who is father to his congregation to be a great father to his family, the ideal. But this minister is so needy that he becomes the opposite of the ideal father.

Other behavioral polarities would include the ignorant professor, the licentious pediatrician, and the meek athlete.

If you add other characters who are opposites to the characters described (for example, the fiercely competitive coach of the meek athlete, the saintly son of the sadistic minister, the brilliant student of the ignorant professor), you create polarities with dramatic possibilities.

This same technique applies to setting as well. Maximizing polarities increases your storytelling options.

CHARACTER

Decisions about character are key in the writing of your screenplay. Not only do we enter the story through the character, we also translate the events of the story through the eyes of the main character.

Consequently, how to position your character in the story is the first decision to be made. The second task is to explore who the character is and how the character can help amplify your idea. The romantic nature of the main character in Robert Enrico's *Incident at Owl Creek* makes his fate all the more tragic. If he were actually a Confederate spy, the story would not have the same resonance. Indeed, if he were a spy, the metaphorical level of the film regarding the tragedy of war would be lost. If he were a spy, the story would be a tale of retribution rather than a humanistic condemnation of war.

The third task is to examine the relationship of the main character to the antagonist. The more powerful this relationship of oppositional characters, the greater the dramatic impact of your story.

Finally, you should examine how the issue of character relates to the question of allegory. Does the character have the capacity to be considered "everyman" or "everywoman"? If the character has this more general quality as well as the other characteristics you have given him, the story is elevated to an allegorical level.

THE DRAMATIC CORE OF THE STORY

You are gripped by your idea, you have found a frame for the story, and you've developed conflict, polarities, and character in the film script. What is the dramatic heart of your story? Until you can answer this question, you won't be able to determine the proportions of scenes to one another. Where should the emphasis be placed? The answer to this question will determine the shape of your story.

In *Incident at Owl Creek*, the core of the story is that the condemned man, although he dreams of freedom and his family, will be executed for the crime of being found near the railroad tracks. His crime, and the punishment for that crime, should inform and shape the whole story. It is the dramatic core of the story,

The dramatic core in Norman McLaren's *Neighbours* is that belligerence, no matter how trivial, is all but impossible to stop once it has begun. There is an escalation to territoriality that goes from possessiveness to competitiveness, to active rivalry, to hostility, and on to murder. Nothing can stop the disagreement until it reaches its logical conclusion: the reciprocal murders of the two neighbors.

There is a drive to the core idea that influences the writing of all scenes. Its energy source is a magnet for the character and his actions. In a sense, the core idea is the engine of the script.

To illustrate the development of the dramatic core, we turn to a treatment by one of our students at New York University, Adisa Lasana Septuri, entitled "The View from Here."[5]

> We are in the Bedford-Stuyvesant section of Brooklyn, the home of Iron Mike Tyson. A community filled with laughter, pain, and hope. MONTAGE OF NEIGHBORHOOD—young men on the basketball court, girls playing hop-scotch, old men sitting on milk cartons, etc. A thirteen-year-old boy named Derrick is leaving his house carrying a football. He pauses a moment to secure his leg brace, and then hurries off. He bumps into a neighbor; they greet, but Derrick is in too much of a hurry to stay long.
>
> Derrick runs over to a group of kids. They are selecting teammates for a game of touch football. Everyone is picked except Derrick—being left out and unable to play, Derrick sits on his porch watching the game from the sidelines.
>
> Unexpectedly, one of the kids twists his ankle, and Derrick gets his golden opportunity to play—although now the kids won't throw the ball to him. After two unsuccessful plays,

Derrick's team decides to throw him the LONG BOMB. As the quarterback releases the football, it goes high in the sky. Derrick runs the length of the block while the football is going higher and higher. As Derrick crosses the street, a car almost runs him over.

The driver comes to a halt just long enough to look up and see the football flying overhead. Next we see Derrick catching a subway train to Manhattan. When he comes out of the subway exit, he looks up and sees the football soaring way up high. We then see Derrick knock a woman down at a bus stop.

We cut back to Derrick in the neighborhood. The football is coming down, and Derrick dives for it. The football just glides off the tips of his fingers, and rolls to the curb. Derrick's face shows grim disappointment. As the kids all gather around him, the air becomes very tense. After two long seconds the kids laugh, encouraging Derrick to do the same.

FADE TO BLACK

The dramatic core idea of *The View from Here* is that a thirteen-year-old boy wants to belong so much that he can run all over the city trying to catch a football finally thrown to him. His desire to belong is so great that the fantasy that a football could be thrown so far seems suddenly believable. Consequently, this football game is not just a football game. His efforts surpass what is realistic. His desire to belong is so great that we accept a reconfiguration of the meaning of "the long bomb."

PLOT POINTS

It's a good idea to write down a list of plot events that might help your story. At this stage you should be as generous as possible in terms of plot. You will not necessarily keep all these events in your story, but the list will help you look for a logic in the plot to surround the dramatic heart of your story. The list will also help you begin to think about proportion between events. Is one event more important to the plot than is another?

Preference should be given to those events that introduce surprise into the plot. Consideration should also be given to those events that reveal character.

ORGANIZING TO TELL YOUR STORY

In organizing events around a core, it is critical to include a rise in action in your story. This may mean the organization within the natural dimensions of the form. For the journey, for example, this may mean that the journey has a beginning, a middle, and a destination.

The rise in action may also be organized in terms of the character and his or her goal. In this case, the story begins with the articulation of the goal, and it ends when the character either achieves his or her goal or fails to achieve it.

The Beginning

Where and how you begin your story will set the tone for the script. It will also be the invitation to the audience to engage with your story. The more compelling the opening, the more likely it is that we will be engaged quickly with your story. This is all the more true with a short script. The opening should maximize the dramatic possibilities of the story.

Middle

The journey has begun, the event is under way. In the middle of your story, you must concentrate on the mechanics of the struggle, the confusion, the desire, so that we understand how difficult the undertaking is for the main character.

What is notable about the middle of the story is that the character's goal seems more difficult to achieve than it did at the beginning of the story. The journey is now more complicated; the event is not what it seemed. There may now be doubt that the character can achieve his or her goal.

End

The concluding section of the screen story should answer the question, did the character achieve his or her goal? Was it as he or she expected? There also should be a sense that the character has in some way changed or gained understanding because of having undertaken the journey or having experienced the event. What has brought him or her to that understanding is of greater dramatic intensity than the struggle of the middle or the articulation of the goal in the beginning.

Climax

One key event takes the character to the summit, and that event is the climax of the story. The event will involve the antagonist and the resolution of the main character's struggle with the antagonist.

THE IMPORTANCE OF SEEKING CREATIVE SOLUTIONS

It is very easy for writers to rely on mechanical solutions to narrative problems. Transforming an idea into a script means attending to dramatic principles and forms; however, too often the writer unwittingly falls into the trap of taking the path of least resistance: the mechanically correct rather than the creatively desirable dramatic solution.

In essence, avoiding mechanical solutions means keeping your awareness of, excitement about, and commitment to the original idea in the forefront. Only by finding energetic and interesting solutions to problems encountered in translating your idea into a short film will you end with a story as exciting and as interesting as your original idea.

THE ROLE OF ENERGY

Your dramatic story needs a level of energy in the script that keeps the viewer primed and receptive to the creative solutions you develop. Energy should come from every source—the frame of your story, the nature of your character, the character's goal, the barriers to that goal.

If you have done your job well, you will not have to write dialogue at the level of a scream in order to simulate energy in the screenplay. The development of polarities and the interjection of an element of surprise will provide the story with energy.

THE ROLE OF INSIGHT

Surprise and energy lead to insight. When you and I discover something about a person, a place, a time, something we never knew or had forgotten, we experience an insight. Just as your main character should experience insight about him or herself through experiences in the script, so too should the audience members gain insight about themselves.

All of us want to learn all the time. It's the great payoff from reading or viewing stories. When they are very good, they teach us, as all positive and negative experiences should.

Insights into people, places, and times give us clues to our own lives—what we want and what we don't want from our lives. Insights are the shared moments between writer and viewer, the point at which we are closest. In script writing, they are the most powerful moments in the act of telling a dramatic story.

EXERCISE 18

Identify two ideas for short films that you will work with in this exercise. One idea should be autobiographical. It should be a painful incident from the past. One approach to articulating this idea is to write a letter to a real person who was not involved in the matter.

A second idea should be drawn from a newspaper, also describing an incident that captures your interest. Use the incident to write a letter to a person who was involved in the incident. Write the letter as if the incident happened to you.

Using these two ideas, choose a frame or genre for each story. Once you have decided upon a genre, answer the following questions or complete the tasks below:

1. Do you want an intense or distancing treatment of this story?
2. Name five strategies to intensify your story.
3. Name five strategies to distance us from your story.
4. Identify five potential conflicts in each of your stories.
5. Identify five polarities that you will use in each story,
6. What is the most important idea in your story?
7. How does this idea relate to each of the conflicts in your story?
8. List ten events or plot points in your story.
9. Organize those events along a rising action.
10. Which event best opens your story?
11. Which event best closes your story?
12. What is the climax of your story?
13. Add three surprises suitable to your story.

NOTES

1. Margaret Drabble, ed., *The Oxford Companion to English Literature*, 5th ed. (New York: Oxford University Press, 1985), 335.
2. Two collections of such tales are Yaffa Eliach's *Hasidic Tales of the Holocaust* (New York: Random House, 1988) and Bernard Gotfryde's *Anton the Dove Fancier and Other Tales of the Holocaust* (New York: Washington Square Press, 1990).
3. Jerome Stern, *Making Shapely Fiction* (New York: Dell, 1991).
4. For an elaborate treatment of this relationship, see K. Dancyger and J. Rush, *Alternative Scriptwriting* (Boston: Focal Press, 1991), 154.
5. Adisa Lasana Septuri, "The View from Here," Graduate Department of Film and Television, New York University, New York, 1990.

10

CHARACTERIZATION STRATEGIES

Who is your story about? Why have you chosen this person? The answers to these key questions will go far toward helping you write your short script.

The first impulse of writers of short films is not to spend much time on the characters. The thinking is that because you have less time, you therefore need less characterization. This is totally wrong. In fact, your short film relies principally on character. Unlike in the long film, there is little time to deal with the complexity of relationships, but the viewers must feel that your main character has a complexity appropriate to the type of story you choose to tell. For example, in *Incident at Owl Creek*, it is true that we don't have a profound understanding of all the dimensions of the principal character, but we fully understand his desire to live rather than to die. Similarly, we understand the two men in *Two Men and a Wardrobe* to be naive in a cynical world—but at least they believe in something! In both cases we understand and empathize with the characters in the context of their goals. Short films, therefore, do not tend to develop complex relationships between characters, but they do rely on complex characters.

Another feature of characterization in the short film is the speed with which the main character must be established. Again, time constraints mean that the writing has to exercise considerable economy in characterization. Here the suggestions of E. M. Forster in his *Aspects of the Novel* are relevant. Forster speaks of *flat* characters and *rounded* characters. Flat characters, he says, in their purest form are constructed around a single idea or quality; one advantage of flat characters is that they are easily recognized whenever they appear. Rounded characters, however, are more complex and, unlike the flat ones, are capable of surprising us. A rounded character has the incalculability of life about him or her and is a more unpredictable character.[1]

Flat characters, because they are readily recognizable, are often the starting point for the writer. Two naive men, one Southern gentleman, a young urban boy—these are all at one level stereotypes. Again, the advantage is that they are readily identifiable. It is for the writer to shift them slightly so as, while not losing the benefit of recognition by the audience, to gain an edge of surprise by having the character ever so slightly rounded. A third aspect of character development draws on the Aristotelian position that character is habitual behavior. To put it another way, we are what we do.[2] The characters in screenplays are also defined by their actions.

Working with Konstantin Stanislavsky's ideas, we begin to add a dynamism to those actions. Stanislavsky suggests that the inner life of the character is concealed by the outer circumstances of his or her life.[3] If Aristotle suggests that action defines character, Stanislavsky suggests that the energy of character is often a by-product of the tension between what the character *wants* to do and what he feels he *should* do in a given situation. Elia Kazan, the great director of theater and film, used this dynamic tension and suggested how the character could externalize these complex feelings. As a director, he looks to turn psychology into behavior.[4] This means transforming what a character is thinking and feeling into physical action. If Aristotle emphasizes behavior as character, and Stanislavsky links that behavior to an inner life (that may be at odds with external circumstances), Kazan points out the dominance of inner life as the more complex—or for character, more *true*—source of character. The relationship between inner feeling and outer action is very useful for the writer, because it is those outer actions that define character.

POSITIONING THE CHARACTER

In most forms of storytelling, there are a variety of options available to the storyteller as to the position of the main character in the story. A *third-person* position makes the character an observer; a *second-person* position places the character in the role of guide through the story; finally, the *first-person* position places the character in the middle of the narrative; the story is happening *to* the character.

In prose, poetry, the short story, long pieces of fiction, and plays, all of these choices can work and not be detrimental to our experience of the story. In film, however, the story works best when the first-person approach is taken, so that the character is positioned in the middle of the story.

To illustrate, let's explore what happens when the character is presented in the third person. In this type of story, the plot evolves, and the character watches it evolve. The character does not suffer because of the plot. The character may alter his or her views because of what he or she sees happen, but the character does not have a great deal at stake. The question then is, what is the influence on us when we see the story as observers, watching the story just as the main character watches the story?

Watching the story results in a diminution of dramatic opportunity. What conflict can the main character have, beyond a difference of opinion? The main character as voyeur does not have his or her goal directly challenged. Characters in the third person may modify their goals because of what they see, but there is no direct challenge in the narrative to their goals, because they do not come into contact with the other characters in the story. The result is that conflict, if it does exist between the main character and other forces or characters in the story, remains cerebral rather than emotional, and the dramatic tension in the story diminishes.

Why other forms of storytelling can succeed using a main character positioned in the third person has to do with the possibility in the other forms of having more than one *voice*. It is not unusual in a play or a poem to be aware of the author's voice as well as the character's voice. In film, the author's voice must be subsumed under the voice of the main character. The reason for this is that in a play, a suspension of disbelief is necessary in order to accept the play as an experience. This is also the case in a poem, although in a poem the reader has far more control over the experience than he does when attending a play. A poem is privately read; it can be discarded at any point or picked up at any point. Once a performed play begins, although viewers can choose not to stay, if they do stay the actors and director hold greater control over the experience than the viewer does. Suspension of disbelief and control influence the readers and the viewers to accept the form and its characteristics.

In film, on the other hand, the story looks real. Far less suspension of disbelief is necessary, and the viewer has no control over the place or nature of the story. Consequently, the invitation to the viewer is to engage directly with the story. The main character offers us the most direct access to the story, and so the viewer enters the story through the main character. Multiple voices confuse us and impede identification with the main character. First-person identification is the most powerful. The third person, a form not as involving as first person, is used in film satire.

We may be aware as viewers of short film of the voice of the author, but the voice is generally secondary to our relationship with the main character. Authors, filmmakers, and writers whose views are not subsumed under the main character's are accused of being "stylists" or, worse, pretentious filmmakers. Both labels imply a failure to engage the viewer in the film narrative. The route to that engagement is through the main character.

What happens if the writer attempts a second-person position, the position of character as interpreter? There are film stories in which the main character shares first and second-person point of view. In John Osborne's screenplay of *Tom Jones*, the main character is generally a conventional first-person main character but occasionally a second-person main character: at those moments, he turns directly to the screen and addresses the audience.

The same technique of using the main character to narrate is found in Stanley Kubrick's *A Clockwork Orange*. Whether it is a direct onscreen second-person appeal to the audience or the use of the main character as an offscreen narrator, the result is to alter our relationship with the main character, from one of involvement to one where we step out of the relationship and reflect upon it. This distancing device serves to generate empathy for Alex in *A Clockwork Orange*.[5] In *Tom Jones*, however, the technique does nothing but draw attention to itself. In this sense, the Brechtian device of alienating us from the character in order to reflect upon the subtextual political or social commentary does not work. It is a style that is counterproductive to the dramatic elements of the story, much as the third-person position is.

The second-person position, then, is a risk for the writer. The danger is that the writer can fracture our relationship with the story. The gain can be that the writer succeeds in commenting upon the character, his or her behavior, and his or her view of society.

The best approach to the main character is in the first-person position, where the character is in the middle of the story. Events happen to the character. Barriers exist in the story that challenge the character's goals. In this classical situation, the position of the character best serves the narrative purpose of the film script, and the writer can take advantage of the mechanics of conflict, polarities, and a rising action in order to engage the viewer most effectively in the screen story.

The Main Character and Secondary Characters

The main character's positioning in the story is only one issue of positioning you will have to consider. The second concern has to do with the positioning of the secondary characters in relation to the main character. The reason that this is crucial is that only through interaction with the other characters does the main character move through the plot. The rungs of the dramatic ladder are, in a sense, built with the secondary characters. The issue for the writer, then, is how to deploy the secondary characters for maximum impact in the story.

Given the issue of scale in the short film, writers employ fewer secondary characters than in the long film. The amount of time devoted to developing the secondary characters is also far less. Although this may mean disproportionate reliance on stereotypes for the secondary characters, a more productive approach is to relate the secondary characters to their functions in the plot of the film. They have specific purposes in the plot, so complex characterization is far less important in their case.

In this sense, the secondary characters may be considered catalysts for the plot. Generally, there are two types of secondary characters: those who propel the main character toward his or her goal and those who stand as barriers to the achievement of that goal. In *Incident at Owl Creek*, the Union soldiers are clearly barriers to the main character's achieving his goal. His wife is also a secondary character, but one who helps move the main character toward his goal.

The Main Character and the Antagonist

One particular secondary character, the antagonist, acts as the greatest barrier to the main character. In *Incident at Owl Creek*, this is the Union officer in charge at the execution.

It is the complexity and dynamics of the relationship between the antagonist and the protagonist that is the dramatic core of the film narrative. The more powerful that relationship, the more powerful the screen story.

This relationship is important enough to merit further discussion here. In the longer film, the relationship of the main character to the antagonist is used to create a heroic dimension in the main character. The greater the adversary, the greater the hero. However, heroic action is less credible in the short film, because of its scale. Consequently, the antagonist has to fulfill other narrative goals. The antagonist is the principle barrier to the main character as presented in the plot. The characterization of the antagonist, however, is not used to amplify the character of the protagonist. The relationship is no less important than it is in the long film, but by necessity it is different.

What is the narrative goal of the antagonist? The antagonist must provide a level of opposition to the main character that makes the main character's goal difficult. To illustrate, let's take a look at the great student film by George Lucas, *THX 1138*. The main character in this futuristic film is a human being who is trying to escape his life as a drone in an underground world controlled by technology. In the main character's particular journey there is no one character who fulfills the role of antagonist. Rather there is a plethora of control devices, computer driven and machine operated. In this world, computers, as an expression of technology, are the enemies of human beings. As a group, they function as the antagonist of *THX 1138*. They are the masters from whom the main character is trying to escape.

In the plot of the film, the difficulty of mastering the computers, because of the scope of technology they can call upon, makes it seem almost impossible for the main character to escape. They oppose all forms of humanness. The antagonists require total submission by the main character; the protagonist requires freedom from the tyranny of the machines. Here the classic science fiction struggle between humanity and technology works, because the protagonist-antagonist relationship is at the very core of the dramatic idea. Short films work best when the protagonist-antagonist relationship drives the plot of the screen story

CHARACTERIZATION

The full range of physical and behavioral characteristics should be employed to develop your story. The physical looks of character can help your story. Height, weight, age, gender, together with cultural and professional characteristics, flesh out the look of a character. The more specific you can be about the character, the more likely those qualities can be helpful in your story.

If your story concerns peer relationships, the emphasis on appearance becomes very important. Recall the young African-American boy in Adisa Lasana Septuri's *The View from Here*, described in the last chapter. The fact that the boy has a limp and that the other boys are playing football presents a situation where the main character has a physical impediment to his being accepted by his peer group.

We can imagine other stories where the physical characteristics of the main character are central to the story. For example, let's imagine a story of a first-time director who gets his chance when his mentor is fired. This story is vitalized by the youth of the main character and his relationship with the older mentor. Another story of powerful forces in place to oppose the main character might be one of the (physically) shortsighted bureaucrat who begins to have visions of a new way of doing business. Here sight and poor sight are key physical elements.

Behavioral characteristics can be as important as physical ones. In *Silence of the Lambs*, Hannibal Lechter (played by Anthony Hopkins) is a brilliant, but insane, psychiatrist who is a great danger to his patients. The behavioral quality of madness in a man who society especially expects to be sane is an excellent example of how behavioral characteristics can be used in a dramatically dynamic manner.

Behavior needn't be as extreme as that of Hannibal Lechter. It can be less obvious; here Psychology 240 becomes useful. In a recent classroom discussion, students voiced considerable dissatisfaction about a character in Joe Eszterhas's *Music Box*. The problem was that the character was a good father and grandfather and seemingly a good citizen of his adopted country. He was also tremendously fit for a senior citizen. The flaw was that he had been a Nazi collaborator in Hungary and had killed ruthlessly. The students were dissatisfied that the character in the screen story did not own up and confess his past to his own daughter, the protagonist of the story, who defends him legally and emotionally until the evidence becomes irrefutable.

How could the character lie so deftly even to his own daughter? The answer is that the behavior he exhibits is that of a sociopath. He believes in all sincerity what he says—but in the next breath he can be caught up in a lie, which he will deny with indignation. What the students were confronted with in this character was a behavioral characteristic that was right at the character's dramatic core. Lying was at the core of this character's behavior. Without it, the plot and the main character's dilemma would have been far less interesting.

Behavioral characteristics run the full gamut of human behavior. They require that writers be sufficiently observant to use these characteristics for effect.

In both physical and behavioral characterizations, writers tend to use extremes. Extremes are not only more useful dramatically, they are also more memorable for the audience. We are gripped by extremes for an obvious reason: they are more sensational than middle-range qualities. Film stories are extremely well suited to the sensational.

Singular Qualities of Character

The behavioral and physical qualities of characters are important dimensions. However, they do not necessarily link character to goal. Here a sense of purpose is necessary. It is critical that writers link the character to a goal powerfully, in order to animate the plot.

Different writers will speak of *intentional* characters or *energized* characters. It doesn't matter which term you use. What is important is that there be a palpable internal quality that pushes your character in a particular direction. This drive is as important to your story as the dominant behavioral or physical qualities you have given your character. The drive is the fuel for the plot. Without it your character is passive, acted upon rather than reacted to. A passive character can work in a short film, but by choosing a reactive character you flatten the conflict and position your character as much as an observer as a participant. The result can be counterproductive in dramatic terms. The active, obsessed main character is the most useful in the narrative. Once the plot begins, there is a natural tension between plot and character that will carry the audience more easily through the story.

Drawing Out the Character

Writers may use several other devices to make a character more vivid for an audience. The quality most often used to engage us with the character is humor. Whether the character uses humor to deal with his or her situation or whether the humor arises from the character's response in a situation, humor plays a critical role.

A second device is to allow the character to step out of his or her public self in an opportunity for private revelation. While the audience primarily sees the character in action in the world, the writer can introduce the private dimension, by putting the character into a vulnerable situation. We expect a particular response from the character based on our experience of the character so far. If, instead, we see a vulnerable or more private, less-anticipated response or side to the character, the writer has succeeded in setting up the kind of paradox that yields sympathy for the character. We feel the character has shared a private moment with us, the viewers; the relationship between character and viewer is thereafter transformed.

A third device writers use to draw us into a character is the role played by the antagonist. The more powerful the antagonist's resistance and hence power, the more likely we will empathize with the plight of the main character. All of us have had goals thwarted by people or events. We understand the position of the main character, and we will empathize with him or her.

It is critical that the character try to move toward his or her goal, but it is just as critical that the writer draw us into his or her struggle.

The Importance of Research

It should be clear by this point that the writer not only must have a clear understanding of the craft of writing but also should be a student of human behavior. To understand behavior is to be able to use action purposefully in a story. We are not suggesting that you rush off and do a Ph.D. in psychology. We are, however, suggesting that you become curious about human behavior.

We suggest that you make notes and observations of behavior. When you observe a young child pinching a dog, speculate as to why. You don't have to be right about the reason, but you should formulate a reason that makes sense to you. Why does your doctor write prescriptions with a fountain pen? Why does the grocery clerk double-check the punched-in prices and the bagged groceries? Why does the professor arrive late every week for class? Why does the surgeon doze off as soon as he sits down at lunch?

The questions are endless, and only by observing, asking, and understanding will you begin to be able to employ human behavior characteristics in a dramatic way. The key here is research. It doesn't matter if the script you are working on is a work of fiction. The characters in your story have to attain a certain credibility, and so your powers of observation will be called upon to make the characters interesting and believable.

Your research can be observational or based on others' observations and conclusions. Whether you depend on the library or the lunch bar as your research center, the key is to use those resources to help your storytelling. If you are open to behavior, your stories will improve markedly.

How much research is enough? Put it this way: when it comes to human behavior, we are all students always. There is never enough information. There are only the deadlines, self-imposed and real, to suggest it's time to make the film.

Achieving Believability

The drive of the character can be interpreted as manic energy, or it can be interpreted as a drive to fill a deep-seated need. In either case, the comprehension of the drive is the first step toward the audience's believing the character and believing *in* the character. Also, by understanding motivation the writer can begin to imagine the physical and behavioral characteristics of the main character.

It is critical for the writer to use a character who has both physical and behavioral qualities that aid the story. If the emphasis is on one element over the other, the characterization may be too flat, and believability will be compromised. If both coexist in balance, the main character is more rounded and more useful.

Just as the dramatic possibilities are optimized when the writer places the character in the middle of the story, believability will be enhanced if the writer places the character appropriately in the scene. Place your character in a situation that will optimize believability.

The character's behavior in the scene should be an indirect expression of his or her character. Characters whose behavior can be expressed as "get me out of this scene" are not only less credible but not very interesting. Taking the opposite strategy, that of describing a character who wishes nothing better than to be there but acts as if he or she doesn't, we have a tension between character and action that is purposeful to the process of characterization. Simply put, the tension between thought and action creates the sense of being caught, possibly trapped. The tension is recognizable as all too human, and implicitly the character seems more credible.

Finally, the specifics of the character's speech in pattern and dialect can enhance believability. We all come from a specific place, belong to a family, and live in a particular time. It's not simply a matter of giving the Scotsman a Scottish accent. The words of his region, the phrases of his profession, the influence of his father, and so on, all will influence his speech. If the writer has been specific about the qualities of speech (here the research is important), we will believe the character.

In this phase of writing, it is helpful for you to develop a full character sketch, with as much specificity as possible. Include details such as birth order, colloquialisms, and turns of phrase specific to the time period. Middle children, for example, tend to be overlooked; they may talk a lot to be noticed. The meaning of what they say is less important than the degree that they talk in order to get attention. You should note gender, age, and profession, paying specific attention to how these elements might influence speech.

Achieving Complexity

Characters may have drive as well as numerous other characteristics that make them believable. They may employ humor to be charming and use language that tells us they are working-class Scots from the far north of the British Isles. But there remain a number of steps in the writing process before we view the character as a complex human being—inscrutable, fascinating, real. In order to achieve complexity, the writer needs a character who is a person as well as a symbol, in a sense a character who is both a type and an archetype. Start with the signature of the character. By signature we mean identifiable *signage*. Some characters have a particular phrase identified with them; others have a marked behavior or response to situations. Whether it is a phrase or a behavior, signage is very useful in marketing your character.

It is also the first step in the creation of a more complex character. The next step is to give your character a repetitive behavior pattern. This may be habitual behavior or opportunities to reinforce verbal or behavioral signage. In either case, you should introduce this early in the story and reinforce it as the story proceeds.

Repetitive behavior, particularly in situations of stress, is understandable and will both identify and humanize your character. Excellent examples of habitual behavior include eating and greeting people in a particular manner, a compulsive need for human contact, such as touching, always mailing letters from the same postbox, and always taking the same route to work. The key element here is that repetitive behavior, particularly with respect to everyday events, suggests the power of the emotions over the power of reason.

Repetitive behavior also suggests an underlying feeling. The contrast between the emotional and the rational conveys the idea that both levels are constant and in conflict. The behavior also implies that the emotions are winning out. The resulting impression is of a character struggling with him or herself, and the repetitive behavior suggests he or she is failing. This process creates the sense that the character is a more complicated person than he or she might seem. The impression is very useful to the writer. It deepens the credibility of the character.

Perhaps the most challenging dimension for the writer is to create a character who is both an individual and an archetype. At what point does the little boy in *The Red Balloon* become every little boy? At what point do the two men who carry the wardrobe in *Two Men and a Wardrobe* become everyman? In both films the repetitive behavior of the characters is excellent habitual signage, but we have to turn to the plots to illustrate how the archetype is achieved. Neither film employs a realistic tone. To put it another way, the antirealistic impulse to fantasy runs freely in the narrative. How else can we explain the devotion of these two men to a wardrobe? Or that the balloon takes on more human characteristics than many of the humans in *The Red Balloon?*

Realism suggests that a balloon can't be human and that slavish devotion to a wardrobe is either extreme anxiety or sheer madness. An antirealistic approach, on the other hand, tolerates the humanized balloon and the devotion to a dresser. When a balloon becomes the stand-in for a human, the discovery of the little boy in each of us is not far behind. Fantasy in the plot is the first prerequisite in creating a character who is both a *type* and an *archetype.*

A second prerequisite for the creation of an archetype is to frame the story in a genre that favors such a use of character. Satire, the fable, and the morality tale all use character in such a way that an archetype is very useful in supporting the core idea.

Finally, the catalytic event that begins the plot can be a tool in creating an archetype, if it is an event with which the audience can readily identify: the delivery of a letter mailed four years earlier from a post office seven blocks away; the arrival of a draft notice; the traffic gridlock that prevents the character from arriving for the job interview; or the long-anticipated date to the semiformal. All of these catalytic events create a situation each of us can identify with.

What is the advantage of creating a character who is both type and archetype? Essentially, there is the layer of complexity arising from the kind of identification the viewers have with the situation of the character. When an archetype is created, the space for symbolism becomes even greater, and consequently the meaning of the film can be more layered than is first apparent.

We turn now to the two extreme forms of complex characters: the *comic* character and the *tragic* character.

The Comic Character

The comic character and the tragic character are essentially negative versions of one another. The comic character is, however, more flexible, in that the writer can employ irony through the character. The comic character will also allow you a range of feeling much broader than the tragic character will allow. For example, you can present the comic character as a clown who reflects on his or her behavior, or as a fool who can reflect on the behavior of those around him or her as well. Although you may present both characters as victims, they are far less victims than is the tragic character. There are even narrative circumstances under which the writer can present the fool as a hero, at least in relative terms.

The comic character also has potential for a measure of charisma or appeal, because he or she tends to stand apart from peers, whether as a result of their scorn or by his or her choice.

Finally, the benefits of humor in the narrative accrue more readily when the main character is a comic character. The result may be charm, or it may be biting satire. In either case, the comic character tends to energize the narrative in a variety of positive ways.

The Tragic Character

The tragic character tends to be presented as a victim of the narrative. In fables, morality tales, and satire, as well as other types of stories, it is useful to have a tragic main character.

The challenge for the writer, however, is to show the main character struggling not to be a victim. Without that struggle, the narrative is flattened. It is also useful to *overdevelop* the narrative, so that the odds against the main character seem overwhelming. When the plot proceeds like an avalanche, we will have some empathy for the main character as he faces the inevitable.

Finally, the tragic character needn't be sacrificed in vain. To "redeem" that sacrifice, you need a witness, a secondary character, in the narrative, someone who will proceed with life differently after having observed the main character's struggle—a person, in other words, who absorbs the lesson of the narrative. When the main character is a victim, we subtly shift our allegiance to the witness, thus surviving for another day.

EXERCISE 19

1. List ten objects you own that are meaningful to you, objects you would not want to give up. Characterize these objects briefly—for instance, my grandfather's jackknife, the piece of blue glass I found at Jones Beach, and so on. Choose the five most important. Write any changes in the descriptions you would like.
2. Pick a fairy tale and picture the main character. Describe his or her life. Imagine the possessions that might be meaningful to him or her. List five of these in the same way, as in Number 1. For instance, in "Little Red Riding Hood" you might list the following: the red-hooded cape my mother made for me; my new patent leather shoes; the little clock my grandmother gave to me for my birthday; my jump rope; my collections of stones from the forest.
3. Write a short paragraph in which your character is alone in a room, then perhaps outside, and in some way handles, wears, or uses each of the objects. Remember to use present tense, as in all scriptwriting, and be sure to describe only what you can see and hear. Do not include thoughts or feelings—these must be expressed in the handling of the objects. Remember also that character can be fleshed out by habitual behavior; here is a chance to show us how your protagonist is when alone.
4. After you've finished the last two exercises, read them aloud and try to answer the following questions from the evidence on the page: Does your character enjoy life? Is your character active physically? Is your character reflective? Is your character sensuous? Is your character sad or uneasy? Is your character eager to find new ways of doing things?

The goal here is to understand as much as possible about your character before you begin to write your script.

NOTES

1. E. M. Forster, *Aspects of the Novel* (New York: Harcourt Brace, 1956).
2. Aristotle, *Poetics*, ed. Francis Fergusson, trans. and introduction by S. H. Butcher (New York: Hill and Wang, 1961), 62.

3. Konstantin Stanislavsky, *Creating a Role*, ed. Hermine I. Popper (New York: Routledge, Chapman & Hall, 1961).
4. Elia Kazan, notebook on directing *A Streetcar Named Desire*. See also Elia Kazan, *A Life* (New York: Alfred A. Knopf, 1988).
5. As a thoroughly despicable main character, he needs all the empathy he can get if we are to, in any way, identify with him, whether as a young person, a rebel, or a victim.

11

DIALOGUE STRATEGIES

Like every other dimension of the short film, dialogue has to be exercised with economy and purposefulness. There is no time for lengthy speeches or excessive exposition. Perhaps the most useful strategy with dialogue is to view it as another opportunity to further the emotional drive of your screen story. In this sense, dialogue should be as animated, intentional, and active as the visual dimension of your story. Consider dialogue as much a part of the action of the script as the visualized actions.

The underlying premise here is that language can create a sense of activity and intensity of the kind that one usually associates exclusively with visual action. Dialogue and visuals must be partners in the short script; our goal in this chapter is to show you how to make them partners. Before we do so, however we will begin with the warning: don't use *too much* dialogue. This may seem to contradict the previous assertion, but a few illustrations will clarify and contextualize the caution.

What if a film were made up entirely of dialogue? It could work, but the energy, characterization, maturation, and plotting would all come from the same source: the dialogue. Unless that dialogue were tremendously vital, we in the audience might not engage with the screen story as readily as we would if there were visual variety. We also would tire or tune out, sound and dialogue overload would take place, in part because the viewer needs more time to interpret sound than visuals. The danger here is that the screen story will bore or tire the viewer.

Even in a less extreme case, in which dialogue was not exclusive of other elements but simply excessive, there would still be an imbalance, too much aural stimulation and not enough visual.

The writer needs to find a proper balance between dialogue and visuals in order to provide viewers with the variety they need to interpret what is being said and seen, and to be stimulated by both.

THE PURPOSES OF DIALOGUE

Good dialogue, in the most general sense, gives the speaking characters credibility. Writers know this intuitively; they wince every time they hear bad dialogue. The message registers: I don't believe this character. Without this credibility all else fails, since disbelief in character quickly leads to disbelief in plot and in the other dramatic elements of the script. Consequently, the writer does not want to fail with dialogue.

In addition, dialogue can characterize. When characters register their responses to situations, they characterize themselves as bigots or big shots, as highly anxious or supremely confident. Speech is only one path to an understanding of character, but it provides the writer with a complement to visualized behavior. It is through the mix of visual behavior and verbal behavior that we gain an understanding of character.

Dialogue also advances plot. Although, as mentioned earlier, dialogue should not entirely replace visual action but aid and complement it, effectively placed dialogue often lessens the need for visual action. For example, imagine a scene in which we stand before an awesome mountain, watching people climb. We can't see the peak; it is hidden in the mist and clouds. The visual option is to watch them climb. To show how daunting the task is, we can emphasize the difficulty of the climb visually. After sufficient screen time, we will understand the plot: they are trying to go all the way to the summit.

An alternative approach using visuals and dialogue would have the two climbers engage in the following dialogue at the foot of the mountain:

```
                    CHARACTER 1
     We have about six hours of light.

                    CHARACTER 2
     You have your boots, I have my Bible.

                    CHARACTER 1
     Let's go. Heaven is waiting.

  They look up at the mist, and then begin to climb.
```

The purpose of the dialogue is to tell us they want to climb all the way to a peak neither can see. The reference to heaven alludes to the goal but does not state it directly—although to do so is also an option.

Another goal of dialogue is to modulate the tension in a scene. This is usually done with humor. Since this is a very important function, we will deal with it later in the chapter, after discussing issues of character and plot in relation to dialogue.

DIALOGUE AND CHARACTER

It is in the specific details of dialogue that the writer develops credibility. Everyone is a member of a family, a community, a country. Speech patterns and phrases are often associated with particular communities. It's not simply a matter of dialect; it's also the slang and the level of formality or informality that differs from one community to the next. The writer who has done research will know that. The members of the audience who know people who "speak that way" will recognize those particulars of speech.

Age and gender will also influence a character's choice of words. And what about profession? A lawyer does not have the same speech pattern as a baseball player; a young lawyer from Regina, Saskatchewan, will not share the same phraseology with an older lawyer from Manhattan; again, an African-American female lawyer from Santa Rosa will speak differently from the lawyer from Manhattan.

So every factor—age, gender, race, profession, regional association—will alter speech. If the goal is credibility of character, what that character says will help us believe in who the character is and where the story might be located.

The emotional makeup of a character is also crucial for credibility; dialogue plays a role in this, because it is here that character and plot meet. The reason is not always apparent, so let's be explicit: it is the emotional reasons that motivate a character toward a goal, a place, a person and that make the journey dramatic. "I want," "I need," "I must" are the modus operandi of every dramatic form, including the short film. So we turn now to that meeting point of dialogue, character, and emotion—the plot.

DIALOGUE AND PLOT

Dialogue marries character and plot, by demonstrating the emotional motivation of the characters, whether directly or indirectly. The writer articulates the characters' feelings through the particular goal in a scene.

Once the writer determines that the scene's purpose is to suggest that the characters want to climb to the peak of a mountain, for example, or that they will wait endlessly for the Long Island commuter train, the central issue for the dialogue becomes clear: how does the character who has a goal feel about the barriers to attaining that goal? That feeling is what should fuel the dialogue.

The writer's choice of words will make it easier to relate emotion to plot. Direct, active words convey more feeling than indirect, passive words. Too many words can be a barrier as well. The conditional tense distances the audience, as does the past tense. That is not to say that a reminiscence about the past can't be emotional; rather, the writer should try to keep the action in the present and in development, and that means active, present-tense dialogue. The more immediate the dialogue is, the more emotional and the more surprising the story will be.

Remember, when dialogue intended to develop plot is separated from character, emotion is lost, and the dialogue becomes no more than descriptive. For dialogue to be vital to the plot, it must be related to the desires of the character as he or she moves through the plot. Dialogue is only dynamic when it forwards the plot.

DIALOGUE AS TRANSITION

Dialogue can be very useful in providing transitions between scenes. One of the problems the writer faces is the task of "collapsing" a story that may take place over a long time and in a number of geographical locations into a script less than thirty minutes long. Even the story of one day or one moment, as in the case of Enrico's *Incident at Owl Creek,* requires transitions to convince us of the dramatic use of time, and place of the script. Changes of time and place occur in the story "An Occurrence at Owl Creek Bridge," making it seem to take place over a full day, whereas this thirty-minute film refers only to the last five minutes in the life of the main character. The writer has to convince us of the dramatic time, creating a sense of real time by punctuating the end of the action.

Writers can facilitate transitions by simply repeating a phrase. In *Citizen Kane,* the repetition of "Merry Christmas" and "Happy New Year" allows us to leap twenty years into the future. Of course, the time shift can be more modest. Either way the writer can use repetition to alert the viewer that one scene or location is related to the next.

A more direct approach is simply to tell the audience in one scene where we will be in the next. When the two climbers in our imaginary film tell us they want to go to the peak of the mountain, we are prepared for the following scene on the mountainside or at the peak. The dialogue here can be as pleasing as you want it to be. If this climb is but one of a series of climbs, in a series of locations, the dialogue can alert us specifically to the next mountain range or the next phase in this journey. Once alerted, we are prepared for the transition in place or time and will go along.

Because of the dramatic collapse of real time and place in the screen story, dialogue is very important; it prepares the transitions so that we can more readily accept and enter the time and place frames of the screenplay. Without those transitions, we would be lost—or worse, indifferent to the screen story.

DIALOGUE TO INTENSIFY TENSION

Just as dialogue is the expression of the emotions of the character in terms of arching toward a goal, it is also the barometer of that arc as the character moves through a scene. Perhaps the best way to understand this notion is to consider that every scene has an arc from the point where we understand the character's goal to the point where the character either succeeds or fails in achieving that goal. In either case, the scene should be shaped by a growing anticipation of achieving the goal, or of the tension between the character and the barrier to success. As the character tries more forcefully to achieve the goal, the tension should grow. Once we know the fate of the character in terms of the goal, that tension is resolved. Dialogue plays a critical role in the articulation of that growing tension.

As with other dramatic elements, the writer should not rely solely on the dialogue to create that tension. Visual action, interaction between characters, as well as the nature of the setting can and should contribute to the scene. If these elements are well considered, they free the dialogue to be less direct and more effective—expressing feeling in a more oblique way. Direct dialogue would be obviously purposeful, less masked, and consequently less effective. For example, returning to our mountain-climbing scene, we see that the scene already has an overlay of religiosity, in terms of the devotion of one of the characters and of the irreverence of the other. The failing light introduces an element of danger. If we also introduce another factor, a twisted ankle, we develop a physical barrier to the goal. We have then as barriers a personal tension, over religion, between the climbers; a visual danger, the loss of light; and a physical danger, a twisted ankle. There would be an obvious visual explanation for the danger or tension in the scene. This is more effective (and less direct) than their speaking about the danger of the climb, the time, and their health.

As you might imagine, there are any number of other external factors we could introduce to raise the tension in the scene. But working with the factors we have named—personal differences, the loss of daylight, and an injury—we can construct a scene that progresses through a series of stresses, from the least stressful to the most. These factors can be elements in the dialogue throughout the scene, but when we want to increase the tension, we should shift that dialogue to a factor that understandably yields more tension. For example, references to discarding sunglasses might humorously imply concern about the impending nightfall. The irony increases tension.

The most dangerous factor in the climb to the peak is the loss of daylight. If the personal injury were to worsen, they would stop the climbing. The personal differences are always there regardless, but the daylight, whatever they do or say, will be running out as they progress through the scene. Therefore, in order to increase the tension in the scene, the writer can focus the dialogue on the loss of daylight, such as the reference to sunglasses. By shifting the focus between the three factors, the writer can modulate and make more effective the rising tension.

DIALOGUE TO RELIEVE TENSION

Dialogue can also be used equally effectively to relieve tension. The writer must keep in mind the arc of the tension as it builds throughout the scene. In order to reduce tension, the writer can employ humor at strategic points.

Humor should not be as direct as a character suddenly stopping to tell a joke. Although this approach might work, it tends to take the viewer out of the scene. Relief of tension in a scene should keep us in the scene but simply drop the stress level of its characters.

Humor is useful when it surprises and disarms us. As with the other dramatic elements, it can be derived from a visual action. More often, however, it comes out of the reaction of a character to a visual situation. A reference to escalators by a climber who has a physical injury and is attempting to climb a mountain is a surprise, which helps to relieve tension for the audience. Such a reference is an improbable wish, one that can also give voice to the stress the character feels during the climb.

Humor can range from the aggressive to the absurd. Often writers will have one character in a scene say the wrong thing, tell a joke, or voice a funny complaint that relieves the tension. In this sense, character can be the source of humor. Often that character is the most anxious, the character who carries feelings on his or her sleeve.

NARRATION

Narration occurs more frequently in the short film than in the longer dramatic form. The most obvious reason is the best one: there is too little time available to the writer to allow the action to develop on its own. Whether to frame the story or to establish the point of view toward the narrative events, writers of short films often will resort to a narrator.

The narrator may be onscreen, like the grandmother in Lisa Shapiro's *Another Story* (the script is reprinted in the Appendix). Or the narrator may be offscreen, a guide or interpreter for the story. The actual dramatic needs of the story will determine whether the narration will be *interior* or *exterior*.

Interior Narration

Interior narration is a private monologue on the events of the story. Perhaps it's easiest to think of it as a confession by the narrator to the viewer. Writers resort to interior dialogue to foster intimacy, deepen emotion, or offer revelations in the narrative. Some writers believe that a counterpoint of visual and voice strengthens both. In this case, objective visuals are undermined by a subjective narrator. The interior voice whispers an interpretation that clashes with visuals that are not intimate but, instead, formal.

Where an intimate, closer relationship between the character and the audience is the goal, the interior narration can act as window between viewer and screen story.

In order to intensify a sense of inner voice, some writers will resort to a poetic narration. Others will use the language of passion, in preference to the language of science. The dialogue would include words such as "love," "want," and "possess" rather than "respect," "conclude," and "contain." Whatever the approach, the writer chooses language that emphasizes intimacy, feelings, sharing, and insight.

Exterior Narration

An external or distant voice is useful when the writer wants to distance us from, or present an alternate view to, the visual drama. Many approaches can distance the viewer, but most often the writer will borrow from journalism and use an "on-the-air" narrator or offscreen voice. The purpose is not only to distance the viewer but also to lend an air of credibility to the proceedings.

If the drama is presented as reportage rather than fiction, the audience will develop a different relationship with the dramatic material. This is not always a relationship of respect; the journalistic narration can also undermine the credibility of the drama, or supersede it with a new reality. In either case, the exterior narration introduces another voice into the drama. If that voice is purposeful, it can strengthen the dramatic impact of the script.

The specific language of the exterior narration tends to be objective, journalistic, even scientific. The narration is organized to enhance credibility, perhaps a credibility not present in the visuals. Consequently the past tense, conditional verbs, and subjunctive phrases all support the distancing goals of the exterior narration. Too much subjectivity and passion undermines belief; a sense of believability derives from information, usually statistical or scientific.

SILENCE

Now that we have discussed narration, we need to note that the visual and dramatic dimensions of the script may become crowded. It is worth considering the absence of dialogue and narration, particularly where one or both have been used in the script.

When a silence is juxtaposed with a scene filled with sound, that silence, momentary or protracted, can be deafening in its dramatic impact. Just as the counterpoint of visual and sound can heighten the drama, so too can a counterpoint of sound and silence. Let's turn back to our climbers on the mountain. They have personal differences, one of them has a physical injury, and as they climb they are quickly losing light. We spoke of the growing tension conveyed in the dialogue, particularly around the issue of impending darkness. A way of using silence effectively would be to shift to silence at that moment when darkness arrives. Suddenly there is no more dialogue, and the characters' sudden silence screams out their fear. Silences can be as powerful as dialogue and narration.

DIALOGUE AND REALISM

Dialogue as sound is the most immediate device with which the writer creates a tone for the film. The writer can choose to use dialogue to convince viewers that what they are experiencing is real, or to undermine deliberately the film's sense of reality. In either case, dialogue is the most immediate vehicle to achieve these ends, but the writer has only a brief time to capitalize on that first impression.

In order to deepen the impression of realism, the writer must flesh out and capitalize on the dialogue. This means doing in-depth research and making informed decisions as to time, place, age, gender, race, education, physical qualities, and behavioral characteristics. Every factor about character will and should influence what the character says. Each time the character speaks, that sense of realism should be deepened. There is no better way to convince an audience to believe in your characters than through what they say. How realistic and credible your characters are will influence the audience's response to the characters and their story. That's how important dialogue is!

You have to decide what level of realism suits your story, and it is to this issue that we now turn.

THE LEVEL OF REALISM

Many short film genres do not rely on an absolute sense of realism. Perhaps only the mockumentary requires a sense of belief that lasts until the very end of the story. The other genres (the fable, for example) require some realism, but not so much that it crowds out the fantastic, the supernatural, from the screen story.

Dialogue can be useful here. In an animated film where the donkey speaks of going to Harvard and the frog speaks of going to MIT, we see visually how absurd the notion is, but if the dialogue is sincere and intelligent, on one level we will believe the donkey and the frog. Here, where visually it's difficult to see past the animals before us, the writer must use the dialogue to interject a sense of realism and sincerity.

In genres such as the fable and the parable, the balancing between realism and fantasy is the challenge for the writer. Here too the dialogue is critical, to introduce that balance. If the language is too objectified, it will flatten out the fantastic dimension of the parable; if the language is too passionate, subjective, it will also undermine the parable, by seeming to be too much from the viewpoint of the particular character.

CONCLUDING REMARKS

In this chapter, we have suggested a variety of strategies regarding the uses of dialogue in the short film. Dialogue can be a highly charged expression of emotion, or it can be a vehicle for moderation in the story. But when in doubt about the use of dialogue, the writer can always rely less on it. If you set up the visual action and the interplay of characters, the drama will unfold with or without words. Many people are intimidated by writing words; they think of Shakespeare and freeze when it comes to the dialogue.

If that is your concern, simply use less dialogue and, where you use it, keep it simple. It might not help you as much as you would like, but simple dialogue won't hurt you either. Too many scripts are ruined by inappropriate or excessive reliance on dialogue. Our message is that you can always get away with less dialogue. This is an option you might think about; if you want to go for broke, reread this chapter.

PART III

GENRES: FORMING THE STORY

The term *genre* often conjures up images of gangsters, Western heroes, or monsters. In fact, the term is applicable to all stories. Genre is nothing more than the form, the envelope, that encloses the characters and structure of the story. Of course gangster films, Westerns, and horror films are particular genres. But so are war films, biographical films, science fiction films, and a wide variety of comedies.

In this section of the book we are going to look at four *meta-genres*, those genres that transcend the more specific genres and yet include them. For example, every sports film, every gangster film, every screwball comedy has in it a layer of melodrama. Although we will be using long films to contextualize the different genres, we will look only at meta-genres that are suitable to the short film. These meta-genres embrace the particularities of the short film—its relation to the short story and to the photograph, as well as the link of the short film to nonnarrative forms—poetry and abstract art.

Now let's turn to those meta-genres and show how they will be useful to your writing a short film.

12

THE MELODRAMA

Perhaps its best to start this chapter with a bit of fact and fiction about melodrama. First the fiction.

Over the years, the term *melodrama* has increasingly taken on a negative implication. It is associated with soap opera, exclusively with romantic women's stories, and with a dramatic device best characterized as exaggeration (as opposed to realism, or a story that is simply more believable). Although all of the above about melodrama have a hint of truth, each is too narrow an approach to melodrama, and each keeps us away from the usefulness of melodrama as a form.

Turning to the positive, what then do we mean by the term melodrama? A good starting point is to suggest that melodrama at its most basic concerns itself with stories that are essentially realistic. Within that general description, melodrama can be a story about ordinary people in ordinary situations as well as a domestic story about a king (Lear) or a prince (Hamlet). Melodrama can be a relationship story of the privileged (James Cameron's *Titanic*) or of the famous (Michael Frayn's *Copenhagen*). All are melodramas. Melodramas can be presented in the form of a novel (Judith Guest's *Ordinary People*), a play (Arthur Miller's *A View from the Bridge*) or as a film (Joseph Mankiewicz's *All about Eve*). It can be a long film or it can be a short one.

In order to understand the form, we will first look at its characteristics in the long film. So much teaching about writing is based on the long film; we will use it as a baseline and then modify the ways in which it presents itself in the short film. This approach should avoid the confusion that inevitably arises when one assumes that the long and short film are the same, with the sole exception of length.

GENERAL CHARACTERISTICS OF MELODRAMA

Realistic People in Realistic Situations

Melodramas, unlike fables, are stories that may have happened, or that at least in the mind of the audience could have happened. That means that the supernatural and the fabulous are the subjects, or surround, of other genres. In the melodrama the story is about you or me, or our grandparents, or about someone we believe exists or did exist. This recognizability affects every element of the melodrama—its characters, its shape, its tone. Although not all forms of drama are accurate renderings of reality (rather, they are exaggerated forms of reality), melodrama is essentially constrained by this notion of recognizability and consequently believability.

To get more concrete, melodramas on television, such as *ER* or *Chicago Hope*, focus on the lives of doctors and patients. Hospital bureaucracy, societal problems, love affairs, and the struggle for life are the story elements of these successful series. The characters are well defined, differentiated, and above all, very human. Hope, fear, passion, commitment, power, and powerlessness define the characters and their goals. But key to our involvement is that we in the audience know these people; they are you and me.

This quality of the melodrama is recognizable in the most highly acclaimed films of the past few years—*Titanic*, *Shine*, *The English Patient*, and *Slam* are all melodramas. Looking back over famous melodramas, the subject matter echoes these recent successes. Ambition is at the heart of *All about Eve*. Family violence is the core issue of Lee Tamahori's *Once Were Warriors*. The consequences of divorce are the subject of Robert Benton's *Kramer vs Kramer*. Racism is the core of Robert Milligan's *To Kill a Mockingbird*, as it is of Euzhan Palcy's *A Dry White Season*.

The key element all these films share is that they treat the core issue realistically, and the characters who inhabit the story are realistic.

The Dominance of Relationships as a Story Element

There are genres that are dominated by plot—the action-adventure film, the western, the war film. Other genres, such as melodramas, are dominated by character. What this means is that melodramas key in on relationships on a level that is both understandable and appealing to us.

In George Stevens's *A Place in the Sun* (1952), the main character deeply explores two love relationships, one with a working-class coworker, the other with a privileged debutante. These relationships dominate the story. In Peter Yates's *Breaking Away* (1979), the main character explores his relationships with his peers (a group of working-class mates who do not go to college) and a relationship with a privileged college student. In order to pursue this latter relationship, he pretends to be a college student as well. To hide more deeply his true identity from her, he also pretends to be Italian.

In Anthony Minghella's *Truly, Madly, Deeply,* the main character struggles between loyalty to a dead lover and the life urge to form a relationship with a man who is alive and capable of a future. Her struggle is very much between remaining rooted in a tragic past and risking a viable future.

The Nature of the Struggle for the Main Character

Melodramas are marked by a very particular struggle for the main character. Essentially that struggle can be characterized as the struggle of a powerless main character against the power structure. I should add that the definition of powerlessness has to be viewed in a very liberal way. For example, a king may be on the surface very powerful, indeed all-powerful, but if he is as old as King Lear is, he will be faced with a power structure that is young, vibrant, and confident that it is "coming into power." In this sense an aged King Lear is powerless.

More understandable is the young child in a family drama. Relative to his adult parents, the child is powerless. So too is a woman in a culture where male dominance prevails. Consequently, a story like Mike Nichols's *Working Girl* is one of a bright woman trying to make her way in a workplace that is a male power structure. To complicate this story, Nichols places a high-status woman at the head of the company. The main character's working-class roots make class the overlay to the female/male power grid. Consequently the female, working-class main character has two layers of the power structure to contend with.

Whether the main character is dealing with gender, class, race, or age, the key element to the melodrama is that the main character's struggle is always against the power structure.

How Plot Is Used in Melodrama

In genres such as the action-adventure and the situation comedy, the plot enables the main character to achieve his or her goal. In the melodrama, the plot is set *against* the main character and his or her goal.

In *Titanic,* the voyage of the liner and its consequent sinking is the plot that conspires against the main character's struggle to choose love (played by Leonardo DiCaprio) or money (Billy Zane). Her goal is thwarted by the sinking of the ship. Similarly the plot, the death of the working class lover, and Charles Eastman's subsequent trial for murder in *A Place in the Sun* thwarts his goal to have as his love interest the rich debutante (Elizabeth Taylor). A last example is *Breaking Away*. The bicycle race that concludes the film offers the main character a chance to win the race, but in doing so he loses the college girl with whom he was infatuated. To win he has to drop his pretense. No longer a foreign student, no longer a college student, he acknowledges his working-class self. He wins the race (plot) but loses the girl (goal).

The Adaptability of Melodrama

Although melodrama tends to be a character-driven proceeding, whether without plot (*Truly, Madly, Deeply*) or with plot (*A Place in the Sun*), it is not rigidly so. The form can be adapted if the story benefits. Specific examples will illustrate.

George Miller's *Lorenzo's Oil* is a melodrama in which the mother, and to an extent the father, are powerless main characters, who do not accept that their son is afflicted with a fatal illness. Rather than accept his fate they fight the medical establishment (power structure), which views their son as raw material for scientific experiments, experiments that will enhance the doctors' reputations but not save the son. The parents decide to explore science for solutions to halt the disease, and in the end they are successful. *Lorenzo's Oil* uses plot in the way the thriller uses plot—to victimize. By eluding the victimization of the plot (the disease), mother and father are victorious, and they save their son (their goal). In *Lorenzo's Oil*, the adaptation of the structure of the thriller makes this melodrama unusual and powerful.

The same adaptation of plot and the thriller form makes Christopher Morahan's *Paper Mask* an unusual melodrama. The main character's goal is to pretend that he is a doctor. The threat this poses to his patients, his friends, and to himself creates the tension that relentlessly moves us through this story.

Other examples of this particular adaptation include Volker Schlondorff's *The Lost Honor of Katerina Blum* and Reinhard Hauff's *A Knife in the Head*. Other unusual adaptations that involve mixing forms are the western-melodrama (Maggie Greenwald's *The Battle of Little Jo*), the crime story-melodrama (Jules Dassin's *Night and the City*), and the war film–melodrama (Steven Spielberg's *Schindler's List*).

Melodrama Explores Psychologically More Complex Issues than Other Genres

Because the melodrama is essentially character-driven, and because all stories require us to form a relationship with the main character, it is critical that we understand and identify with the issues they face. This means that the issue must be primal, not peripheral. Consequently, it has to be an issue that touches us quickly and deeply; it should be an issue close to each of us.

Family relations are complex, and they are the key to many of the critical issues in melodrama. Acceptance and rejection within the family, particularly between parent and child, is at the heart of many of the great melodramas—Elia Kazan's *East of Eden*, Ingmar Bergman's *Autumn Sonata*, Kazan's *Splendor in the Grass*. The problems of commitment and autonomy are at the core of melodramas like these, which focus on problematic marriages—Irvin Kershner's *Loving*, Paul Mazursky's *Enemies: A Love Story*,

Phil Kauffman's *Henry and June*. An identity crisis is at the heart of Yates's *Breaking Away* and of Steve Kloves's *The Fabulous Baker Boys*. Conformity vs. individuality is the central issue in Milos Forman's *One Flew over the Cuckoo's Nest* and Tony Richardson's *The Loneliness of the Long Distance Runner*. Issues of loss, gender, sexuality, ambition, jealousy, envy, all are prime subject-matter for the melodrama.

What is important here is that these issues not be treated casually. The more deeply they lie in the heart of the story, the more likely we are to deeply engage with the story.

Melodrama Is Adaptable to the Issues of the Day

One of the most notable qualities about melodrama is how the form can be used to embrace the key social, economic, and political issues of the day. When the downturn of coal mining was a central concern of British society, films such as John Ford's *How Green Was My Valley* and Carol Reed's *The Stars Look Down* were produced. Today, sexual abuse and incest, particularly concerning children, is a powerful issue. Films like John Smith's *The Boys of St. Vincent*, Angelica Huston's *Bastard out of Carolina*, Tod Solondz's *Happiness*, and Lee Tamahori's *Once Were Warriors* all attest to the power of this issue in the public consciousness.

Women's issues, children's issues, education, religion, morality, amorality, immorality, the lives of politicians, priests, pundits—if they are questions of the day, they quickly become the material of melodrama.

This impulse is most pronounced in television, both series television and TV movies, but it is also a phenomenon of feature films. One of the reasons melodrama is so gripping for audiences is this very malleability.

Melodrama Is the Fundamental Layer of Many Genres

A biography of T. E. Lawrence or Jake La Motta, or an epic screen treatment of the religious-secular struggle of Thomas More or of the political-personal struggle of Yuri Zhivago—each of these stories has a layer of melodrama. In fact, it is the layer of melodrama that humanizes and dramatizes the story.

To be more specific, the plot of David Lean's *Lawrence of Arabia* is the story of the Arab revolt against its Turkish rulers. Lawrence led the revolt, essentially a sideshow in the larger world war of 1914–18. The progress of that revolt and its outcome is the plot of *Lawrence of Arabia*. The melodrama layer is the story of T. E. Lawrence, bastard of a British nobleman, a man who sees himself as an outsider in British society. This outsider affiliates himself with a group of outsiders, Bedouin tribesmen. He unites them and is united with them, one outsider leading other outsiders against the power structure (the Ottoman Turks and the British, two distinct empires). Of course he wins the battle but loses the war: the Arabs merely change masters, from the Turks to the British, and Lawrence has been their instrument. In a sense the melodrama is the story of Lawrence's search for a new identity. It is a new identity, but sadly it lasts only for a short while. Once the revolt is over, there is no place for Lawrence. He must return to his own again, to be an outsider (and soon die).

This same pattern shapes David Lean's *Dr. Zhivago*. The plot is the Russian Revolution of 1917 and how its success was the ruination of the individual and of the family unit. The melodramatic layer of the film centers around Yuri Zhivago's relationships; the Revolution always undermines the only thing he truly values, love—embodied in an intimate relationship first with his wife, then with Lara. In the end the personal losses and sacrifices are so great that Yuri is literally heartsick. Does he die of a heart attack or of a broken heart? Choose whichever interpretation you wish. The key issue here is that melodrama is the fundamental layer in biographical, sports, war, gangster, and epic films.

MOTIFS

To be more specific about melodrama, it is useful to look at eight motifs that characterize the genre. Those motifs are:[1]

Main character and goal
Antagonist
Catalytic event
Resolution
Dramatic arc
Narrative style
Narrative shape
Tone

In order to illustrate how the motifs operate we will look at three case studies—Antonio Bird's *Priest* (1995), Steve Kloves's *Fabulous Baker Boys* (1989), and Mike Van Diem's *Character* (1994).

Priest

The main character and his goal. The main character is a young priest, new to a poor parish. His goal is to be the spiritual leader of the community. What he does not realize is that in a poor community life is practical, and difficult. There is little room here for spirituality.

The *antagonist*. The young priest is his own antagonist. He struggles with his issues as a man—sexuality and gender. As a gay man he struggles not only with the issue of celibacy but also with anti-gay sentiment.

The catalytic event. The young priest comes to this new community.

The dramatic arc. The dramatic arc in a melodrama is always an interior journey. The young priest learns how to be a better priest by acknowledging that he is also a man.

The resolution. The priest accepts himself, and the community accepts him.

The narrative style. This particular story has both a plot (foreground story) and a character layer (background story). The background story gravitates around the issue of the priest as spiritual leader and of the man as a sexual being. The presence of another "sexual" priest in the same parish is enabling, although that priest is heterosexual. That priest is also socially and politically active in the community. The plot relates to incest shared with the main character in the confessional. What is his responsibility to the young girl and to her family? In the end he acts on behalf of the girl, against her father.

The narrative shape. The factor of time is not inherently critical in the melodrama.

The tone. The tone is realistic, as expected in the melodrama.

To offer a final comment on *Priest*: the priest on first appearance is a powerful figure in the community. By making him a gay priest, the screen writer makes him one of the powerless minority who struggle for power in the society. Making him sexually active presents him as a character in the minority also in the power structure of the Catholic Church.

The Fabulous Baker Boys

The main character and his goal. The main character is the younger brother in a fraternal musical act. His goal is not to grow up but to remain frustrated, irresponsible, and unhappy.

The antagonist. Although one's first impulse is to suggest that the controlling, tight older brother is the antagonist, he is not. The main character is his own antagonist. As so often in melodrama, he is his own worst enemy.

The catalytic event. The musical act is failing, and the older brother decides they need a singer. They find one who, although she is inexperienced, may be too much for either brother to handle.

The dramatic arc. The journey of the main character in this story is the journey from passive unhappiness to a willingness to take a chance on his real goal—to be a jazz musician. His inner journey is from risk aversion to risk taking, from dependence upon his older brother to independence.

The resolution. The main character will take a chance, strike out on his own, and try to develop a career.

The narrative style. The Fabulous Baker Boys is all character; there is no plot to speak of. The two relationships that are explored are the two brothers (a relationship that represents dependence for the main character) and that of the main character and the female singer. She represents independence. Although their relationship ends, we leave the main character in a hopeful, if apprehensive, state.

The narrative shape. Beyond the fact that we join the story at a low point in the brothers' career, time is not an important factor in this story.

The tone. As we expect, the tone in this film is realistic, in line with genre expectations.

A final note: since there is no plot in this film, the energy in the story comes from the complexity of the characters and the vivid dialogue.

Character

The main character and his goal. This story, set in 1920s Rotterdam, Holland, is a coming-of-age story of a young man. His goal is to survive an upbringing of deprivation and suffering.

The antagonist. The antagonist of the story is the biological father, a man who never acknowledges him. When the young man needs his help, he offers it only under very punitive conditions.

The catalytic event. The catalytic event is the rape of a maid (the main character's mother). When she discovers she is pregnant, she leaves the employ of the rapist, the main character's birth father.

The dramatic arc. The journey of this main character is very challenging. Both parents are cold emotionally, and his father is cruel as well. His journey is one of survival. He does survive both parents, but he pays a very high personal price.

The narrative style. The background story is dominated by the main character's relationships with his parents. Fortunately, the plot enables him to overcome the negative qualities of his parents. The plot is about self-improvement and education. Initially he teaches himself English. Later he trains to become a lawyer. Although the path to self-improvement means reliance on his father for money, the main character does manage to become a lawyer. At this point he tells his father that they will never see each other again. He no longer needs him. The father claims to have made the main character the success he is. This idea enrages the main character, but we in the audience have to wonder whether the father's claim has merit.

The narrative shape. Mike Van Diem chooses to frame his story with a murder (the father) and an interrogation of the son. The story is then narrated by the son. The story covers the preceding thirty years.

The tone. The tone of the story is realistic, in keeping with the genre.

A note on *Character*: by choosing a murder story-frame, Van Diehm catapults us into the story. The strategy energizes what would otherwise have followed a slower chronological structure.

WRITING DEVICES

There are a number of requisite mechanics that will enable you to shape your story as a melodrama. The analogy here is to a car or to a building. Both have to be functional; both can be creative; but without those mechanics in place, neither will be either functional or creative. So it is with your story—and so we turn to those writing devices that are the mechanics of the melodrama.

Your Character Should Have a Goal

A character without a goal, a passive character, is rudderless, subject to the goals of others and to the plot. Although a melodrama can work with a passive character (Steve Soderbergh's *Sex, Lies and Videotape* and Gus Van Sant's *My Own Private Idaho* are examples), for the most part melodramas work best when the main character is active and goal directed.

What is an adequate goal for a character in a melodrama? Two extreme examples will illustrate the parameters for a purposeful goal. The first is the desire to escape Central Casting, for the main character in Peter Weir's *The Truman Story*. The problem here is that the character realizes his goal only after a third of the story has elapsed; once he articulates that goal, he spends the balance of the story achieving it. Once the conceit of his world—his life is a twenty-four-hour-a-day television show, complete with the artifice of a set and cast that pretends to be his town, with his house and his wife—is unmasked, there are no more barriers of understanding for the character to achieve. Only the act of achieving freedom will do. We watch him achieve his freedom, as earlier we watched the artifice of his life. The problem here is that the goal, once acknowledged, is too flat in its struggle with the plot (his life as television). The trajectory is not developmental, and therefore it is limited.

At the other extreme is the main character in Mike Figgis's *Leaving Las Vegas*. Here an alcoholic decides in the first five minutes of the story that he wants to drink himself to death. In the next hundred minutes, he manages to do so. He does meet another character, a prostitute, who tries to save him, but this relationship is filler. He knows what he wants and proceeds relentlessly to do it. Again the problem is that there is no trajectory to the goal; the story itself is linear, in the horizontal sense.

Both of these main characters have a goal, but the goal results in too flat a story. Either the goal or the plot has to give amplitude to the story. What we find is helpful in giving amplitude to a story is the mechanical device of triangulation.

Triangulation

Triangulation is a device whereby the main character explores two opposing relationships. Those two relationships can be viewed as the two opposing choices. They can also be viewed as two opposing means for the character to achieve his or her goal. In either case, the exploration of these two relationships gives the melodrama amplitude. It prevents the drama from flattening out, as occurs in *Leaving Las Vegas* and in *The Truman Story*.

To illustrate how triangulation works, we turn first to a simple structure (no plot)—the film *Truly, Madly, Deeply*. A woman has lost her lover. Her goal is not to refuse to accept the loss, to hold on to her grief. The two relationships that are fully explored in this particular triangulation are the woman's relationship with her dead lover (he comes back as a ghost) and her relationship with a new suitor. The first relationship maintains her goal, and the second challenges it. In the end she opts for a live lover and a future, and it is the ghost that in the end says goodbye to her.

In *Once Were Warriors*, the main character is the wife-mother in a Maori family. Her goal is to keep her family intact. This is no small feat with a violent husband, an eldest son inducted into a gang, and a middle son removed into a juvenile home. The two relationships that oppose each other are the relationship with her husband and that with her children. She cannot have both, and so her goal of an intact family is challenged on both sides of the triangle. In the end she has to reconstitute her family without her husband.

It is possible in the melodrama to have more than one triangle, although one triangle will always take primacy over the others. The presence of more than one triangle simply complicates the story further. This is especially important in *Sex, Lies and Videotape*, a melodrama where the main character is passive, without a goal until the last third of the story.

The primary triangle is between the main character (her husband) and the guest (her husband's friend Graham). Her husband represents the unfaithful, untruthful, manipulative mate, while Graham is truthful, interested in her, and not at all manipulative. These two male-mate choices represent the primary triangle in the story. A secondary triangle is the triangle of the main character, her husband, and her sister. Both her husband and her sister are betraying her, and it is the resolution of this triangle that prompts the main character finally to act: she discovers that the two have been having an affair and have been so bold as to make love in her bedroom. A third triangle is the main character, her sister, and the male guest. It is the experience of being videotaped by him talking about sex that prompts the sister to reject the husband, and eventually the main character to choose (via videotape) to awaken sexually and to leave her husband for the guest. These three triangulations form the actual progression, the train tracks of the journey of the main character.

Use Plot against the Main Character's Goal

Just as triangulation provides a method to build the dramatic arc of the story, plot can be used to make the climb steeper and consequently more gripping. It should be said again that it is not necessary for a melodrama to have a plot, but if you choose to use plot, it should be used in a particular fashion. In the melodrama, plot tends to be used against the character and his goal. The flip side to this is the situation comedy, where the plot is used in the opposite way, to enable the character to achieve his goal. Having stated the ground rule, we should also mention that inventive writers alter those rules. A case in point is Woody Allen's *Crimes and Misdemeanors*. Allen mixes both melodrama and situation comedy in these tales of two characters—an opthalmologist and a documentary filmmaker. The goal of the main character in the melodrama is to maintain his life situation and status. His mistress threatens to upset the status quo, by telling all to his wife. The plot is the murder of his mistress. In classic melodrama, the plot should lead to the downfall of the main character. Instead, in this story the plot enables the character to achieve his goal.

The second story about the documentary filmmaker is a situation comedy. The character's goal is to produce ethically worthy documentary films that will give him the status he feels he deserves. Unhappy in his marriage, the character is offered the opportunity to produce a TV biography of a Hollywood TV producer (his wife's brother). This plot should bring him the money to make his worthy projects. It also introduces him to a woman he believes will elevate him out of his unhappy marriage. Again, Allen upsets our expectations. The plot undermines the filmmaker, dooming him to failure on all fronts. Indeed even his ethical goal of a worthy production is thwarted, by the death of his subject by suicide.

Woody Allen's film is unusual; generally, genre expectations are met as described earlier in this chapter. Plot should work against the main character and his goal. Two additional examples will illustrate how this works. Paul Thomas Anderson's *Boogie Nights* is the story of a man whose goal is to gain recognition or, in a more modest sense, acknowledgment that he has value in his family and in his community. The plot that he looks to as the opportunity for recognition is a career as a star in pornographic movies. Although initially his star rises, and his career could be deemed a success, he quickly falls, and the plot becomes the means to his devaluation. In the end he is a victim of the plot.

Robert Redford's *Quiz Show* provides a second example. Here too the plot, success on a quiz show, proves the undoing of the character and his goal. The main character is an upper-class intellectual, scion of an academic family. The quiz show, popular across the nation, has taken to providing the answers to its "popular contestants" in order to prolong their week-to-week appearances, which in turn maintain its popularity and ratings. When the fraud of the show is uncovered, the main character's status turns to humiliation. His father and his university both are appalled, and the censure that follows denies the character of the goal he believed he had attained. *Quiz Show* was based on an actual incident that occurred on *The $64,000 Question*, a game show in the 1950s.

The tension between the character's goal and the plot can be as important as the triangulation in making the melodrama dramatically viable.

Resolution Or No Resolution

Generally melodramas resolve when the main character either achieves his or her goal or fails to do so. For the majority of melodramas, the issue of resolution has been the end point of the story. However, a number of storytellers have begun to opt for no resolution—or to put it another way, for an open-ended ending. Films such as Spike Lee's *She's Gotta Have It* and Atom Egoyan's *Exotica* have opted for a two-act structure, essentially relinquishing the resolution that comes in the third act of a story. Of course, the inspiration for the open-ended ending is older, rooted at the artistic edge of melodrama, particularly in Europe. Many of the European classics—Federico Fellini's *8½*, Michelangelo Antonioni's *L'Eclipse*, François Truffaut's *400 Blows*—are melodramas that opt not to resolve their stories.

The choice, then, that the contemporary writer faces is whether to follow the linear progression of story to its resolution or to opt for an open-ended conclusion. The choice has serious consequences for the reception of the film. Clearly, the majority of audiences are accustomed to resolution; they expect it, and in certain ways they are comforted by it. The absence of resolution can be disquieting, even troubling.

If you choose to avoid resolution, it will be helpful if the dialogue and characterizations are especially vigorous. The more you can do to engage your audience, the greater their tolerance for the journey of the film, in this case a journey without resolutions.

The Potential for Tragedy

At the extreme, melodrama can achieve the status of tragedy. To be successful it does not have to strive for tragedy, but at its best as a genre it does so. Some examples will illustrate this peak of the genre. William Wyler's *The Heiress*, George Stevens's *A Place in the Sun*, Elia Kazan's *East of Eden*, Robert

Rossen's *The Hustler*, Martin Ritt's *Hud*—all are melodramas that achieve this status. More contemporary examples include Nikita Mikhalkhov's *Burnt by the Sun*, Emir Kusterica's *Time of the Gypsies*, Ingmar Bergman's *Autumn Sonata*, Mike Leigh's *Secrets and Lies*.

What distinguishes these stories from other melodramas is the scale of their stories. The main character in the triangulation has choices that are so extreme as to create a profound sense of loss should one or the other relationship fail. The plot additionally ratchets up what is at stake for the main characters. What is at stake are the core issues—their dignity and their lives. The greater the risk taken by the main character, the greater potential that the story can achieve tragedy.

Use Structure to Meet the Needs of the Story

Structure is the servant of story, although much that has been written about screenwriting these past two decades might lead you to believe otherwise.

The key to story is character—its nature, its dilemma, and above all its goal. If you know these, the structural options become cleaner. In melodrama the key structural layer is the character layer, the background story. If you use this layer and triangulate the key relationships quite early in the story (the first act), you will have used structure well. Act I has other requirements as well—to join the story at a critical moment and to introduce a catalytic event, one that prompts the character to begin his or her inner journey (some writers refer to the catalytic event as the "point of attack"—what you call it matters less than the attention you pay to it). Finally, you need a turning point at the end of the first act, to open up the story—and yes, if there is a plot, it is often also introduced in Act I.

Having introduced the notion of plot, we should consolidate the idea that melodrama can proceed without a layer of plot. If however you opt for plot, it can be introduced later. In *A Place in the Sun* it is introduced in Act II, which is fine. Some stories opt to introduce it later. In Robert Young's *Dominick and Eugene*, the plot is introduced in Act III; this is not so fine. Its too late to be credible.

Act II, the act of confrontation and struggle, is often where relationships are explored most fully. By the end of the act, the main character has made a choice. Act III follows the character moving toward that choice. In Act III both plot and the background story are resolved.

Does Realism as a Tone Suit Your Story?

The genre expectation in melodrama is that the tone will be realistic. It is quite rare that the choice veers from realism; increasingly, however, filmmakers are opting to move away from this expectation. For example, Hanif Kureishi, the writer of *My Beautiful Launderette*, opts to mix realism with irony. Consequently this melodrama about a young man who is Pakistani by birth, British by citizenship, and gay by choice deploys irony quite often. It does so particularly toward Pakistanis who have become exceedingly assimilated, as well as those who have not assimilated at all. Kureishi is thoroughly realistic about the main character's love relationship—a working-class "Brit" with no affectations.

Other examples of melodrama where irony coexists with realism as a tone are Clara Law's *Floating Life*, *Exotica*, and Hal Hartley's *The Simple Truth*.

THE SHORT FILM

As stated earlier, the broad qualities of the melodrama are most clearly apparent in the long film. However many of these qualities are present in the short film. There are, however, key areas where the mechanics are different, and it is to those differences that we now turn.

THE DIFFERENCES

The most useful way to proceed to highlight those differences is to describe them and then illustrate how they manifest themselves in a short film.

Main Character and Goal

In the short film, the goal must be more urgent than in a long one. The short film is all about compression. There is no time to explore relationships in as elaborate a manner as is appropriate in the long film. By making the goal of the main character more urgent means that there is less time for characterization. A choice must be made quickly in the short film. Consequently, characterizations of the secondary relationships are quick, even stereotypical. More time is consequently available to experience the main character's reaching for his or her goal.

Structure

There are numerous differences between the long and short film in terms of structure. Most obviously, the proportion of Acts I, II, and III, generally held to be 1:2:1 (thirty minutes to sixty minutes to thirty minutes), simply does not apply. Act I is more likely to be five minutes in a short film. There will be no middle act: there will be Act II or III, depending on the writer's choice of a resolution or an open ending. If the option for resolution is taken, the structure is Act I–Act III, in feature-film terms. If a more open-ended script is the choice, the structure looks like Act I–Act II of the feature film.

There are other differences. In Act I in the feature film there are key points—the critical moment (where you join the story), the catalytic event (where you kick-start the story), and the first major plot point (the end of Act I). In the short film, all three can be the same; at the very least, the catalytic event and the first major plot point are the same. The catalytic event can occur five minutes into the script, at which point the first act is over. In the next act we rush to resolution (Act III), or we explore options (Act II). Then the script ends, with a resolution or not. The second act, whether it be an Act II or Act III, is quite lengthy relative to the first act.

Plot

The deployment of plot is in one way similar to the presentation in the long film. That is to say, a short melodrama can proceed without a plot and remain effective. If, however, you choose to deploy plot, its utilization is similar to the use of character and goal in the short film. If you use plot, the likelihood is that it will play a dominant role in the script. There are short films, such as *The Lady in Waiting* (see Appendix), where a very modest plot is used; the New York blackout is more a plot device than plot proper, but it is nevertheless the plot of *The Lady in Waiting*. More often, however, when a plot is used it dominates the short script. Because it does so, it bears down on the main character and his or her goal with particular intensity. If it does not oppose the main character's goal, the script as a whole softens under the intensity of a character's pursuit, with too little resistance offered to that pursuit. The result is a loss of credibility in the character. This is so for melodrama.

Its useful to look for a moment at the situation comedy, which is the "positive" (in photographic terms) of the melodrama. This means that elements such as plot will be used in the opposite way than in melodrama. In Matthew Huffman's film *Secret Santa*, it is Christmastime. The seven-year-old main character simply wants not to be bullied and belittled by a larger classmate. That's his goal. The plot enables him to achieve that goal, as follows. A bank robbery is carried out by six men wearing Santa Claus outfits. One escapes, injured in his hurry to get away. He is found by the seven-year-old, who believes he has found Santa Claus. He takes him home, where the robber hides in the basement. This is the catalytic event. In the second act the boy befriends "Santa" and convinces him to have words with the bully. "Santa" tells the bully to be good—or no presents this year. The bully complies: the main character achieves his goal. ("Santa" is caught climbing out of the basement window.) Here the plot—robbery and its aftermath—enables the main character to achieve his goal.

Tone

Generally the tone of the long-form melodrama is realistic. There are ways to move away from the expected tone-mixing genres, certainly, but for the most part the genre dictates a realistic tone.

The short film has a much wider tolerance for moving off of realism. Because of the urgency of the character and his goal, or conversely because of the intensity of the plot, subjectivity and irony both have a place in the melodrama. In this sense the short film more readily offers the writer the option to enlist his or her voice directly in the script.

CASE STUDIES

These case studies will illustrate how short films which are melodramas use character, structure, and tone.

Case Studies in Character

In Elke Rosthal's *My Name Is Rabbit . . .*, a young woman returns to visit the father she has not seen since she was a child. As a child, she had been a witness to her mother's death in a car accident; her father had been driving. The current visit does not go well. Her father, an alcoholic, is inappropriately affectionate with her. He's sexually jealous of a friend she has made at work. In fact, the visit is a disaster, but it does prompt her to recall her early life. She remembers his temper and his possessiveness toward her mother. As the story ends, she is left with a conscious feeling of her guilt for her mother's death. She felt guilty because the accident occurred when her father swerved to avoid hitting a rabbit. He had always called her Rabbit.

In *My name Is Rabbit*, the character pursues her goal of a relationship with a father who is a mystery to her. Although she discovers that a relationship is impossible, her pursuit is understandable and earnest. Because she is modest, her father's over-the-top drinking and salaciousness is all the more shocking. By the end of the film we understand that it is the father, rather than Rabbit, who bears the responsibility for the family tragedy.

In Christian Taylor's *The Lady in Waiting*, Miss Peach is a character whose goal, to the last, is to be the loyal servant. The man she served, the man she loved, had left a request after his death: a love letter to be delivered personally in New York. Unrequited love and a powerful sense of duty mix as Miss Peach goes to New York to deliver the letter. This journey is interrupted by a power failure. Stuck in an elevator, Miss Peach meets Scarlett, a black transvestite. They manage to get out of the elevator and into the apartment of the woman she has come to see and deliver her master's letter. But the owner is not at home, and so Miss Peach and Scarlett get acquainted. The blackout has paralyzed the city, and there is nowhere else to go. As the two learn about one another, Miss Peach realizes that her self-esteem will have to come from herself, as Scarlett has long ago learned. These two are the sole characters of *The Lady in Waiting*, and it is their relationship, as two marginalized people from different backgrounds, that helps Miss Peach to move beyond her goal, the delivery of the letter.

Case Studies in Structure

Both Christian Taylor's *The Lady in Waiting* and Susan Emerling's *The Wounding* (see the appendices), proceed in an Act I–Act II structure, essentially resulting in open-ended conclusions.

In the case of *The Lady in Waiting*, the critical moment—take this letter to New York—is not the same as the catalytic event, or turning point between acts. The turning point here is when the elevator stops as a result of the power outage. Act II is dominated by the exploration of the relationship between Miss Peach and Scarlett. From the elevator, to the apartment, to the parting of their ways, the focus is on how Scarlett influences Miss Peach. The story is character driven; it has little plot (the power outage). The end is open, leaving us hopeful that Miss Peach will feel better about herself. She remains, however, marginalized.

The Wounding follows a similar pattern. Act I is brief. An adolescent, Julie, plays with dolls, with which she acts out an imaginary home life. We quickly move to real life: Julie's mother is having a party. But in this first act, the focus in on Julie and her mother. Her mother is vain and not very interested in Julie. Act II focuses on the party downstairs—her mother and these three men proceed to drink a great deal. Sheila, the mother, is quite seductive and flirtatious. The men vary in age. Julie becomes a witness, powerless to influence anyone's behavior. Later in the night, Julie seeks refuge in a bath. Her mother has an argument with the oldest of the men. Aggression, accusation, and drunkenness have replaced the flirtatiousness. Sheila fires a shotgun at the man. He leaves, as do the others. None of the men had been reliable; their goals had been sexual. All the mother now has is her daughter—and now Julie has to care for her, an alcoholic. All Julie wants is a home, but all she has is an alcoholic mother. The script ends at the party's aftermath, with all the signals of a failed home.

As in *The Lady in Waiting, The Wounding* focuses on relationships, specifically their insufficiency for the adolescent main character. The ending is open ended. We know this will not be the last evening like this, and we wonder how Julie will survive.

Graham Justice's *A Children's Story* exemplifies the Act I/Act III structure. The main character is a six-year-old girl. The film opens with children being very playful on a school bus. The driver tells them to settle down, not to show each other their underwear. In the following scene a school psychologist looks into a parallel incident, where the driver was inappropriately friendly with the children. The act ends with the driver being arrested for molesting the main character. In the next act, the investigation continues. We learn that the main character has had "numerous fathers." The community is pressing for conviction of the driver. This requires the testimony of the main character. As the psychologist tries to learn more via play therapy, the main character is fearful about releasing a secret. Ultimately, though, she inadvertently reveals that it is the mother's current lover who has been molesting her. The script ends with the driver freed, again presented as a true and caring friend to the main character.

In *A Children's Story*, the discovery of the true antagonist and his consequent arrest brings the story to resolution. In this sense, the long act resembles Act III of a feature film.

A Case Study in Plot

Graham Justice's *A Children's Story* also provides us with an example of the deployment of plot in the short film. In the classic sense of melodrama, plot works in opposition to the main character's goal. In *A Children's Story*, the goal of the main character is to keep the family secret of sexual abuse. She does so out of fear of losing her mother's love. The plot—the investigation into the case of sexual abuse—puts continual pressure (via the school psychologist) on the main character. As the investigation progresses, so does the pressure to reveal the secret.

As expected in a melodrama with plot, there will be resolution and, accordingly, an Act I/Act III structure. There also will be twists and turns—thus the catalytic event, the arrest of the driver, and the resolution, the arrest of the mother's lover. What also needs to be mentioned is that the presence of plot diminishes the level of characterization in the screenplay as well as the screenplay's dependence on the dialogue for energy. In plot-driven melodramas the characterizations are often stereotypes, and the energy in the screenplay derives from the twists and turns of plot.

Case Studies in Tone

Generally the tone of the short melodrama is realistic. Susan Emerling's *The Wounding*, Christian Taylor's *The Lady in Waiting*, and Graham Justice's *A Children's Story* are each presented realistically. This means recognizable characters in recognizable situations. The consequence is a dramatic arc for the main character that does not veer from the expected.

Having confirmed the expected tone of the genre, it's important to reaffirm that tone in the short film has a wider latitude than does tone in the long-form melodrama. Two examples will illustrate the point. Ayanna Elliot's *Tough* is a story of a teenager. The story is simple, "a day in the life." But it's a special day—the first day she menstruates. She is on the verge of womanhood. Also, her father (divorced from her mother) is to take her out for the day. The incidents in the story are as follows. She has a vicious argument with her mother. Her mother is more attentive to her female lover than she is to her daughter's anxiety about menstruation. The main character decides to move out. Her father does not realize it, but the main character is now planning to be with him for more than the day. The main character insists on bringing her girlfriend along. The father insists on bringing *his* new girlfriend along. Needless to say, parenting is not the order of the day—rather, who can be more childish, the adults or the children, is the goal.

In order to make her point about "who is the parent here," Ayanna Elliot uses humor and irony. If there is a consistent tone to *Tough,* it is irony. The tone is effective in making her point about parenting. It is, however, quite different than the tone in Susan Emerling's *The Wounding,* a story with a similar main character in a similar circumstance.

Emily Weissman's *Pocketful of Stones* offers a very different tone as well. *Pocketful of Stones* opens with the admission of the main character, in her late teens, into a hospital. She has attempted suicide; a failed relationship has driven her to the act. The story focuses on her hospital stay. Will she get better or worse? The story ends with her more withdrawn than ever and confined to the hospital. In between, we learn that her goal is to get out of the hospital. Although rebellious to authority (the nurse), she is nevertheless somewhat reality based. She develops a relationship with a young man, also a patient. Through his influence and control, she is coaxed into self-mutilating behavior, and she becomes increasingly withdrawn, then aggressive. She goes from talking with the psychiatrist about a release plan, to behavior troubling enough to preclude release. At the end of the story she is worse off than she had been at the beginning.

The tone in *Pocketful of Stones* is expressionistic, even nightmarish, emphasizing her emotional, subjective state. By doing so, Emily Weissman puts us in her place—time is obliterated, authority figures are monsters, the hospital is a war zone. By resorting to an exceedingly subjective tone, Emily Weissman avoids the case-study approach and takes us inside mental illness. The result is very powerful. Here again, moving away from the expected tone creates a powerful and fresh experience. Here tone makes the short film quite an original experience.

Summation

The key issue in writing melodrama in the short film is that there are classic commonalties between the long and short forms—the nature of the struggle for the main character, the main character powerless against the power structure, the recognizability of character and situation, the characters living the lives we do, and of course the narrative approach, which is essentially realist.

Where the long and short forms differ goes beyond length. Compression means faster characterization and less characters and plot. It also means a structural choice—for an Act I–II approach or an Act I/III approach. The short film also allows the writer latitude in the area of tone. Like the short story, metaphor and poetics can work in the short melodrama in a way that greater characterization and plot tend to disallow in the long film. The key in all your considerations about the short film is to be aware of these similarities and differences.

13

THE DOCUDRAMA

On one level, that of content, docudrama has much in common with melodrama. Many dramatic qualities, the nature of the struggle, the positioning of the main character, and the tone are similar. But on the issue of *style*, the manner of presentation of the story, they differ. The docudrama is concerned with a particular kind of style, a style that assures an aura of veracity. This style may be present in the melodrama, but it is never as central a feature as it is in the docudrama.

The docudrama has its roots in the documentary. The sense of actuality in Robert Flaherty's *Nanook of the North* and *Man of Aran* conveyed the idea of cultures quickly giving way to modern urban life. Equally important, however, these documentaries took editorial positions about those cultures, advocacy positions that were romantic but also represented a wish that the pattern of these cultures passing were not so inevitable a by-product of modernization. These two elements—actuality and a social, or political, perspective on the life situation of the participants—link the documentary directly to the docudrama.

Whether anarchistic (Vertov's *Man with a Movie Camera*) or fascist (Leni Riefenstahl's *Triumph of the Will*), the documentary quickly became a form whose agenda was principally educational and propagandistic rather than entertaining. This quality too became a link to the docudrama.

Style became more pronounced in the '50s, in the documentaries of Lindsay Anderson ("Momma Don't Allow"), Karel Reisz ("Everyday except Christmas"), and Tony Richardson ("Direct Cinema"). This was even more the case in the "cinema verité" explosion in the documentary filmmakers of the '60s (Leacock, Pennebaker, the Maysles brothers). But no examples of the style sacrificed those original intentions—actuality, education, political goals. Also, the style crossed over into the feature film—Haskell Wexler's *Medium Cool* and Michael Ritchie's *The Candidate*. In the extreme, that style is represented in the recent "Dogma 95" films, particularly Von Trier's *Breaking the Waves* and Vinterberg's *The Celebration*. But none of the work has given up those original documentary intentions—to share with the audience a real experience, and to educate more than to entertain. The docudrama represents the consciousness of style fused with dramatic principles to share a story the writer-directors feel is important.

GENERAL CHARACTERISTICS

The Centrality of Actuality

At the heart of the docudrama is the *sense of actuality*. Whether the focus is on real people, a real place, or a historical event, the docudrama trades on this sense—it happened to real people, in a real place and time. This may mean in essence a biography, or a place, person, or period. This may also mean that the deployment of style, as well as of the dramatic components, will focus on that veracity.

This will also mean that time will be allotted to supporting the sense of actuality—details, habits, and customs will all be specific to the topic. This does not, however, necessarily mean that the focus will be on the famous or highborn, although both have provided ample material for the docudrama. It means that at whatever level, rich or poor, famous or obscure, the focus of the narrative will be as much taken up with the "anthropology" of the place and time as it will with the dramatic properties of the event or person. Films such John Madden's *Mrs. Brown* and Michael Winterbottom's *Jude* are ultimately concerned with a portrait of nineteenth-century Victorian England, even though one is concerned with a monarch, the other with an educated laborer. In both, the sense of time and place often seems more important than character.

The Dominance of Place and Time over Character

In the melodrama, the character and his goal seem to transcend time and place. The reason is that at its heart melodrama is about psychology, behavior, and interior issues; in a sense, the dramatic arc of the main character is an inner journey. Consequently, the externalities of time and place are subsidiary to the internal dynamics of character. Mike Van Diem's *Character*, discussed in the previous chapter, is an excellent benchmark. The main character's family life, his ambition, and his self-abnegation far transcend the sense of Rotterdam in the 1920s. We are aware of Rotterdam, its poverty, and its labor unrest, but none of this overrides the interior journey of the main character. In docudrama the reverse is true. Place and time not only transcend character, they are central to the experience of docudrama. In Ken Loach's *Wednesday's Child*, the prevailing ideas of antipsychiatry in the London of the 1960s override the film, considered as a family drama about dysfunction and child-parent relationships. Equally, Michael Ritchie's

Downhill Racer is more about competitive international sports in the 1970s than it is about a particular skier. Why this is the case has everything to do with the goals of the writer or director, an issue we will address later in this section.

The Nature of the Struggle of the Main Character

The struggle for the main character in melodrama dominates the narrative. In the docudrama, the nature of the character's struggle is subordinate to the goal of the story. In addition, here the voice of the author subsumes the elements of story, often for political (as opposed to dramatic) purposes. Also, the heritage of the documentary film overrides dramatic considerations. In Karel Reisz's *Saturday Night and Sunday Morning* the challenge of conformity is more critical than the character's fate, and something similar is true of Tony Richardson's *The Loneliness of the Long Distance Runner*. The idea of female oppression at the hands of male chauvinism far supersedes the portrait of Camille Claudel as an artist in Bruno Nuytten's *Camille Claudel*; further, place and time—turn-of-the-century Paris and its art world—are more critical than the personal relationship between Claudel and Rodin.

The Role of Plot

In the melodrama, plot (if deployed) is a primary barrier to the main character and his or her goal. If the main character and the goal are less important in the docudrama, how is plot used? In Peter Watkin's *Culloden*, the battle itself, the last battle fought on British soil, dominates the narrative. Although there are many characters on both sides of the battle, their vividness does not dominate the story; indeed, there is no single main character. The course of the event, which is the plot, dominates the narrative.

This dynamic does not change when Watkins takes a character as his subject. In his film *Edvard Munch*, the goal of the main character is to pursue his artistic goals. His early career in Norway and Germany is a failure, because of the powerful conservatism of the German art critics. Although Munch finds alliances with other artists and writers, the course of his career, the plot, has a tragic quality. Here too plot seems more important than the interior emotional journey of Munch (so often reflected in the art).

There are stories whose style echoes docudrama. Two such are Von Trier's *Breaking the Waves* and Vinterberg's *The Celebration*; both films, from a story perspective, bridge melodrama and docudrama. Their characters are pursuing an inner journey, as characters do in the melodrama. Yet the writer-directors use style to "educate" or share their views, as do writer-directors in docudrama. These stories are exceptions. More often the docudrama will deploy plot to override the main character and their or his or her goal, or to subsume the main character and goal.

The Relationship of Docudrama to Issues of the Day

Like melodrama, the docudrama is eminently adaptable to the issues of the day. Because as a style it gives the viewer the sense of being there as the story is unfolding, the style evokes the power of television, with its immediacy. Consequently, films such as *The Death of a Princess* are particularly powerful. Much of Ken Loach's work, from *Poor Cow* to *Riff Raff*, has this quality. The docudrama, however, also lends weight to past events, special events, and famous people of the past. Steven Spielberg's techniques for the opening battle scene of *Saving Private Ryan* borrow extensively from the style of the docudrama. He has used the approach not only to memorialize the D day landings on the beaches of Normandy but to give us the feeling that we are on those beaches.

The docudrama form has been used by Peter Watkins in his portrait of Edvard Munch and in his portrayal of the Battle of Culloden. Other styles can be used to portray a battle or an artist: Ed Zwick's Civil War film *Glory* depicts battle in a more formal, ritualistic manner; Vincent Minnelli's portrait of the artist Vincent Van Gogh, in *Lust for Life*, is in its way as romantic as is Zwick's film. Neither is docudrama, yet both are effective films.

The docudrama form is particular and elicits a very specific kind of reaction from its audience. It lends an immediacy to events past and present, an immediacy that is quite unique in its impact on the audience.

The Voice of the Author

Although one interpretation of docudrama is to call it simply classical melodrama with a distinctive style, this is too circumscribed a definition to encompass docudrama fully. Another view is to call docudrama a story form that, by virtue of the author's strongly held views, requires a style powerful enough to act as a pronouncement of those views. To put it more simply, docudrama is a form where it is important to the author to say to the audience, "This story is more important than your average melodrama. I have something to say, and I want you to listen and to watch and to be moved to action by the experience."

In this sense, the choice of a docudrama approach in a film such as Ken Loach's *Land and Freedom*, with its cinema verité style, gives us the sense that we are there on the Republican side during the Spanish Civil War. The style gives a feeling of immediacy to the combat scenes, but the docudrama form also has an impact on the narrative choices Loach makes. On at least three occasions during the film, lengthy debates take place about issues that are in essence matters of dogma—land rights; the role of the Soviet Communist Party and Joseph Stalin in the organization of the Republican side; and military organization—whether formal structure would undermine the paramilitary units, which are presented as ideologically "pure" and therefore true revolutionaries. These lengthy discussions are filmed earnestly and respectfully, as if they were just happening. From a dramatic point of view, these choices make the experience of the film more educational than "emotional," as melodramatic equivalents (*The Sun Also Rises* and *For Whom the Bell Tolls*) would tend to be.

When they wish to achieve a more active voice, a voice that implies a higher level of importance, serving an educational or political goal rather than entertainment, directors choose the docudrama, a form whose style implies, "This is important."

MOTIFS—CASE STUDIES

For docudrama, as for melodrama, it is useful to look at case studies in order to understand the narrative shape of the form. Three case studies will represent a spectrum of subcategories of the docudrama: the personality, Peter Watkins's *Edvard Munch* (1976); the event, Peter Watkins's *Culloden* (1964); and the political portrait, Ken Loach's *Land and Freedom* (1996).

Edvard Munch

The Main Character and His Goal

The main character is Edvard Munch, a young man whose goal is to establish himself as an artist. Growing up in Christiania (the modern Oslo) in the late nineteenth century, Munch struggles to find a form for his inner struggles. The society is conservative, his art is anything but. The profoundly painful struggle of this artist to actualize his work is constantly misunderstood by the public and by professional critics. Spiritually speaking, he is burned at the stake each time he has an exhibition. This pattern reoccurs even in the more bohemian Berlin. The narrative follows the first forty years of his life.

The Antagonist

The antagonist of this story is principally the conservative community of Christiania and the art critics of Norway and Germany. However, to a certain extent it is also Munch himself. Scarred by tragedy (the death of his sister) as a youth, he sees life as a series of personal losses, at the very least disappointment. Since his paintings so often are iterations of that pain, his obsession with art as an expression not of beauty but of something darker understandably causes clashes with a public looking to art as an expression of idealism and hope, not despair.

The Catalytic Event

Watkins continually returns to one critical event in Munch's life, the childhood death of his sister. This catalytic event is referred to throughout the balance of the narrative.

The Dramatic Arc

The dramatic arc follows twenty years of Munch's artistic career. The deeper layer of the arc is Munch's inability in this period to form love relationships.

The Resolution

Having tried numerous forms to express himself, Munch's obsessive productivity finally leads him to be accepted artistically in Germany. On one level he has begun to be recognized as the forerunner of the artistic movement later called Expressionism. On a personal level, however, he suffers a nervous collapse. His human fragility is echoed by the suicide of a younger brother.

The Narrative Style

The narrative proceeds both with a plot (the progress of Munch as an artist) and a background story (his continual failure in personal relationships).

The Narrative Shape

The narrative covers the first forty years of Munch's life. Time itself is not a factor, in dramatic terms.

Tone

The tone of the film, as one would expect, is realistic. Watkins himself narrates the film, as both a commentator and a psychological observer. At times factual, at other times editorial, Watkins is trying to articulate the interior struggle of the artist. He does not romanticize the portrait, but he does link the inner and outer life to suggest that Munch is an explorer—of "interior" space. By introducing a narrator to the story, Watkins can introduce his own views more directly into the story.

Culloden

The Main Character and his Goal

The story proceeds without a main character. The combatants are the Scottish and the English. The leadership in each case is highlighted; however, there is no single character through whom we enter the story. If there is the equivalent of a main character, it is the narrator, in essence a reporter in search of the story. He interviews combatants, the victors as well as the vanquished. He is looking to explain as well as to understand the battle and its aftermath. In this sense the narrator could be considered the main character, with the goal of reporting the story of the last battle to occur on British soil. The narrator, by the way, is Peter Watkins himself. Using the form of the docudrama, he has made himself, and his voice about the battle, the entry point (which is the role of the main character) into the story.

The Antagonist

The antagonist in this story is certainly the imperial forces, from the commander, Prince William of England, down to the English soldiers. They are portrayed as cruel, lusting for Scottish blood. Although Prince Charles, who leads the Scottish rebellion, is rebuked for his indifference to his forces and for his addiction "to his little bottle," he is presented as no worse than an incapable leader of the disunited, underarmed forces that meet the English on the field at Culloden.

The Catalytic Event

Since the entire film is devoted to the events leading up to the battle, the battle itself, and its aftermath, the catalytic event would have to be considered the beginning of the Scottish rebellion that has resulted in the battle. Whether this is the landing of "Bonnie Prince Charlie" from France or some subsequent political coalition, the fact is that the catalytic event, unusual as it is, occurs before the film begins.

The Dramatic Arc

The shape of *Culloden* is the course of the battle itself. There is a lead-up to the battle, and there is an aftermath. However, the major part of the narrative is devoted to the battle itself, its details, and its outcome.

The Resolution

The battle ends with a decisive victory for the English forces. In the aftermath of the battle, the Scottish wounded on the field of battle are executed, and those who are captured are transported for execution in the cities of England or deported to Australia.

The Narrative Style

Culloden is entirely plot. We follow the course of a battle from beginning to end. Since there is no central character, relationships are not developed. Characters are introduced only in terms of their roles in the battle. Their performance and their fates are reported in the narrative.

The Narrative Shape

Because *Culloden* is about a battle, time is important. The film illustrates how quickly and decisively the English forces were able to win the battle. Time also plays a role in how remorselessly and cruelly the vanquished were hunted down and punished for participating in the Scottish rebellion.

Tone

The battle is presented in a cinema verité style. Details of social, economic, and military organization and weaponry are combined with journalistic interviews with the combatants. The presentation is extremely realistic. The narrator, the writer-director Watkins, has clear sympathies for Scottish nationalism; consequently he editorializes about the English leadership and forces in the harshest terms. It is his view that this last battle on English soil destroyed a culture, the remnants of which were consequently dispersed to the far corners of the Empire. The tone of the narration is one of loss. That loss is the sense Peter Watkins wants to leave with us, via the experience of *Culloden*.

Land and Freedom

The Main Character and His Goal

The main character in *Land and Freedom* is a young man, a laborer (and a Communist) from Liverpool. His goal is to live by his beliefs; consequently he joins a militia group fighting on the Republican side during the Spanish Civil War. He is a man of principle trying to live by those principles.

The Antagonist

Superficially, the antagonist would seem to be the Nationalist forces of Gen. Francisco Franco, but this is not a story about the Civil War and its outcome. Rather it is a story, focused on the Spanish conflict, about idealism versus pragmatism as it plays out in the world political arena. Consequently, the forces of pragmatism (the main character would say cynicism) are the real antagonists. This means that Stalin, Stalinism, Communism, or Fascism would all be far more important antagonists than Franco. The forces within, and the corruption within, are the real antagonists.

The Catalytic Event

The main character decides to go to Spain to fight for the Republican cause.

The Dramatic Arc

The arc of the story is the journey of the main character to disillusionment in the very cause in which he enlisted. The story begins with an aura of camaraderie in a particular militia unit. The unit is democratic, its members principled and brave. They succeed in combat. Slowly, however, the unit is fractured by orders from Moscow—a requirement to obey a central command (implied to be controlled by Moscow). Dissension among the group leads some to join the organized army, others to remain in the militia. The final confrontation occurs when Republican soldiers, commanded by a former member of the militia, orders the men of the militia unit to surrender their arms and its leaders to submit to arrest and prosecution. The confrontation ends with the death of a female member of the militia. The group is disbanded, and the main character becomes a man hunted by the very forces who represent the cause he first joined. The implication is that Franco did not win the Spanish Civil War but that the Republicans lost it, by giving up their original principles.

The Resolution

The main character buries his female comrade-in-arms (and in love) and returns to England.

The Narrative Style

Land and Freedom has both a plot as well as a background story. The plot is the experience of the main character as a soldier on the Republican side during the Spanish Civil War. The background story is that of his personal relationship with a woman who is a member of the militia group he joins. Originally a prostitute, she is passionate about the purity of the ideology held by their group. She believes in the egalitarian ideal within the militia and within Spanish society. She is the ultimate idealist. The main character, on the other hand, is a Communist, and when the Party orders the militias to join into regular forces, he obeys (thereby betraying her). His experience with the regular forces fighting in Barcelona is disillusioning, and he eventually rejoins the militia and the woman. When she is killed by Republican soldiers commanded by a former member of the militia, the main character's disillusionment is complete. There is nothing for him to do now but return to England.

The narrative is framed by a modern sequence. At the film's opening, the main character dies of a heart attack. The story unfolds as his granddaughter reads his letters. The film closes with his funeral. The granddaughter empties onto his casket a red bandana filled with Spanish earth gathered from the earlier funeral of his Spanish lover, and so he goes to rest with fragments from his past buried with him.

Tone

The tone is realistic. The introjection of various debates among the militiamen and townspeople, between the militiamen themselves, or with Republican soldiers provides a sense that ideology is what is important here—not people, not their fates, but political ideas and structures that can change everything. The respect for ideology over dramatic principles suggests Loach's priorities. In this sense the details, the style, and the dramatic choices characterize *Land and Freedom* as a docudrama.

WRITING DEVICES

What writing devices will help you shape your story as a docudrama? How do they differ from those of the melodrama? We now turn to those writing devices.

The Kind of Story That Can Benefit from a Docudrama Approach

Every story can be presented in a style that emphasizes veracity, but not every story is suitable for such treatment. The first question you must answer for yourself has to do with your sense of purpose for the story. Is your goal concerned with politics, education, or information, as opposed to entertainment? A second question has to do with the importance of the event or person you are dramatizing. Was the event critical to history, was the person influential? If so, how is the event or person relevant to today's audience? Finally, do you feel it is very important to share your view of this story with the audience? How will it change their lives? How has it changed yours? If the majority of your answers are affirmative, the docudrama may very well be a useful approach to the story.

The Use of Character and Goal

Although the docudrama can proceed without a main character if it chronicles an event, more often there is a main character, and that character does have a goal. The difference between melodrama and docudrama is actually one of point of view: how the main character and his or her goal is deployed differs between the two forms.

In melodrama we enter and experience the story through the main character. In docudrama, however, the point of view—or point of entry to the story—is via the writer-director, whose point of view is not necessarily that of the main character. In fact, the main character and his goal is simply the vehicle by which the writer-director presents his or her views on the story. In *Land and Freedom,* Ken Loach wants to say something about idealism and about how realpolitik destroys the idealism that arises out of hopeful political ideology. He uses the main character and his consequent disillusionment as the vehicle for that idea. In Peter Watkins's *Edvard Munch*, the issue is nonconformity and artistic originality. Munch, an original, was heaped with contempt, even hatred, because of his work. Its not so much Munch as Watkins's ideas about art that are at the heart of this docudrama. In both films the view of the writer-director exists separate from the main character and his goal. The main character and his goal become the lightning rod for the ideas of the writer-director.

The Proximity of the Docudrama to the Documentary

Docudramas are organized dramatically in a manner closer to the documentary than to the melodrama. The melodrama is organized on a three-act structure. It deploys character in a particular way. It may or may not have plot. It may or may not have resolution.

The documentary, on the other hand, is organized like a case. An idea is put forward, then a number of points are argued that make the case. The idea is then restated in the light of the case established.

The documentary tends to be a closed, or resolved, presentation because it is in essence a proven case. Whether about a person or an event, the process will be the same. The case will be made. The docudrama makes a case for the writer-director's views upon a person or event. The writer-director organizes the story around the case structure. If the film concerns a person, the character and his goal constitute the vehicle for the case—so too the course of an event, if the story focuses on one. The shape of the docudrama follows the shape of the documentary rather than that of the melodrama.

Plot Is Used in the Same Manner as the Main Character and His Goal

Plot in the melodrama is used in opposition to the main character and his goal. Since the role (that is, view) of the writer-director is the dominant presence in the docudrama, subsuming the role of the main character and his goal in a melodrama, a parallel process goes on in the deployment of plot. In the docudrama, the dominance of the views of the writer-director subsume plot. Plot serves to illustrate, and make the case for, the views of the writer-director. In *Culloden*, Peter Watkins has particular views on the imperialism of England vis-à-vis Scotland, and Scotland's eighteenth-century venture into nationalism. The plot, the Battle of Culloden, is presented in the light of Watkins's views, and it is those powerfully stated views that we take out of the experience of the film. The plot, then, is the evidence for the case Watkins is making.

Find the Structure That Is Suitable to the Story

Several of the previously mentioned docudramas use narrators. It is by no means mandatory that there be a narrator; however, the device, borrowed from documentary, is commonly used in docudrama. Very often that narrator assumes the journalistic role of reporter, and so the structure proceeds as a piece of reportage (*Culloden*). Another approach to the narrator is to use a diarist. In Loach's *Land and Freedom*, the letters of the main character document the story.

Whether reporter or diarist, the framing device of a shared piece of reportage or a recorded piece of personal history provides an entry point into what is essentially historical material. The presence of the narrator helps shape for the audience what might otherwise be difficult or inaccessible material. The narrator is a useful device to structure the story.

This differs from the playwright's approach, for example, to the Battle of Gallipoli. David Williamson's treatment of events is very dramatic, and we do enter the story through the experience of two main characters. The treatment, however, is very different from the narrator approach earlier described for the docudrama.

The second dimension to the structure of the docudrama is that it can be shaped as a character-driven or a plot-driven narrative. Whichever is chosen, the story, because of its parallel to the documentary, tends to have closure or resolution. In this sense it differs from melodrama, which can proceed either to an open-ended conclusion or to resolution.

Does Realism Have to Be the Tone in the Docudrama?

Even more than the melodrama, the docudrama embraces realism as a style. Consequently, realism is a central feature of the docudrama. One might even say that there realism is the orthodoxy for the docudrama. The realism may be strongly part of the narrative, in terms of the subject. It will certainly pertain to how the subject is treated, a journalistic approach for example. It will be relevant to the stylistic choices as to camera, light, as well as the use of on-air journalistic techniques, those we associate with broadcast journalism.

The exception here is comedic treatment of a subject. Just as the situation comedy is the comedic version of the melodrama, the mockumentary is the comedic version of the docudrama. The same journalistic references are at play. The goal, however, is satiric rather than serious. Rob Reiner's *This Is Spinal Tap* and Christopher Guest's *Waiting for Guffman* are two examples of the mockumentary. The humor arises from the apparently serious intentions of the writer-director. To put it another way, mockery replaces self-importance as the editorial position of the writer-director. Otherwise, the docudrama does not veer from realism.

THE SHORT FILM

Having elaborated the features of the docudrama in the long film, what is the balance between subject matter and style in the short film? Are main character and goal, plot, and tone deployed in a manner that supports the authorial voice? How much if any variance in tone does the short docudrama tolerate? These are questions to which we now turn.

Style in the Short Film

In the short film, the notion that what you are watching is a documentary is even more critical than in the long film. Consequently, the deployment of journalistic techniques, from camera style to on or off-air narration, are critical. In fact, the first narrative responsibility of the writer is to create at least the illusion that what we are watching is real people at real work or leisure. A candid quality, even the sense of "eavesdropping," should inform the writing and the style of performance. This "spontaneity" immediately establishes veracity and seriousness, upon which the writer-director will draw. What is being captured is not so much an enactment as the real thing. This is the central style of the docudrama. It is the primary and foremost key to the success of the docudrama.

The Main Character and the Goal

As in the long film, the main character, with his or her goal, is the vehicle for the ideas of the writer-director. Although the character may be vivid or important, the narrative has to create a large place for the voice of the writer-director. We will look at this issue in detail below, under structure.

The Role of Plot

As with the main character, plot can be vivid; indeed, it can be the principal focus of the narrative. However, the voice of the writer-director has to be a counterweight. The plot, like the main character, has to be secondary to the voice of the write-director in this genre.

Structure

Whether the narrative is plot driven or character driven, the dominant or shaping element of the docudrama is the voice of the writer-director. Whatever opinion is being pursued, it is that view that will shape the narrative. Very much like a documentary, the narrative is shaped as a case to be proven. Plot and character are tools used to illustrate, but the organization and presentation of the narrative, whether through onscreen or offscreen narration, is the principal shaping device. It is here that the voice of the author resides.

Tone

The tone will be emphatically realistic, with as much detail to emphasize realism as possible. This may mean camera style, or it may mean an on-air narrator speaking directly to the audience. The one exception is the mockumentary, where the realism itself is undermined as the viewer gradually realizes that it is realism itself that is being attacked.

Case Study in Character

Matt Mailer's *The Money Shot* chronicles a particular film project. The filmmaker is the central character. He is following two "street kids," both teenagers in trouble. The film opens with the male subject confessing to killing people. He is charming but brutal and very candid about what he does. The female subject also lives a marginalized life—alienated from her mother, she supports herself by prostitution, and she is a drug user. The filmmaker also interviews the young woman's mother and the young man's aunt. Both duck the realities of the two young people's lives. Both refuse to speak about matters too personal to them. In the course of the narrative, the filmmaker crosses the line and gets personally involved with both young people. The young woman overdoses on drugs, and the young man kills a policeman while being filmed. The filmmaker is thrilled to get the incident on film, but when threatened by the young man, who wants the incriminating footage, the filmmaker tries to call his bluff. The young man kills him and takes the film.

The character of the filmmaker is presented first as relentlessly pursuing the truth about life on the streets. Later we see he is a user, interested only in exploiting the situation, the entrapped and dangerous lives of two young people. His cynicism about people and his zeal for exploitation in the end costs him his life.

Matt Mailer is very interested, as others have been (Oliver Stone, in *Natural Born Killers*), in the exploitative power of film. His voice is that the media are two-edged swords. Their power can destroy the lives of the subjects as well as of the observers. This cautionary tale uses the main character and his goal to voice concerns about the media. A more satiric form of this caution was the subject of Paddy Chayevsky's *Network*. The main character and his goal in *The Money Shot* is the primary vehicle for the exploration of Mailer's ideas about exploitation, media, and the power of the media.

Case Study in Place

Helen Besfamilny's *Brighton Blues* is a story about the Brighton Beach area of Brooklyn. The story takes place in the Russian émigré community. The story is a simple one. A Russian wanders into a deli and admires the variety of food. The woman behind the counter is young, an American. He tells her he cannot afford the food, that he spent his money on cigarettes. She invites him out for dinner. Their night together is a bittersweet one. Other émigrés drop in to her apartment while he sleeps off the evening. He leaves but returns to invite her to accompany him to the airport. She refuses, but after he leaves she follows, loaded down with food for him. She goes to the subway station, but they do not see each other. She is alone, and he is gone. This brief description does not capture the despair, loneliness, and the joy these people can experience (but only momentarily).

The film uses a blue filter to present an attitude about Brighton Beach. The cinema verité footage of the deli, the restaurant, the street, and the subway station, as well as the Beach, echo a community in a deep malaise. The emigrés are not home in their new home. But they recreate the sounds and smells and sights that remind them of home—Moscow, Mother Russia. The film has a powerful sense of place and of nostalgia for that other home, far away.

Besfamilny's views about place infuse *Brighton Blues* and share with us a profound sadness about displacement. This is her voice in *Brighton Blues*.

Cast Study in Plot

Ethan Spigland's *Strange Case of Balthazar Hyppolite* tells the story of a film archivist who finds some rare film footage by the filmmaker Balthazar

Hyppolite. The film predates the numerous technological discoveries that helped create the film industry. Consequently it is footage of considerable historic importance. The balance of the film is devoted to searching and reconstructing the footage. In the second part of the film, the main character's love interest in a fellow archivist is introduced. By the end, the footage has been added to, and a new narrative reconsideration of the footage is presented.

Spigland is himself obsessed with obsessive characters. This plot of reconstructing lost footage provides him with the opportunity to explore that characteristic, to observe that love of film and love itself often fuse and, in a sense, combine. The distinction between movie-life and real-life blurs for the character. His structure, essentially a detective story told initially in a serious and later in a mocking tone, is both a paean to film and a mocking commentary on obsession (his and others) with film. The detective style plot allows Spigland to freely editorialize about the purpose and passion of his main character.

A Case Study in Time

Phil Bertelson's *Around the Time* is an interview by a son of his father. What Bertelson is exploring is actually the circumstances of his own birth. This encounter of young adult and middle-aged man is a meeting of two strangers. The conversation triggers the narration by the father of a time a generation earlier, of his relationship with a white woman, and of the sign of the times, the impermanence of interracial relationships. The relationship fails, but the narrator gives us the nervous, excited feel of the early sixties, a time when change was possible, if elusive. By framing the story around the relationship and the time of the relationship, the filmmaker is looking to understand the circumstances of his birth. Bertelson does not condemn or approve his father. He remains dispassionate, the true interviewer of the narrative. Consequently, the sense of time dominates character, goal, and plot. As in the Besfamilny film, the sense of place and time is overwhelmingly the core of the film. All else is secondary.

A Case Study in Tone

Geoffrey Mandel's *Kill the Director* is a mockumentary about production, specifically student production. It uses interview techniques focusing on the director and his crew. The tale is one of continual failure. Crew members leave. The director feigns optimism, and artistic integrity above all is his goal, even in the nude scenes. Eventually all the crew members and actors leave, and the director undresses and films himself as stand-in for the actor. A lamp falls on him and kills him. His crew rallies, finishes the film, and wins numerous awards. It was art after all.

Mandel's film amusingly mocks pretension, film criticism, acting, and directing. Every area is subject to mockery, and the result is a mockumentary that amusingly portrays student film production as disproportionately earnest.

To sum up, docudrama allows the voice of the writer-director to dominate. As a form it uses style to both suggest the importance of the film but also to allow that voice to override and shape the dramatic properties—character, structure and tone.

NOTE

1. As described in K. Dancyger and J. Rush, *Alternative Scriptwriting* (Boston: Focal Press, 1991), 52–54.

14

THE HYPERDRAMA

Hyperdrama is in many ways far from both melodrama and docudrama. Although it maintains the basic structural elements and places a conflictual main character against a plot, hyperdrama is the opposite of the tonal realism and factual realism so central to the other two meta-genres. In this sense, excessive exaggeration, hyperbole, and fantasy all are key ingredients of the hyperdrama. Although the analogy to the fairy tale is too restrictive, the parallels are there—the predominance of elemental moral struggle. In "Little Red Riding Hood," the danger is the unknown, and the moral struggle concerns respect for one's elders. How different is the story in the *Star Wars* trilogy, where respect for one's elders is modernized? In the trilogy, the ultimate elder, the father, no longer deserves respect. What is a child, in this case a son, to do?

Hyperdrama can directly mimic the fairy tale, as does Neil Jordan's *The Company of Wolves* (1984), or it can convert the fairy tale into a horror story, like Vitaly Kanevski's *Freeze Die* (1989). Both focus on a child as the main character, and both embrace a level of incident whose intention is to give moral instruction to the main characters about their relationships with the worlds they find themselves in. The genre, then, has a wide latitude. Also, it has a long history.

Although particular filmmakers have been affiliated with hyperdrama—Luis Buñuel throughout his career, from Spain to Mexico to France—the genre is more often affiliated with humorists, such as Charlie Chaplin and the Marx Brothers. *Modern Times* (1936) is a fable about industrialization and its explicit tendency to mechanize and dehumanize. The many set-pieces in the film have an internal logic, but they are so fabulist in their content that realism is actually beside the point. A similar quality infuses the majority of Chaplin's work, with the exception of *Monsieur Verdoux*, a film that suffers from its link to realism.

At the other extreme, the films of the Marx Brothers dwell on the anarchy that befalls characters beset by life problems—making a living, getting along, organizing action toward a goal. All the character's goals are subverted by the anarchy that allows individual will to reign supreme. In the Marx Brothers' films, such as *Duck Soup*, the truly moral thing to do is take care of yourself at the expense of others, a modern moral interpretation that has made their films popular to this day.

Hyperdrama seems to have taken on new life since *Star Wars*. Although filmmakers like Fellini occasionally drifted into hyperdrama (*Satyricon*), today there are numerous filmmakers whose careers are associated with it. They are notable filmmakers, too—Werner Herzog (*Aguirre, Wrath of God*), Steven Spielberg (*E.T.*), Stanley Kubrick (*A Clockwork Orange*), Robert Zemeckis (*Forrest Gump*), Emir Kusterica (*Underground*), Neil Jordan (*Butcher Boy*), and Lars Von Trier (*Breaking the Waves*). What is also notable is that particular genres—the action-adventure film, the horror film, and the melodrama—are all amended in hyperdrama to incorporate, above all, a moral lesson, which have been powerfully embraced by audiences. In order to understand why, we now turn to the general characteristics that distinguish hyperdrama from other genres.

GENERAL CHARACTERISTICS

The Centrality of the Moral Lesson

At its heart, hyperdrama is a story told in service of a moral lesson. Character, plot, tone, all serve that overriding purpose. The moral lesson might be focused on personal behavior. The main character in Buñuel's *The Criminal Mind of Archibald Cruz* is a character convinced that he committed a crime (murder) as a child. We know that he did not. However, he conducts his life and relationships in an aura of guilt and in the expectation that if he becomes too close to anyone, in a love relationship for example, he will again become a murderer. The moral lesson of Buñuel's film is that we are all prisoners of our childhood experiences, whether they are negative or positive. How useful or not this imprisonment is goes to the core of Buñuel's goal in *The Criminal Mind of Archibald Cruz*.

The moral lesson can be driven by social or community standards, as in the case of Zemeckis's *Forrest Gump*. By community standards, Forrest Gump is slow intellectually, and consequently he does not quite comprehend events around him. He passes through the Hippie Revolution, the Vietnam War, the political upheavals of the '70s, and the rising hopes of the '80s in America. All the while he is a constant—running toward or away from his peers, ingenuous, a Candide in a shark-infested society. In his naiviete, in his faith in people, and in his constancy he actually becomes "the one good person" who can change the lives of others. Here the moral lesson is that communities sometimes are too quick to label their members and consequently limit them and their contributions. The moral lesson is to back away from labeling and limiting.

The moral lesson can also be driven by political goals. The young boy who decides to stop growing, as a political protest to Nazism, in Volker Schlondorff's *The Tin Drum* is making a political statement. The immorality of the regime and its influence on personal codes of conduct is so pervasive that the young boy's moral decision about his own physical stature is both pragmatic and metaphorical. The ideology of Nazism, with its racism and its celebration of Aryanism, is visually assaulted by the main character's stature. He is German, he is imperfect, and yet more moral than his peers.

The engine at the heart of the hyperdrama is the moral lesson. This quality distinguishes the form from other genres.

Realism Is Not Important

Although moral tales can be presented realistically, if hyperdrama is to be dramatically acceptable, realism actually gets in the way. Perhaps a more inclusive description of hyperdrama requires that the fantastic, positive or negative, be integral to the genre. This may mean man-monsters, as in Jordan's *The Company of Wolves*: it might mean the monster within, as in John Frankenheimer's *Seconds*; it might mean the existence of magic, as in John Boorman's *Excalibur* and Ron Howard's *Willow*. It certainly embraces the actualized imagination, as in Jean Claude Lauzon's *Leolo* and Victor Fleming's *The Wizard of Oz*.

Skirting around the issue of realism is the notion that hyperdrama films are really children's films, like *The Lion King* et al. This is not actually the case. Although the main character in Jordan's *The Company of Wolves* is a teenager, the presentation is too violent for children. The film is more a cautionary tale for adults. The same is true for Boorman's treatment of the Arthurian legend in *Excalibur*. Hyperdrama may include films for children, such as *The Wizard of Oz* or *Willow*, but often the subject matter or its treatment is far too extreme or sophisticated for children. The key issue here is that realism plays no part in hyperdrama, whether the intended audience is children or adults. Perhaps it might be more accurate to consider hyperdrama as the genre that speaks to the child in all of us.

Character Is the Vehicle

In melodrama the main character provides the direct means to identify with the outcome of the narrative. In hyperdrama, identification with the main character is less important. The main character is only the means or vehicle for the narrative. Consequently, we experience the character more as an observer rather than the stronger role of participant. We view the main character's alienation and depression in Frankenheimer's *Seconds*, but do we feel deeply about his fate? In a melodrama we would; here we do not. We remain detached from Lauzon's Leolo, a young boy so alienated from his family that he creates a new identity (Italian rather than French-Canadian) rather than be identified with it. As he says, "I dream and therefore I am not [a member of this family]." He is detached, and so too are we.

In Boorman's *Excalibur* we observe Arthur, the idealistic and cuckolded king, but we do not identify with him. We position ourselves far more easily with Merlin the magician, a man above the worldly and otherworldly goings-on of *Excalibur*. We understand, even like, Forrest Gump, but do we identify with him? I think not. In hyperdrama, the main character is the important vehicle for the story, but no more than that.

Plot Is Critical

Consider the plot in hyperdrama as a lengthy journey wherein the main character will encounter many obstacles. The characters may succeed, or they may fail; in one way or another, they will be transformed by the journey. In the *Star Wars* trilogy, the galaxy is the path that will take a son into a confrontation with his father. In *Excalibur*, the journey for Arthur is from a warring, barbaric origin (his birth) to an attempt to establish a just society (Camelot), where nobility and honor will supplant cruelty and betrayal. In *Forrest Gump* the journey is from childhood to parenthood, the twist here being the childlike (simple and pure) quality of the main character. In Kusterica's *Underground*, the journey is from the violence of World War II Yugoslavia to the violence and irrationality, even madness, of the dissolution of the country in the late 1980s—a forty-year descent from hell to a deeper hell.

The journey is substantial, and consequently the amount of plot tends to be considerable. In a sense, the degree of plot in hyperdrama is so great that it makes the main character either a superhero or a "supervictim."

It is important to acknowledge that hyperdramas are not character-driven stories but rather stories dominated by plot.

The Structure of the Plot Is Rife with Ritual

Plot in hyperdrama tends to differ from the deployment of plot in the war film, which tends to be realistic. Indeed the plot in hyperdrama has a very different rhythm from plot in other genres; it is ritualistic and formal rather than familiar or realistic. Some examples will illustrate the point. Battles between good and evil, whether in *Star Wars* or *Excalibur*, tend to be formal—in *Excalibur*, they are orchestrated to Wagner. Those battles, in their details, veer from realism into a formalistic, archetypal struggle analogous to the gunfight in the classic western and the concluding series of executions in *The Godfather Part I*. These ritualized events make these plot points metaphors more than "historical" points in a narrative. It is those rituals that make the character a symbol, a superhero, or a supervictim, rather than a mere mortal.

Ritual is very important in the movement of the plot from realism to a different kind of journey—more symbolic, less simple.

The need to seek out ritualized events also moves the story away from the individual, empathic course of events to the symbolic level, where the character is the means rather than the end.

Tone Is Formal and Fantastic

The tone of hyperdrama has to embrace both the ritualistic and the fantastic—the opposite of realism. Even the poetic tone of the western is insufficient to capture the tone in hyperdrama. Hyperdrama is a form that simulates the children's fairy tale, and as such it has to be filled with an excess (without the pejorative connotations of the word) that embraces the fantastic; "operatic" is a description that comes to mind; "florid" is another. The key is essentially an over-the-top tone that allows to seem plausible a story where anything goes. Ridley Scott's *Legend* is a good example of this "anything goes" tone, and so are Boorman's *Excalibur*, Schlondorff's *The Tin Drum*, and Frankenheimer's *Seconds*.

In a sense, the tone of hyperdrama is as far from the realism of melodrama as you can imagine, plus a bit farther. Even the more formal examples of the style are over the top; they simply have a greater aura of ritual rather than of anarchy. Kubrick's *A Clockwork Orange*, Herzog's *Aguirre, Wrath of God*, and Von Trier's *Breaking the Waves* exemplify this dimension of tone in hyperdrama.

The Authorial Voice

The authorial voice is quite muted in melodrama and overarching in docudrama, but in hyperdrama it is powerful and passionate. After all, the goal of hyperdrama is the moral lesson, with the main character the vehicle for that lesson. In fact, the goal of the writer in hyperdrama is to convey that voice despite the viewer's involvement with the story. That is not to say we do not care for Dorothy in *The Wizard of Oz*. Rather we are much more aware of the writer's views on childhood, play, and the importance of the imagination. At its heart, the film is about the importance of hope in a child's life; this is what we take away from the experience of *The Wizard of Oz*.

The writer views himself or herself as a moralist, exploring moral choices and issuing cautions or recommendations for how we the audience should proceed in the world. This is above all the goal of the writer in hyperdrama. In order to do so the writer looks for the most elemental means—simplicity of character, a basic conflict, and an imaginative journey, which together will make the point for the audience.

Although on one level this may seem pompous (when it does not work), in fact it signals the seriousness of the writer. Given the elemental nature of the lesson, the struggle must be imaginative to convey the moral lesson and to make the vivid connection so necessary for the child in all of us to relate to the story.

Issues of the Day

Because of the serious intent of the writer in hyperdrama, issues of the day have to be used in a particular way. In a sense, issues of the day are powerfully drawn to the melodrama. The "greed is good" mantra in Oliver Stone's 1980s treatment of capitalism in *Wall Street* exemplifies this approach. Hyperdrama, in its over-the-top quality, pushes the issue of the day farther. The result is a film like Taylor Hackford's *The Devil's Advocate* (1997). On the same theme as the Stone film, Hackford's treatment introduces a more proper Devil (to Keanu Reeves' Faustus)—to replace Gordon Gecco from *Wall Street*. The issue is the same, but suddenly our perception of the main character and the dramatic arc is different. What are we to make of the experience? Do we accept it? Do we accept the seriousness of the issues, or do we reframe the experience of *The Devil's Advocate* as cartoonish and more trivial? This is always the danger when hyperdrama deals with topical issues.

A more effective treatment in this respect is Frank Capra's treatment of postwar malaise and responsibility in *It's a Wonderful Life* (1946). When we compare it to a melodramatic treatment of a similar subject in William Wyler's *The Best Years of Our Lives* (1947), we understand better why the melodrama flourished and Capra's film failed at the time: heaven and angels seemed out of place in the immediate postwar period. But today, after fifty years, it is the Capra film that is shown continually and celebrated. The Wyler Academy Award winner film is rarely seen and even more rarely written about.

What all four films mentioned suggest is that hyperdrama has to treat issues of the day in a more urgent manner than does melodrama. The treatment implies that meaning would be lost with a superficial concern with current questions. The result is the introduction of an active, positive deity in *It's a Wonderful Life* and an active, negative deity in *The Devil's Advocate*. Its as if only the interventions of the gods can prevent the society, community, or individual from drowning in the challenges of the day—in *It's a Wonderful Life* an overwhelming sense of responsibility, and in *The Devil's Advocate* overwhelming ambition and personal greed.

MOTIFS—CASE STUDIES

As in the case of the earlier genres, it is useful to look at three case studies in order to understand hyperdrama in a fuller sense. The three case studies we will use are Volker Schlondorff's *The Tin Drum* (1929), John Frankenheimer's *Seconds* (1964), and John Boorman's *Excalibur* (1983).

The Tin Drum

The Main Character and His Goal

Oscar is a young boy born at the end of World War I in the contested Baltic area of Danzig. Part German and part Polish, the zone is neither and both. These national tensions are represented in Oscar's paternity. His mother loves two men, one Polish and the other German. One of the two is his father.

Growing up in this confused familial and national environment, Oscar decides at age five to stop growing. He only gives up this goal after the end of World War II, with his parents dead and the fate of Danzig decided (it is captured by the Russians and becomes part of Soviet-occupied Poland). Now twenty, Oscar begins to grow again. The goal is made more plausible by giving Oscar other eccentricities and characteristics. For instance, he always carries his drum. The drum, and his scream, which shatters glass, are the two means Oscar chooses to use to communicate his feelings.

The Antagonist

There is no single antagonist in *The Tin Drum*. If there is any force that plays this role it would be nationalism, specifically the Nazi form, which in its aggressiveness destroyed people, relationships, communities. The focus in *The Tin Drum* is on one family, on its destruction in the period when its progeny, Oscar, chose stunted growth as a defense against Nazism.

Oscar is not a political character, and his story unfolds in a reactive, emotional, and visceral fashion. Consequently the antagonist, nationalism, manifests itself only in the relationships within his family and in the fate of those who have been kind to him—a Jew, a female Italian dwarf—and of course in the fate of the three people who he considers his parents. In this sense the antagonist is an atmosphere, a distant political entity, rather than single person.

The Catalytic Event

Oscar's birth is the catalytic event of the narrative. In the birth canal he appears already full formed, eyes knowing, the same size he will be when he makes his fateful decision to stop growing. He is presented therefore at birth with a sense of seeing and knowing that one does not associate with a newborn child. This presentation makes credible the act of will that marks the end of his growth. It also positions Oscar as the perennial observer rather than participant in the events that shape his life. Also, because he is presented as a passive observer, in essence the position of the child in society, we observe events as he does, with a detachment unusual given the nature of the events that will follow.

Resolution

The war ends. His German father chokes on his Nazi Party pin and is killed by a Russian. At the burial, Oscar consciously decides that he will resume physical growth. His stepbrother throws a stone, which strikes him. He falls on his father's grave, and he begins to grow once more.

The Dramatic Arc

The journey that Oscar travels is the twenty-year history following World War I. It is a political history wherein Danzig is made a free state, neither German nor Polish. It is an uneasy state, because each minority identifies with its ethnic parent, Germany or Poland respectively. As events shift and German nationalism becomes a force, brownshirts, swastikas, and brutality toward Jews mount. War comes on September 1, 1939; a the battle for the post office becomes the microcosm for German aggression and Polish resistance. The town is quickly occupied. The Germanization of Danzig is rapid, and the rise and fall of German fortunes of war chronicle the history of the town. Finally the Russians overrun the city, and the war is over. This is the plot of *The Tin Drum*.

The background story is the chronicle of Oscar's relationships with his grandmother, his mother, the two fathers, a housekeeper, and finally a troupe of midgets and dwarfs. Only among the dwarfs does Oscar have anything approximating a peer, an adult relationship. In all other cases he is the child reacting against the cruelty and unsettling qualities of the adult world. The relationships never progress very far; they are always inhibited or ended by the progress of the plot.

Narrative Style

The Tin Drum has a great deal of plot, as one would expect in a hyperdrama. But it also has many character scenes. The character layer, however, is never developmental. Oscar is principally the child, and the adults seem transient in his world; they exit, or they die. Only the grandmother provides any continuity for Oscar.

Narrative Shape

Time is not a critical factor in this story. Because the character is resistant to the passage of time (he stops his own physical growth), physical time is in fact suspended as an element in his life. The story itself follows forty-five years of the history of one family in this Baltic region.

Tone

"Fantastic" is the first observation one makes about the tone of this film. Events are extreme. A woman hides a man from the police beneath her expansive four skirts. While she is being questioned by the police in the middle of a potato field, he impregnates her. Later a birth canal is observed by the child who is to be born. Three years later, the main character decides to grow no longer. All these events are fantastic, beyond belief, and yet together they set the moral parameters of this story.

Later the fantastic is joined by the macabre. Oscar's parents observe eels being caught in the sea. A dead horse's head yields the fresh eels that will be dinner. The wife is revolted, and yet later she kills herself by overeating fish. Even later, the father is killed by choking on his Nazi Party pin—he had tried to hide it from a Russian by swallowing it. All these events are symbols of the relationship of life to death in the period of the Third Reich. In the end, all the death symbols—the swastika, the bodies of men and animals—prove to be toxic. They kill all of Oscar's parents.

Seconds

The Main Character and His Goal

The main character is Arthur Hamilton, a fifty-five-year-old banker who no longer finds meaning in his life. Although married, father of a married daughter and a bank vice president, Arthur Hamilton has no enthusiasm for life. As he says about his wife, "We get along." That statement captures his sense of his life. His goal is to change, to be "reborn."

The Antagonist

The company that promises to recreate Arthur Hamilton and totally to alter his life is the antagonist. Although it undertakes extensive plastic surgery and physically relocates him from Westchester to Malibu, the company in fact totally controls his life.

The Catalytic Event

Arthur receives a call from an old friend, who has himself been reborn. This contact begins the process of Arthur's rebirth.

The Resolution

Arthur decides he wants to go back to his old life and so informs the company. Further, he will not cooperate with them to find a replacement for himself. The company destroys Arthur, now called Tony Wilson, using his body to help another reborn client.

Dramatic Arc

The journey that Arthur Hamilton, fifty-five-year-old banker, will take is to be transformed into a thirty-five-year-old artist, Tony Wilson (Rock Hudson), living in Malibu. Much effort is put into acclimatizing Arthur/Tony to his new life. Many company employees and other "reborns" participate. When Arthur/Tony finally feels comfortable in his new life (he has the love of a woman, a relationship), a drunken indiscretion about who he really is breaks the facade. His lover in fact is an employee of the company. His neighbors are all linked to the company. Totally disillusioned, Arthur/Tony returns to Westchester. There he visits his wife under the pretext of securing one of her husband's paintings. There he discovers what his wife thought of her husband—that he had been dead long before he was the victim of a hotel fire (the ruse to cover his transformation from Arthur Hamilton to Tony Wilson). Now he understands—it was not his age, it was his attitude to life. He wants to go back. He is returned to the company in New York, but he is noncooperative. He does not know it, but his fate is sealed—he no longer has any value for the company. It kills him.

Narrative Style

Seconds is plot driven, focusing on Arthur Hamilton's transformation into Tony Wilson and then his desire to become Arthur Hamilton again. Throughout he is a victim of his alienation and his unhappiness. When he wakes up, it's too late.

The character layer of this story is principally the failed relationship with his wife and the developed relationship with a younger woman in Malibu. Only later does he discover she is an employee of the company. The two male relationships that are explored are with his college friend Charlie, the reborn who brings him to the company, and with the paternalistic head of the company. In both cases, Arthur is naive enough to believe what they say.

The character layer throughout demonstrates Arthur's poor judgment. He keeps making false choices. Only his wife seems genuine, strong, and nonmanipulative—and he walks away from that relationship in order to be reborn.

Together these two layers portray how alienation can promote poor judgment and in the end self-destruction.

Tone

The tone of *Seconds* is extreme. Both the urban and rural settings focus on isolation and separateness. Also there is paranoia. He is pursued in Grand Central Station by a faceless man. When he first visits the company, he finds himself in a slaughterhouse. Critical moments are ritualized—the operation, the grape-crushing sequence in Santa Barbara where Arthur/Tony loses his inhibitions, the drunken scene at his home in Malibu. All these scenes are rituals, meant to mark Arthur/Tony's rites of passage. Key in both environments, (his past life setting and his new life setting), is that the tone is excessive and far from realism.

Excalibur

The Main Character and His Goal

The main character in *Excalibur* is Arthur, the king. His goal is to be a good king, a wise king, an effective king—that is, not divisive, as his father was. If the king flourishes, so too will his kingdom.

In order to achieve his goal, he must create a cadre of knights who will share and carry out his goals. He himself must be an example of impeccable personal behavior and bravery in order to inspire his knights and override their personal goals and rivalries. This is no small order in a land where rivalry for power is a way of life.

The Antagonist

Although there is a tangible antagonist for the throne in his son, Mordred, and a tangible antagonist for the affection of his wife Guenevere, in Lancelot, the real antagonist is a more internal one. It is the manifestation of the preconscious history of that time—to give in to lust, revenge, and hatred, to hack and maim rather than to transcend those impulses and become a better, more communally positive kind of person. In the story, Merlin the magician tries to encourage first Arthur's father to higher values, and later Arthur. *Excalibur*, the sword of power, offered by the Lady of the Lake to empower the king against his enemies, can only help the king physically. Emotionally, Arthur (and earlier his father, Uthor), are susceptible to their impulses and their vanity. In the end, it is those qualities that destroy both men. The antagonist then, is the impulsiveness, the weakness, of men within themselves. When these qualities dominate a king's behavior, all the people under him will suffer. If he can transcend these qualities with the help of Merlin and the Lady of the Lake—in effect, of the gods—he can create a better society for all.

The moral tale here is that we have the power within us "to heal or to hack." Which will we choose? In *Excalibur*, Arthur gives in to his vanity and his jealousy, and he is consequently destroyed.

The Catalytic Event

The catalytic event is the birth of Arthur (the new hope). Uthor, who has been given *Excalibur* to consolidate his power, has made peace with his rivals. But it is not long lasting. At the celebration of the peace, he desires his recent enemy's wife. Fighting recurs; Uthor asks for Merlin's help and secures it. But there is a price. Merlin develops a plan—withdraw your troops from the siege of your enemy's castle. The enemy will follow. When he does, Merlin will use his magic to transform Uthor to look like his enemy. Uthor goes to his enemy's wife. She believes him to be her husband, and he rapes her. But Merlin has secured an oath: the child that will be born of that lust will be his. When Arthur is born, Merlin claims the child. He tells Uthor he is not the king who will save his people. Because of how he treated his enemies, no one trusts him. Indeed, Uthor is killed, ambushed as he tries to retrieve his newborn son.

The Resolution

Arthur is killed by Mordred, his son, and there is no hope in the land (the Dark Ages will continue). *Excalibur* is returned to the Lady of the Lake, to be resurrected when man is more worthy of its power.

The Dramatic Arc

Excalibur is an intergenerational story, but it principally focuses on Arthur and his kingship. His journey is one of growing power and idealization (the creation of the Round Table). But it is also marked by his failures as a man—his idealization of Lancelot and the consequent loss of his wife, his desire for revenge arising out of jealousy, the consequent power vacuum, and his insensitivity to his family—Morgana, Arthur's half-sister, and Mordred. His behavior fuels the flames and prompts Mordred to raise an army against him. Arthur's kingship is one of hope and later disillusionment. His interior journey parallels this arc.

Narrative Style

There is, as expected, a great deal of plot in *Excalibur*—the history of the efforts to unite the land (England) under one king and to pacify the warring factions. The elements of that plot, the effort of Merlin to help Arthur secure power, the contribution of the gods (the sword Excalibur), the sibling rivalry between Morgana and Arthur for power, all contribute to the evolving plot.

The character layer of the story has to do with Arthur's deep trust of men (Lancelot, the knights, Merlin), and his deeper capacity to be deceived by the women in his life (Guenevere, Morgana). The nobility that Arthur ascribes to his male relationships has its converse in the guile and capacity for guile in the women. Clearly Arthur needs both values to succeed as king, but they elude him, and in the end he fails. His idealism is out of place in the world he occupies, and so he fails to reach his goal.

Narrative Shape

Time is not a critical factor in this story. We move through three generations in the course of the story; in the end real progress has been temporary and elusive. This seems to be the role time plays. Arthur's time is a time of possibilities, and even temporary achievement and progress, but in the end that promise remains for a future generation to fulfill.

Tone

The tone of *Excalibur* is operatic, excessive (in a noncritical sense). There is an intensity to it that suggests the barbarism, the violence, that is the alternative to Arthur's Camelot. In every way the tone is expressionistic, over the top—once again, far from realism.

WRITING DEVICES

The Kind of Story That Can Benefit from Hyperdrama

There are many stories that can be framed in terms of a moral tale, but not every story can carry the excessive elements of hyperdrama. Stories that are factual, or too recent in terms of their relationship to a specific historical or cultural event, are difficult to render as hyperdrama.

This, however, leaves many options. Stories about children often lend themselves to the moral tale. They also lend themselves to excess and fantasy. A good example here is Peter Brook's *Lord of the Flies*. Novels such as Orwell's *Animal Farm* have their filmic equivalent in George Miller's *Babe in the City*. Stories about animals, such as the above mentioned, are naturals for hyperdrama. So too stories set as fables. Even a film like Warren Beatty's *Heaven Can Wait* becomes hyperdrama when issues of birth, rebirth, angels, and Heaven become active elements of the narrative. Finally, stories about mythical figures or periods, such as Vincent Ward's *The Navigator*, work well as hyperdrama. In these stories the characters are either archetypal or metaphors serving the moral tale that is at the heart of the narrative.

The Use of Character and a Goal

Character in hyperdrama has to be a vehicle for the story rather than a source of identification for the viewer. We have to stand apart from the character. Consequently, it's not important that we care deeply about the character. But it is important for us to understand the character and why they do what they choose to do.

The goal for the character, on the other hand, is crucial. If Little Red Riding Hood is not eager to go through that forest, her story and its moral will simply have no impact. The vigor of the character's striving toward the goal is very important in hyperdrama. The characters and their goals are internally far more complex than they seem to be on the surface. That passion, that commitment to a goal, is vital. Without it, the resistance to that goal offered by the plot will not be enough to qualify the main character as a superhero or a supervictim. The goal is the key here. But again, identification, recognizability as we find it in melodrama, is not necessary and may even prove counterproductive in hyperdrama.

The Use of Plot to Create a Superhero

Moral tales and fables function on a mythic level. In this respect, writers and teachers of scriptwriting who ascribe to Joseph Campbell's ideas about storytelling are right.[1] A main character goes on a mythic journey. He faces many challenges and setbacks. The journey, once completed, makes him a hero. In hyperdrama this heroic position is in the end a by-product of the scale of the plot. Whether that plot is a war, a difficult journey, or the challenges of the plot, the ritualization of the confrontations with the opposing forces, make the character a hero. Think of Mad Max in George Miller's three "Mad Max" films;[2] think also of Lindsay Anderson's *O Lucky Man* (1974).

The larger the scale of the plot, the more likely we will experience the main character in a way in keeping with the genre's expectations.

The Proximity of Hyperdrama to Children's Fairy Tales

If you think of the story form of the fairy tale, it will help you fashion your story as hyperdrama.

The story is narrated by someone. It is told as a cautionary tale, a life lesson, so that the child will see in the fate of the character a warning to him or herself. But that tale will be told with considerable imagination; the writer does have to grip the child's imagination. Also, the resolution has to contain the message, the moral, the reason for the telling. Always, the teller, the narrator, is outside the story (as we are), looking in. This is the approach so often used in children's fairy tales, and it is useful in conceptualizing a story in the hyperdrama form.

Think for a moment of children's fairy tales—the stories of the Brothers Grimm, of Hans Christian Anderson, of noses that grow long when lies are told, of children too innocent or naive not to follow a pied piper—and you have the driving force behind the hyperdrama. The fairy tale is a life lesson, a moral tale wherein the moral is the driving force for the telling of the story. A narrator or storyteller will take us through the cautionary tale.

The Search for Structure

The search for structure finds a shape in the moral lesson that is intended. The story of Excalibur, the Arthur-Guinevere-Lancelot story, is told quite often. The same story has been told as a love story (Cornel Wilde's *The Sword of Lancelot*), as an action-adventure (David Zucker's *First Knight*), and as a musical (Joshua Logan's *Camelot*). John Boorman's treatment of the story as hyperdrama arises out of a structural choice to make the story a cautionary tale of idealism (of what might be in the future, and of more primitive values—vanity, violence, impulse). Here Camelot is an ideal, albeit temporary, created by King Arthur. His ideal kingdom is destroyed by his rage and jealousy at Lancelot and Guenevere, and his consequent loss of faith in his original goals. The story is really about the importance of an ideal in the forging of a more secure future. It is also about the importance of leadership. As first Merlin and later Parsifal reminds Arthur, the king and the land are one. If the king is strong, idealistic, and wise, the land will flourish. If he is lost, the land will be lost.

The moral lesson forms the structure. In the tale of Icarus, the man who would fly, the moral lesson is that excessive hubris is self-destructive. In that story the structure is that if a man has an idea, he can fly. He creates wings and indeed he does fly, but in doing so, he comes too close to the sun. The wax that has held the wings together melts from its proximity to the sun, and Icarus falls to his death. The lesson to be conveyed will help you form the structure for your story.

The Role of the Catalytic Event

Where you start your story will help you elevate your main character to the status the genre needs. The intervention of angels and Heaven in George Bailey's attempted suicide is the catalytic event that elevates Capra's *It's a Wonderful Life* to the requisite importance and meaning the genre requires. In Lars von Trier's *Breaking the Waves*, the wedding of a character disdained by the entire community sets the boundaries for the meaning of sacrificial love the wife has for her crippled husband. The main character is a limited, low-status person, and yet her love heals her husband.

The catalytic event provides the narrative the elasticity it needs to make the moral lesson effective. Without it, the narrative would flatten or be too realistic for hyperdrama.

Tone

There is no question, you need to create an over-the-top tone for this form or genre. In this form the authorial voice is not gentle; it screams a warning to the viewer. Consequently, the tone you should seek is one of excess; naturalism is what you work *against*. Zemeckis uses irony in *Forrest Gump*, Kusterica uses absurdity in *Underground*, and Buñuel uses both absurdity and irony in *The Criminal Mind of Archibald Cruz*. This is where you have to take your story if it is to take advantage of the strengths of hyperdrama.

THE SHORT FILM

The short film is actually a more natural form for hyperdrama. The long film, with its complexity of character and relationships, is more immediately compatible with realism. The short film, with its relationship to the short story, the poem, the photograph, and the painting, is a more metaphorical form, and consequently it adapts easily to hyperdrama.

Style in the Short Film

There is simplicity in a moral tale. All elements—character, plot, and tone—put the unfolding of a narrative in the service of the moral. Metaphor, exaggeration, nonnatural events and characters can all be brought to bear on the moral purpose of the story. Even a filmmaker as grounded in realism as Bergman found in *Seventh Seal* (1956), for example, that he had to move away from realism. The moral tale—no man can escape mortality—is his subject, and so death and a plot specifically about the spread of Bubonic Plague, the Black Death, are his instruments.

The purpose of the narrative, a moral tale, dictates an imaginative, non-naturalistic treatment of the subject. This is the first observation we can make about the short film. This sort of style is more readily found in the short film than in the feature film.

The Main Character and His Goal

As in the long film, the main character and their goal serve the moral rather than inviting identification. The character tends to be a vehicle, even in stories where he becomes a superhero (*Star Wars*). The voice of the writer-director, his or her affiliation to the moral rather than to the character, distances us from character. Nevertheless, the main character does have a well-defined goal, and it carries him or her forward into the narrative.

The Role of Plot

Plot is very important in hyperdrama. The plot provides the scale of the story. Unlike in other genres, it is critical to the success of the narrative. In the short film the plot will have far more effect than character. The resulting sketchiness of the characters helps the metaphorical presentation of the narrative.

Structure

The first important element to the structure is the presence of a narrator, someone who will tell the story. In Lisa Shapiro's *Another Story*, it will be the grandmother. In Juan Carlos Martinez-Zaldivar's *The Story of a Red Rose*, it will be a narrator-storyteller who is not visible but acts as the aural guide to the story.

A second observation about structure is that there is very rapid characterization, and the plot is introduced quickly. The plot is presented in the form of a journey, a journey whose purpose is to illustrate the author's moral.

Tone

As in the long film, the tone is quite unconstricted by realism. The tone is quite free—it can be fantastic, or it can be very dark. In both cases, the tone has to make credible events and characters that do not exist in our everyday lives. The presentation of the material should sharpen the passion the author feels regarding the moral tale that underlies the narrative.

A Case Study in Character

Lisa Shapiro's *Another Story*, reprinted in the Appendix to this book, is a cautionary tale about individual differences and how those in power treat those who are different. A grandmother tells a story to her two granddaughters.

In an undefined place in the past, there are two young girls (the age of the two hearers of their grandmother's story). The period seems medieval. The small girls do not like wearing mittens over their black fingernails. One day they are arrested by the knights of the king—because they have black fingernails. They are imprisoned. In prison, one sister saves the other. The story ends with the epilogue: the evil king is overthrown and those with black fingernails no longer have to be afraid. Back in the present, the question is asked whether the story is real and where the grandmother heard it. The film ends with an image of the concentration camp numbers tattooed onto the grandmother's arm; we realize that the story was a fable based on her Holocaust experience.

The characterizations here are simple: the grandmother and the two girls are the principals. There are knights and parents, but all of their characterizations remain on the level of symbol. The grandmother exudes warmth, and the children exude energy and curiosity. Beyond that, everyone is a symbol serving the plot.

Case Study in the Role of the Antagonist

Dead Letters Don't Die, by Anais Granofsky and Michael Swanhaus, is a modern fable about hope and hopelessness. The main character, a postal worker, is always hopeful. His boss, the woman he loves from her letters, and the Santa Claus character all represent urban cynicism. They fulfill the role of antagonist, not in the sense that the main character hates them, but rather in terms of the social and psychological attitude they represent. They have given up hope. People who are hopeless represent the antagonist. The plot, the effort to save the world by throwing money from the top of the Empire State Building, is not a success. So Fupper's conversion of Amanda, the effort to rescue her, to offer her his love, becomes Fupper's offer of hope. To save one person without hope is to save the world. This is the moral of the Granofsky/Swanhaus screenplay. It is unusual in that we care about the fate of those who represent hopelessness, the antagonists in the narrative.

Case Study in Plot and Tone

Juan Carlos Martinez-Zaldivar's *The Story of the Red Rose* is based on a fairy tale by Oscar Wilde. Every effort is made to be faithful to the fairy tale. This is the story of how red roses were created, and it depends on the interplay of humans with creatures who are partially human, partially nymphlike, called "nighting birds." The time is the distant past. A scientific human pursues the Infanta (princess). She asks of him a red rose to match her dress at the ball where they will dance together (if her request is met). But red roses do not exist. She has set him an impossible task.

He has captured a female nighting bird, Sirah, and killed another, a male. He studies them anatomically. Rather than sacrifice the female nighting bird, he frees her. She loves him for it and tries to be more human, but he is consumed by the Infanta.

Sirah approaches first the yellow rose bush and then the white rose bush in her quest—how to create a red rose. The white rose bush tells her that there is only one way. The white rose bush gives her a white rose; she must plunge the rose deep into her heart, and her blood will dye the white rose red. He asks if it is for a human. She acknowledges it and sacrifices her life to create the necessary rose.

The human finds the rose and her body. He buries her. He rushes with the rose to the Infanta, but he is rebuffed. Someone else has offered her rubies. The scientist is crushed, but red roses grow from Sirah's grave, and this is how red roses began to grow.

The plot of *The Story of the Red Rose* is Sirah's search for a way to create a red rose. The plot is a journey that leads her from love to self-sacrifice and death. The moral is implied that only through self-sacrifice and love can true beauty (the red rose) be created. As we expect in hyperdrama, the plot far outweighs the characterizations of Sirah, the scientist-human, and the Infanta.

In terms of tone, this fairy tale is marked by beauty, violence, grace, and sacrifice. Its characters are paradoxical—the humans are not graceful, but the half-humans (the nighting birds) and the white bush are honest and filled with grace. Naturalness is nowhere to be seen. A formal, ritualistic quality shapes the nonnaturalistic tone and fills the story with beauty and horror, as suits the moral.

Hyperdrama requires such excess to assure the foregrounding of the moral (the voice of the author) over any identification with the character in the narrative.

NOTES

1. J. Campbell, *Hero with 1000 Faces*. (New York: World, 1965.)
2. *Mad Max, Road Warrior, Beyond Thunderdome.*

15

THE EXPERIMENTAL DRAMA

Experimental drama, often called *experimental narrative*, should not be confused with the more specifically nonnarrative experimental film or video. The experimental film or video is often entirely taken up with an issue of style. In the extreme (in more than one Norman McLaren film), the film can concern itself with the variations of movements of abstract lines or shapes. There, line or shape gave a visual dimension to an abstract musical piece. The narrative intention is at best remote; more often in such work it is not a factor. In the experimental drama, in contrast, narrative intention does have a role. However, the form or the style of the piece is as important as—in some cases more important than—the narrative.

Today, the most common expression of the experimental drama is the music video, but its roots are deep, often affiliated with the most important names in film history. Dziga Vertov's *The Man with a Movie Camera* (1928) playfully explores a day in the life of a cameraman, but its style, which explores every conceivable camera angle and plays with projection and special effects (for instance, the cinema seats rise and fall in unison), creates the energy and playfulness of the filmmaking process. The style is very much more memorable than the content. So it is also in Alexander Dovschenko's *Earth* (1930) and Luis Buñuel's *Un Chien d'Andalou* (1928). The latter film, which Buñuel made with the painter Salvador Dali, illustrates the experimental drama's link to the other arts as well as to the intellectual currents of the day. The anarchistic style of the Buñuel-Dali film attempts to appeal to the unconscious with a series of visual shocks—an eye being slit, two bleeding donkeys being dragged atop a piano and in turn dragging two ensnared priests, insects crawling out from a hole in a human hand, and so on. There is a narrative of sorts, but it is continually subverted by these shock images. The result is a powerful if unclear experience.

Here too there is a clue to the nature of experimental drama. It follows a nonlinear pattern as opposed to a linear time or character-arc frame. The usual elements that shape a story—a goal-directed main character, a plot—

and a traditional genre all tend to be subverted in the experimental drama. We are left with the powerful stylistic elements of the experience.

Other notable figures who have worked with experimental drama are Maya Daren (*Meshes in the Afternoon*, 1943), Chris Marker (*La Jetée*, 1962), Andrei Tarkovsky (*The Mirror*, 1974), Miklos Jansco (*The Round-up*, 1965), Alan Resnais (*Last Year at Marienbad*, 1961), and Krystof Kieslowski (*The Double Life of Veronique*, 1992). More recently, such filmmakers as Sally Potter (*Orlando*) in England, Patricia Rozema (*I Even Heard the Mermaid's Singing*) in Canada, and Jane Campion (*Sweetie*) in Australia have joined others like Julie Dash (*Daughters of the Dust*) and Su Friedrich (*Sink Or Swim*) in the United States to produce what are essentially experimental dramas. Terence Davies (*Distant Voices, Still Lives*) in England, Atom Egoyan (*Exotica*) in Canada, and Quentin Tarantino (*Pulp Fiction*) in the United States all are equally interested in the experimental drama.

GENERAL CHARACTERISTICS

Nonlinearity

The key to experimental narrative is the desire to avoid conventional narrative. Conventional narrative is essentially a character-driven or plot-driven story with a beginning, middle, and end. In conventional narrative, the main character may or may not achieve his or her goal, but the drive to achieve the goal carries us through the story to a resolution. A nonlinear story may eschew a single main character, or a plot, or a resolution, or all of the above. In the experimental narrative, the energy of the story comes from the style the writer-director chooses to use to compensate the audience for the loss of linear direction through the story. Many experimental narratives have no plot, some have no defined character. Consequently, the conventional dramatic tools—conflict, polarities—are less at play. In experimental narrative, form or style is as important as, and often more important than, content. Consequently a nonlinear form is more able to capture the essence of experimental narrative than is the usual set of dramatic tools deployed in more conventional or linear narrative.

A Distinct Style

A style is effective when it helps the narrative it is trying to tell. A style is notable when there is an innovative, as opposed to derivative, feel to the energy it injects into the story. The consequence of the latter point is that experimental drama works best for those who are innovative with their stories.

Borrowed styles are obvious, and because the narrative content is often modest, the borrowed style fails to capture the audience it seeks. The consequence is that the shelf life of an experimental narrative filmmaker tends to be short. There are exceptions—Buñuel, Tarkovsky—but they are few. More often the filmmaker turns to more conventional approaches to promote a lengthier career. The shift of Quentin Tarantino from *Pulp Fiction* to *Jackie Brown* exemplifies this pattern. But what is a distinct style? The distinct style so often associated with experimental narrative is difficult for the filmmaker to sustain over a career. Generally content considerations triumph, and the primacy of style wanes.

When Richard Lester made *A Hard Day's Night* in 1965, he was looking for a style that would capture the energy and anarchy of the Beatles. He knew their strength was their music and their individualism, so he sought out a style that would capture those qualities. In essentially the first MTV-style major film, Lester created a series of set pieces unified by the song of the same title. Within that unity he would go anywhere, show anything, shifting tone or point of view. The key was to recreate the energy of the Beatles. He used multiple cameras, a series of running gags, and an absurdist attitude—and the rest is history. The MTV style in Oliver Stone's *Natural Born Killers* is a direct descendant of Lester's film; however it broadens the stylistic palate to include variances in the style of the set pieces, and the pace, now thirty years later, has picked up considerably.

The style in Atom Egoyan's *Exotica* (1994) is probing. The story, set principally in a sex bar named Exotica, follows multiple characters. All are wounded; all are sexually confused. Egoyan uses a restless style, probing for understanding, finding principally the characters' obsessions, delusions, and smoke screens. It's as if he is looking for an opening but the characters avoid it. It is only at the end that he (and we) find that opening; until then it is the probing, eroticized style that maintains the energy in the story.

The style may focus on stills, as in Chris Marker's *La Jetée*; it may focus on long takes, as in Miklos Jansco's *The Round-up*; it may focus on haunting images, as in Michaelangelo Antonioni's *The Passenger*; or it may be driven by a fascination with a particular piece of music, the use of the Mamas and Papas' "California Dreamin'" in Won Kar-Wai's *Chungking Express*; or it may contain all of the above characteristics. Whatever the mix, the distinct style of the experimental drama infuses a powerful energy into the narrative.

Linkages to the Other Arts

More than any of the other genres in this section, the experimental drama takes up the other arts, both for inspiration and for affiliation. All of the arts struggle with the issues of form and content. But the experimental drama, unlike melodrama and the docudrama does not affiliate itself with realism. Indeed it probes with style to find psychological meaning, as opposed to a sociological realism. The work of Buñuel and Dali, for example, links directly to Dalí's paintings, his "dream works." Chris Marker's *La Jetée* links to the tension between photojournalism and fiction. Federico Fellini's *Satyricon* links Dante's *Divine Comedy* with the paintings of Heironymous Bosch. Dovschenko's *Earth* and Bertolucci's *Sheltering Sky* link to the epic poetry of the Far East and the Middle East, respectively. Peter Brook's *Marat/Sade* has everything to do with his own ideas and plays about space as used in the theater.

The key point here is that the experimental drama links to other arts to draw inspiration and to use the affiliation to point up the style chosen for the narrative. Because film has principally been seen as a popular art form, this linkage to the other arts places the goals of the experimental drama in closer proximity to their goals. Those goals may be literary, or they may be related to painting or music. Whichever art it might be, the linkage lends a seriousness of intention to the experimental drama.

The Intellectual Concept

Not only is experimental drama tied to the other arts, but it is also linked directly to intellectual concepts. That is not to say that other genre are not concerned with ideas; rather, the role of an intellectual concept is far more central in experimental drama than it is in other genres. A few examples will illustrate the point. Freud's ideas about sexuality and aggression are influential in the imager in Buñuel/Dalí's *Un Chien d'Andalou*. They are even more central in Daren's *Meshes in the Afternoon*. Erik Erikson's stages of development mix with Jung's archetypal ideas in Friedrich's *Sink Or Swim* (1989). Her self-reflective autobiography and its structure are also influenced by her father's anthropological background. The structure of the film, made up of chapters, echoes an anthropological diary of growing up, from conception to adulthood.

The experimental drama links both to the other arts and to an intellectual concept. These linkages help define the structure of the experimental drama.

The Abstraction of Character

Character is far less important in experimental drama than in any other genre. As in hyperdrama, the character is a vehicle for the ideas of the writer-director. Whereas in hyperdrama the character has a goal, however, in experimental drama the character has no apparent goal. Consequently he or she is clearly present in the narrative for the purposes of the writer rather than of the narrative. Identification is not at all likely; we follow characters in Antonioni's *The Passenger* without sympathy or apparent reason, except that they are in the narrative. In a film like *Exotica*, there are too many characters, and consequently we follow each of them. Again, the absence of an apparent goal precludes identification, and we view them from the outside looking in, rather than from the inside looking out. The complexity or believability of these characters is less at play, because the style and form of the narrative generates enough energy to keep us with the story.

Perhaps the farthest we can go with these characters is to describe them as obsessed, to see their behavior as habitual (they reject themselves a good deal). These observations make us curious as to the why of their desire and the consequent self-abnegation. Unlike in hyperdrama, where the character serves a moral purpose or goal, no such purpose is obvious for the characters in experimental drama. They serve various purposes, the most obvious being to give us someone to follow through the narrative. Beyond that they are abstract figures—often troubled, always mysterious. Only the style directs us to their habits and to their obsessions, often commenting on both.

The Absence of Plot

With no goal for the character, there is no purpose to plot. Since the dramatic dynamic is main character and goal against plot, the absence of one negates the usefulness of the other.

The result is that the dramatic shape of the experimental drama is entirely shaped by the style rather than the conventional character-driven arc. This can leave us with a diminution of energy. It can leave us confused. It can leave us bored. The challenge for the writer is to deploy style in a playful or energetic manner to offset the absence of a key dramatic device, plot.

The Reliance on Pattern

What is required when plot and character are downplayed is a style that invites involvement from the audience, that creates a pattern substituting for the functions of plot and character. In *Exotica* we follow each of the five characters through a gradual revelation of their sexual confusion and the sources of their despair. In *Sink Or Swim*, the pattern is literary—chapters unfolding chronologically. In *A Hard Day's Night* the pattern is the songs, with the in-between made up of narrative bits—the ongoing concern about Paul's grandfather, the grandfather's unending appetite for adventure, Ringo's inferiority complex, and so. In *Natural Born Killers* the pattern is the frequent references to television. Pattern is the grid along which we begin to find structure, which in turn will lead to meaning. It needs to be said, however, that meaning in the experimental drama can be elusive, or not concrete. We may be left with no more than a feeling at the end of the experience of the experimental drama. Nevertheless, it is the pattern that gives us our first direction toward meaning.

Ritualized Tone

Just as hyperdrama uses ritualization of the action to create metaphor, experimental drama uses the organization of the details, aural and visual, to develop a tone that creates metaphor. The tone may be poetic, as in *Satyricon*; it may be beautifully mysterious and menacing, as in *The Passenger*; it may be hallucinatory, as in *The Double Life of Veronique*; it may be epic and inhumane, as in *The Round-up*. Whichever tone the filmmaker chooses, that tone will tend to have a formal quality that ritualizes the behavior of the characters or creates a metaphor about the sense of place. In Egoyan's *Calendar*, Armenia is every homeland. In *Chungking Express*, Hong Kong is every ultra-urban city, throwing people together and yet making each the loneliest person in the world. The characters in *Exotica* are not simply wounded or confused individuals; they are refugees, running way from twentieth-century alienation.

The ritual of tone, with its formal repetitions of details and sounds, creates the metaphors of people and places that are at the heart of the experimental drama.

The Voice of the Author

If most forms of drama (like melodrama, for example) are deliberate, purposeful, focusing on an emotional experience for the audience, no such contained experience is the goal of the writer of experimental drama. The feeling sought might be too diffuse or too intense to be dealt with directly. Consequently, the author seeks out a more indirect or meditative experience for his audience. The writer might feel as much passion as the writer of the docudrama, but that passion is not as directly accessible to the writer of the experimental drama. Whereas the writer of the docudrama uses form to say "This is important," the writer of the experimental drama uses the form in a more exploratory way. In a sense, the writer is in the position of the poet rather than the popular prose writer—it is in the cadences of the words that a feeling will emerge. Metaphor, image, and feeling substitute for the dramatic tools the docudrama writer uses—character, plot, and structure. There is nevertheless a voice, a definite will to convey a feeling, to share an insight, but what is being shared is not a moral tale, as in hyperdrama, or a political or social polemic, as in docudrama. It may be very simple or complex, but it is very personal and always surprising.

Motifs—Case Studies

In the case of experimental drama, the presentation of the motifs is at considerable variance from that of the other genres. The three case studies will illustrate those differences. We will look at Atom Egoyan's *Calendar* (1993), Wong Kar-Wai's *Chungking Express* (1994), and Clara Law's *Autumn Moon* (1992).

Calendar

Main Character and Goal

The main character in *Calendar* is a photographer. He goes to Armenia, ostensibly to photograph churches for a calendar. He travels with his wife and a driver. While in Armenia we see only his point of view, never him. He asks questions, he reacts, but never in a sympathetic manner. His wife acts as the translator for the driver, explaining the history of the sites. The photographer appears rigid, defensive, and eventually jealous of the developing relationship between his wife and the driver. On a deeper level, he seems to be reacting against her acceptance of being both Armenian and Canadian (after all, she speaks the language). He on the other hand seems a stranger in Armenia, certainly separated from any sense of identification with the place.

Interspersed with the Armenian sequence is a later sequence, which takes place in Canada. The photographer has dinners with a number of women, all from ethnic minorities; each excuses herself when he pours the last glass of red wine. They ask if they can make a phone call. They each do so. Each speaks (apparently to lovers) in their mother tongue—French, German, Finnish, Arabic. As they do, he ruminates on writing to his wife (in Armenia) or to his foster child (also in Armenia). The scene moves back and forth in time from Armenia to Canada.

The Antagonist

There is no overt antagonist in *Calendar*. However, to the extent that the main character is torn between his Armenian origins and his Canadian self, he is his own antagonist. The film seeks no resolution, but the issue of identity—the struggle between the identity deriving from the mother country and that deriving from the host country—is the premise in *Calendar*.

Catalytic Event

Going to Armenia to photograph churches is the catalytic event.

Resolution

There is no real resolution in *Calendar*. Although his wife has stayed in Armenia and he has returned to Canada, we do not know if the marriage is ended or simply in trouble. Nor do we know if the wife has remained with the Armenian driver.

Dramatic Arc

The story progresses back and forth through time rather than along an arc. The Armenian sequence has two distinct parts—traveling, and photographing. Each is presented differently in terms of visual style, but the proximity of the travel footage contrasts sharply with the more distant images of the photography footage. The photographer's point of view unites the two, and the wife is prominent in both. These Armenian sequences contrast with the stillness and the focus on the photographer in the Canadian sequences. Repetition of images, points of view, and style mark each sequence.

Narrative Style

The conventional descriptions of plot-driven or character-driven structures do not really apply to *Calendar*. There is a journey to photograph churches for a calendar, but the character's struggle is not so much with the pictures as his resistance to being in Armenia. He is there physically, but emotionally he is consistently backing away. Back in Canada we see the actual calendar (the published calendar serves as a transition device between the visit to take the pictures and the present in Canada). In Canada, the character tries to relate to women (as his guests), but each rejects him. The fact that they speak their language on the phone implies that his bland Canadian presentation does not engage them. Consequently there is no development in the relationship dimension of the narrative.

Rather, we have the patterns in the past (Armenia). In fact, having taken the pictures he went to take (and thus achieved success), he appears to fail on all fronts—with his wife in Armenia and with these various women in Canada.

Narrative Shape

Physical time is a factor, but the sense of alienation in the main character contrasts with the spiritual well-being of his wife. In this sense, psychological time for the main character stands still.

Tone

The tone of *Calendar* is formal and emphasizes the spiritual value of continuity (his origins in Armenia) and the alienation of displacement (he now lives in Canada). This is an intellectual premise, to which Egoyan gives roots by using himself and his wife as two of the principal actors. The style reflects the fact that Armenia and Canada are very different—Armenia is exterior, open, while Canada is interior and closed. The Armenian sequence is marked by movement; the Canadian sequences are marked by stasis—no change.

Chungking Express

Main Character and Goal

The main character is a policeman who has no luck in his love life. He lives and works in ultra-urban Hong Kong. In a city so densely populated, he seems desperately lonely. He is not antisocial; he simply seems destined to be alone. He has particular habits—he drinks coffee and eats salads and food from a small take-out restaurant. The proprietor is as much as philosopher of relationships as he is a good salesman. He recommends numerous women. One of his employees, his cousin, a very eccentric young woman addicted to records of the American group Mamas and Papas, takes an interest in the policeman. In the middle of the narrative, she takes over the story. In this sense she is also a main character. Her overt goal seems to be to develop a relationship with the policeman, but she does not. Instead, using a key a girlfriend who had rejected him had returned in a letter, she enters his apartment and begins to populate it with fish and other bits of life. When he discovers her in the apartment, she runs off. When he asks her for a date, she does not agree. She runs off to California—the Mamas and Papas song she admires most is "California Dreamin'"! A year later she returns. The policeman has taken over the restaurant from her cousin. The story ends, posing the question, will these two people, clearly attracted to one another, get together? As to the goal of these two characters—clearly both are lonely, but their ambivalence prevents them from getting together.

The Antagonist

The antagonist of this film is the modern ultra-urban existence that fixes people in their places, leaving them fantasies and a not-very-attractive reality. The result is alienated people, unable to reach out to one another. In this sense, the characters are their own antagonists.

Catalytic Event

The two characters meet.

Resolution

The two characters are in front of the restaurant where they had met. Whether they will become a couple remains undefined. In this sense the ending is hopeful, but it is too open ended to imply a definite resolution.

Dramatic Arc

The dramatic arc for each character is an expression of their ambivalent drawing together. For the policeman, the continuum is where he eats, initially at the fast-food restaurant, later at a distant restaurant, and finally setting up his own restaurant. It is as if food and its consumption brings him into contact with women. It is at the distant restaurant that he keeps bumping into the other main character. He then helps her carry produce to the fast-food restaurant. For him, food in all forms mediates male-female relations.

For the woman, the dramatic arc is her growing interest in the policeman. But that interest takes the form first of taking a key out of a letter left for him and letting herself into his apartment. She then develops a relationship with him through her visitations to the apartment. That relationship ends when he finds her at the apartment. He tries now to move the relationship to a more conventional male-female footing. She sidesteps the opportunity and follows her dream—she goes to California, but she leaves him a note—that she will return a year later to the fast-food shop (implying that the date he had asked for is merely postponed). When she returns, now a stewardess and more conventional in appearance, he also has changed profession—he will open a fast-food restaurant on the site of her cousin's restaurant. The film ends with the question open as to whether these two ambivalent people will get together.

Narrative Style

There is no plot in *Chungking Express*. However, there is a character layer. What is unusual about the character layer is that we do not know the two main characters any more at the end of the narrative than we did at the outset. She is a hippie, and he is a policeman. She likes American music, and he likes to eat. He is unlucky with women, and she seems indifferent to men. This is all we know, but all these opposites are explored. The usual development would be to move toward knowing these people and watch them come together in a relationship. The arc is far more tentative here. They keep coming closer and then drifting geographically farther apart. In this sense *Chungking Express* looks initially like a conventional relationship story, but finally it is not.

Narrative Shape

Time is noted but is not critical in this story.

Tone

The time of *Chungking Express* suggests motion and yet stands still. Both characters are always eating or doing something symptomatic of the ultra-urban city, hustling and bustling, and yet Wong Kar-Wai introduces many elements that make them seem immobile. The use of freeze frames as the policeman is running not only slows him down but freezes him in time. The lack of interest of the young woman in her job illustrates how she too is immune from the Hong Kong style. She is the opposite of a hustler—she is looking *not* to do her work. Her level of distraction promotes a sense of indifference to the prevailing values of the city. In many ways the two characters are isolated from their environment.

Much is also made of how people personalize their space—the restaurant, his apartment, her fixation with listening to music when she is supposed to be working. This personalization takes on the character of personal ritual, and although it makes them both seem troubled, it does unite them in our eyes. As one might expect in experimental drama, this creates a psychological sense of Hong Kong, a subjective suitable to these two people.

Autumn Moon

There are two main characters in *Autumn Moon*. The story takes place in Hong Kong, but in this film the city is pictured as a city of skyscrapers and sea. Each is fascinating and offers the two characters a formal space to occupy.

The female character is a fifteen-year-old girl who lives with her grandmother. Her parents and brother have already emigrated to Canada. Whether she is finishing her schooling or waiting for the passing of her grandmother, she is very much in between—being in Hong Kong and being in Canada, being a child and being a woman, being Chinese and being a new generation of internationalists (her favorite food is McDonald's), between being happy and being disappointed in life. She has no discernible, specific goal that drives her through the narrative.

The male character is older, possibly thirty, Japanese, a tourist. He too is in between—between being single and committed, between being material and being spiritual, between being cynical and being curious, between being unfeeling and being feeling. He too has no discernible goal that carries him through the narrative. He does not speak Chinese, and she does not speak Japanese. The two of them converse in English.

Autumn Moon carries us through the course of their unorthodox friendship.

Antagonist

There is no apparent antagonist in the narrative. If anything, they are two products of traditional family-oriented cultures and yet both seem uprooted, floating, without benefit of tradition. They are two modernists, and in this sense they may be their own antagonists. No other characters represent clear antagonists, although there are two important secondary characters, one in each of their lives. The girl's grandmother, who is utterly traditional, is the only character who proceeds with confidence through the story.

For the man's part, he meets the older sister of a former lover from Japan. She too is uprooted, divorced, a modern, unhappy person. They become lovers, but lovers of convenience, and neither of them seems to be able to benefit generally from the intimacy.

The Catalytic Event

The two characters meet.

Resolution

The ending is open ended. Although the two characters have benefited from the friendship of each other, it is clear that the girl will go to Canada and that he will return to Japan. He is more feeling that he was, but spiritually neither seems more rooted than they were.

Dramatic Arc

Beyond the course of the relationship, there is no clear dramatic arc. Within that relationship, the young girl explores a relationship with a male classmate. They are attracted to one another and arrange a tryst but are reprimanded by an adult. He may be a policeman, but he seems more a truant officer. Neither is in any case capable of moving the relationship away from the link of school work and future career. The Japanese tourist, who calls himself Tokyo, also progresses along the line of a male-female relationship. But the narrowly sexual band of that relationship seems as frustrating as the asexual band of the young girl's relationship. The friendship itself between the two seems richer than their individual attempts at relationships. The term "richer," however, implies satisfaction, and that might be too strong a term for the outcome of their relationship. The young girl makes sure his appetite is satiated—she invites him home for her grandmother's authentic cooking. But beyond the cursory hanging out together—visiting her grandmother in the hospital and so on, there is no apparent arc to the relationship.

Narrative Style

The young girl is happy and outgoing, he is introverted and caustic. Beyond that we do not get to know either character very well. Consequently, in the character layer of this story there is no clear developmental quality. Each character seems pleased for the relationship, but one cannot go much further. There is no plot.

Narrative Shape

Just as the character seem suspended between epochs, time too seems suspended. In any case, without linearity, time is not important in the narrative.

Tone

There is a cool, ironic tone to *Autumn Moon*. Although there are moments of deep feeling—his confession to the Japanese woman about his inability to feel, his cruel description of the preferable anatomy of her sister—more frequently the film takes the point of view of voyeur, looking from the outside in on these characters. His constantly video filming supports this sense.

The stylized sense of the city—flat rather than deep—also abstracts the sense of Hong Kong.

WRITING DEVICES

What Kind of Story Benefits from Experimental Drama?

Unconventional stories are the first source for experimental drama. Generally, the stories tend to be exploratory—stories of identity, stories of alienation, meditations on a time or place. Vincent Ward's film *The Navigator* looks at a medieval period, Clara Law's *Autumn Moon* looks at Hong Kong—a place where change and tradition meet and, in the 1990s, conflict. Because experimental drama sidesteps plot, stories of character dominate. Because the genre favors open-ended or nonlinear stories, the preference is for tone, to make up for the absence of resolution.

The Link to Poetry

Poetry can be nonrhythmic or rhythmic, it may relate to content, or it may emphasize form. There is a freedom in poetry that surprises. It relates to the organization of words, patterns, rather than to single images. So too it is with the experimental drama.

If you consider your drama as if it were a visual poem, you will strive for the feeling of a relationship or place, or both, and not unduly re-reference the story back to a conventional mode. The key with experimental drama is that sense of liberation. You are doing something different, and when it works you are a poet, working in the medium of film.

A Simple Idea

Large scale simply works against the experimental drama, so think in very simple, elemental terms. If you limit the parameters of the story and strive for a feeling, you will be on the right road for experimental drama. Keeping the idea simple—two people, a particular place—will help you limit the narrative in such a way that you do not accidentally lapse into a more traditional narrative. Experimental drama does not require a lot of story, so simplify.

How to Use Character

Since plot is not a factor in the experimental drama, the use of character becomes very important.

On one level, the writer must keep a playful attitude toward character. The men in both *Chungking Express* and *Autumn Moon* are depressed, and yet the way the writer-director works with them produces an appealing side to each man. It is important that the women differ in each story; the larger the contrast, the better. In *Autumn Moon* the woman is a girl, fifteen years old, as unspoiled as the man is spoiled. In *Chungking Express*, the woman is an as unpredictable and off the wall as the man is predictable and conservative. The larger the gap, the more play enters the narrative, the more creative the writer can be.

We also should be dealing with the characters in a personal way. We are close to all these characters. They are vulnerable, and yet they remain somewhat inscrutable. They are vulnerable and mysterious. The writer does not want us to know these people any better than they know themselves. As they struggle to understand, so do we. This is an important element of the charm of experimental drama. The narrative and the style are used to attempt to gain understanding into the character. Change may or may not happen; it is less relevant than the exploration, the internal struggle.

Finding a Structure

One observable aspect about the experimental drama is that no two structures are alike. We can say the story tends to be nonlinear, but beyond that few structures resemble one another.

There are shaping devices—a tourist from Japan comes to Hong Kong. What will he find? Can he relate to the Chinese? He finds a Chinese girl, and they strike up a relationship. That relationship is unpredictable. The vehicle they use to communicate is English. In *Chungking Express* it's another unlikely coupling.

The relationship in both cases becomes the shaping device. In *Exotica*, a place is the shaping structure. In Milcho Manchevski's *Before the Rain*, an idea—racial hatred kills love—is the shaping idea. Shaping devices become a means to create a structure. The shaping device, however is not linear—ergo the unpredictability of the experimental drama.

Tone and Voice

This is a form where your voice can be truly unique. The form, the substance, the people, and the structure all will be interpreted through tone. The tone can be poetic, ironic, or expressive, but it should be specific, to help us understand why you are drawn to the characters or place of your story. The tone is the critical mode in which you will transmit your ideas, so in a sense, if you choose the experimental drama, it is your most important decision.

CASE STUDY IN CHARACTER: *SLEEPING BEAUTIES*

In Karyn Kusama's *Sleeping Beauties* (reprinted in the Appendix), two adolescent sisters prepare for bed. They smoke a cigarette and share a fantasy about a young man on a motorbike who will come and take them away. They go to sleep. They hold hands, thereby acknowledging the love between them. Such a motorcycle rider actually does appear, and the dominant sister decides that the more modest sister should join him. She does so. The one who is left behind feels abandoned. Her sister returns. They climb into the same bed, but the dominant sister is unsettled. Was this a dream or an actual occurrence? Was it the beginning of a rift in the relationship? Is fantasy an antidote to the life they live at home?

The key issue in this three-character drama is that the focus is on the two sisters. One is dominant, and the other is pliant—a leader and a follower. But what happens to the relationship when the follower leaves? Will she return? Will the roles be reversed? These are the issues that are explored in *Sleeping Beauties*. The male is simply "the male," but the two young women are characterized, if in a very polarized fashion. They are not fleshed out beyond those extremes. The leader initiates—smoking, ordering the pliant sister to join the bike rider—and the pliant sister does as she is told. Will this change? The ending is open ended, unresolved, leaving us with the puzzle—will she or will she not?

CASE STUDY IN PLACE: *EMPIRE OF THE MOON*

Empire of the Moon, by John Haptas and Kristine Samuelson (1991) is about Paris. The point of view is that of the tourist, the tourist coming to Paris, the tourist discovering the mysterious beauty of Paris, its inscrutable quality. In order to capture the mystery of that beauty, the filmmakers use a mixture of documentary images and abstracted images—parts of buildings, the light of the moon moving across tree-lined residential areas, the artificial lights of the tourist boats that peddle the story of Paris as they glide up and down the Seine. Many of the great sites—the Eiffel Tower, the glass pyramid leading into the Louvre, the Louvre itself, the beautiful train stations, all make up the images of Paris. The tourists come from every corner of the world.

In order to shape their notion of Paris, the filmmakers use a variety of shaping devices—five narrators, readings from Baudelaire and Gertrude Stein about Paris, and the nature of the tourist—some happy to be photographed as visitors, others probing, searching for some mystery, a formula that will alter the part of their life they feel needs altering—art, relationships, ideas.

The key to this experimental narrative is that the beautiful mystery of Paris, the Empire of the Moon, is inscrutable but valuable to each of us who need such a place in our lives.

A CASE STUDY IN STRUCTURE: *RIVER OF THINGS*

River of Things, by Katharine and Mick Hurbis-Cherrier, is based on four poems by Pablo Neruda. The filmmakers present four odes based on the poems: an Ode to Things, an Ode to the Spoon, an Ode to a Bar of Soap, and an Ode to the Table. The film is formally structured by these four odes. Not all are similar in length or tone. Ode to Things, for example, the most naturalistic of the four, is the only one to focus on a relationship—a married couple. It is also linear in its progression—it follows them from the beginning of their day to its end. The poem itself forms their observational-style dialogue. Their dialogue about things is self-reflexive. This is also the longest of the four odes. The next three odes focus differently; Ode to the Spoon is less natural and focuses on the ironic dialectic between functionality and artfulness. Although each of the episodes is playful, this second ode drifts away from the naturalism of the first episode. Spoons move on their own; they become animate. The pace of the second ode is more rapid.

Ode to a Bar of Soap slows down. It remains playful but introduces fantasy and absurdity into the act of the morning bath. Images of chocolate cake and of a bar of soap transformed into an elusive fish in the tub make this sequence the most nonnaturalistic of the four. But as in the first two, the narration is a voice-over. In the last of the odes, Ode to the Table, the narration is sung, as a choral piece. The goal is to make the table the hub for every human activity—functional, sexual, artistic. Many people, a chorus of people, participate around the table in order to give it the centrality the ode implies. The tone is serious, sober, important. The playfulness diminishes.

The overall structure of *River of Things* comes from the Neruda poems. But a secondary structure comes from the tone—a playful attitude toward the narratives of each of the odes. Although the structures is loose, it is nevertheless present, and it shapes the rueful observation of Neruda with a tonal appreciation of those elements in life that we ignore but whose functionality Neruda and the filmmakers laud.

A CASE STUDY IN TONE: *ECLIPSE*

Jason Ruscio's *Eclipse* (1995) provides a powerful experience in tone. Set in an unspecified time and place, the only live character is a young boy, aged twelve or thirteen. Through the course of the narrative there are a series of flashbacks that tell us he is the sole survivor of a massacre. His mother was killed by soldiers. Now he surveys the farm where he lived, he sits by the pit where his mother died, he finds a dead soldier and, holding his gun, fantasizes killing him. Finally he leaves home, following a railroad track until he is found by partisans and taken in.

The tone of *Eclipse* is elegiac, principally about loss. Its nonspecificity with respect to any historical time and place allows us to roam and to believe it is about Bosnia or the Holocaust. In fact, the tone allows us to generalize and speculate about all tragic loss, historical or current. The filmmaker takes a formal approach to his images. The consequence is to create two rituals—one for loss, the other for the will to live. *Eclipse* is a powerful, wordless film that remains with the viewer for a long time. The tone is the central reason for its power.

A CASE STUDY IN VOICE: *ALL THAT'S LEFT: SPECULATIONS ON A LOST LIFE*

Katharine Hurbis Cherrier's *All That's Left: Speculations on a Lost Life* gives us an opportunity to focus on the most lingering aspect of the experimental drama—its exceedingly personal nature. It's not simply the nature of the subject matter that makes it personal; rather, it is the approach taken.

All That's Left is a reminiscence of the filmmaker's aunt. Using a number of photographs of her aunt, children, her husbands, and her mother, together with images of the leaves on trees and other distinctly rural images, the filmmaker tells the story of her aunt's life. It is a simple life, a life of responsibility toward children and foster children, toward two men who were not ideal husbands, and toward her sister, for whom she acted as a mother. Four generations of children are nurtured by the aunt, from her own sister to her two children, her grandchildren when the parents no longer were willing to care for them, and for foster children. As the filmmaker repeats more than once, her aunt's life was a simple life.

The narration, spoken by the filmmaker, searches for meaning. Indeed, the whole film probes for values and meaning. In a poetic, simple way the filmmaker finds that meaning in the profound sense of giving her aunt exhibited. Using text as well as image, the film is a diary, an investigation, but most of all a processing of loss. The voice of the filmmaker reflects all of these and in a sense internalizes the deep values her aunt represents. Consequently, the film has an unusual level of feeling. The author's voice elevates this film, but its hard to imagine the same material working in the other genres. The facts of the aunt's life could take the story toward the tale of another woman, an abused, self-sacrificing woman, away from the poetry of the life presented as experimental drama.

APPENDIX
SHORT SCREENPLAYS

The enclosed five short screenplays present a cross section of student work at New York University. All the scripts have been produced and exhibited. Four of the scripts were written in the undergraduate program and one in the graduate program. One is the product of a collaboration. We chose these scripts for their quality and diversity in subject matter and approach.

These five screenplays offer a great range of subjects. In *Another Story*, Lisa Wood Shapiro offers a parable that is abstract and speaks to issues of memory and tolerance. Karyn Kusama in *Sleeping Beauties* also offers a parable, this time about memory and awakening sexuality.

Christian Taylor in his script *The Lady in Waiting* explores stereotypes and lost opportunities. Susan Emerling in her script *The Wounding* explores the issue of sexual abuse in the life of a young girl. All four of these films deal seriously with the lives of the women who are their major characters. Finally, Anais Granofsky and Michael Swanhaus in *Dead Letters Don't Die* write about loss and the capacity of love to help renew life.

All of these screenplays are serious, but none could have succeeded on that alone. Charm and creative solutions to characterization, to providing catalytic action, or to bringing about resolution are hallmarks of each of these screenplays. They are models of the short film script and provide the reader with appropriate examples of the format used in scriptwriting.

ANOTHER STORY

by Lisa Wood Shapiro

FADE IN:

1. EXT. THE BACKYARD OF A COUNTRY COTTAGE—DAY
THROUGH THE LIGHT WE SEE THE FRAME OF BRANCHES A SMALL COTTAGE WITH A LARGE PICTURE WINDOW. WE CAN SEE TWO LITTLE GIRLS PERCHED IN THE LOWER CORNER OF THE WINDOW.

ANNA

I hate rain.

MERYL

I really really really hate rain.

ANNA

(whispering, after a long pause)

I hate rain. . . .

2. INT. LIVING ROOM OF COTTAGE—DAY

The rain is creating a HYPNOTIC RHYTHM on the roof. Two little girls are sitting on a cushion-padded bench with their elbows on the window sill. The taller girl is about seven years old with long blond hair; her name is ANNA. The short girl is just a year younger with long flowing golden hair; her name is MERYL. Through the doorway into the small kitchen is NIVY. She is a handsome woman in her late sixties/early seventies. She is stylishly dressed, with intricate silver earrings. WE CAN HEAR THE CRACKLE OF THE FIRE IN THE FIREPLACE. The fireplace casts a warm glow over the living room, which is oak paneled with an Oriental rug tossed on its hardwood floor. Nivy is making hot chocolate.

MERYL

(carefully computing her words)

I hate school. . . .

(pause)

I hate liver,

(giggling)

I hate bedtime. . . .

Anna throws Meryl a hard look.

ANNA

I hate bees. . . . I hate spelling. . . . I hate liver.

MERYL

(interrupting)

I already said liver.

ANNA
(emphatic)
I can say it too.

MERYL
You always do that, Anna. Always!

Anna looks hurt as she watches Meryl. Meryl just stares out the window.

ANNA
(slightly mumbles)
All I said was liver.

Nivy pours the boiling water into the mugs.

ANNA
Meryl. . . . oh Meryl. . . .

Meryl doesn't look over.

ANNA
(excited)
I hate that girl Yuki with the funny eyes. . . . Meryl look . . . who am I?

Meryl finally looks over. Anna has pulled her eyes into a very distorted look. She pulls them into slants. Meryl laughs.

MERYL
Yeah. . . .

Meryl is giggling out of control. Meryl makes her eyes like Anna's. They are delighted at themselves. Nivy stares at the two girls. She would like to scold them, but thinks of a strategy more sophisticated than scolding. She begins the business of preparing the tray of hot chocolate.

ANNA
(changing her eyes with her fingers)
No! They're like this!

They both giggle. Nivy enters the living room with the tray of hot chocolate. She places the tray on the coffee table.

NIVY
(with a slight Czech accent)
Anna, Meryl. Hot chocolates are ready.

Anna saunters over. Meryl stays over by the windowsill.

NIVY

Meryl why don't you join us. I want to tell a story.

MERYL

Is there a princess in the story?

NIVY

(carefully)

No . . . there isn't a princess, but there is a girl named Meryl.

Meryl slowly walks over and sits down on the floor in front of Nivy and Anna. Nivy opens a tin and sprinkles some mini-marshmallows into each cup. Both girls take the mug closest to them. Nivy takes a sip.

NIVY

(settling herself on the couch)

Once upon a time there were two young sisters. . . .

WE SLOWLY MOVE IN ON ANNA'S FACE.

ANNA

(interrupting)

Like us?

NIVY

Yes, like you two.

NIVY

Their names were Meryl and Anna. . . .

DISSOLVE:

3. EXT. MOUNTAINS AND VALLEYS—DAY

NIVY

They lived in olden times in a land far, far away where the hills kissed the clouds and it was always almost spring, there lived a King.

4. EXT. CASTLE BY THE WATER—DAY

NIVY

(V.O.)

But he was a devious king, full of evil intentions.

5. EXT. WATERFALL

In the distance, women are seen washing clothes in the water.

NIVY

(V.O.)
One day he banished them deep into the Great Woods to face their own fate.

6. EXT. PATH IN THE FOREST—DAY

NIVY

(V.O.)
And do you know the days turned into years and those subjects learned to live with nature. They prospered and lived in peace.

7. EXT. DIRT ROAD ON THE EDGE OF THE FOREST—DAY
A man pulls his GOAT down a muddied path. WE SEE THREE LARGE KNIGHTS DRESSED IN BLACK RIDE UP ON HORSEBACK. They stop when they reach the peasant. The knight closest to the old man points at the man's hands, which are covered by gloves. The man, who is very humble, takes off the gloves revealing that he has black fingernails. He looks up at the dark knight with humility. A flash of terror registers on the man's face. TIGHT ON THE DARK KNIGHT. WE SEE A CLOSE-UP OF A SWORD AS IT GOES UP. CLOSE-UP ON THE BULL AS WE HEAR THE SOUND OF THE SWORD CRASH DOWN.

8. EXT. FOREST—DAY
The sunbeams seep through the green leaves and fall upon the forest. WE CAN SEE A WOMAN IN A COLORFUL DRESS WALK THROUGH THE FOREST. She is Rachel (25 years old). Rachel is carrying two buckets of water attached to a yoke that goes across her shoulders. Though it appears to be spring, she is wearing gloves. SHE IS HUMMING VERY SOFTLY. WE HEAR IN THE DISTANCE A MAN SCREAMING, SOUNDS WE CANNOT MAKE OUT, AND CHILDREN SCREAMING. SHE QUICKLY MOVES THROUGH THE FOREST. She is frightened. She comes upon a small fairy-tale house with a thin stream of smoke rising from its chimney. Through the clearing mist WE SEE ANNA AND MERYL COME RUNNING OUT OF THE HOUSE. WE SEE THEY ARE THE SAME GIRLS EXCEPT THEY ARE DRESSED IN FAIRY-TALE CLOTHING. Both girls wear mittens. They are screaming and take refuge in their mother's skirt. Rachel looks up and sees a man with a scary mask running out of the house. For a moment, the mask is threatening and ominous, then we realize it is play. This is ADAM (30 years old). He is hunched over pretending to be an animal. He studies Rachel carefully and pulls off his mask. The two girls peek out at them.

RACHEL

Adam . . . you frightened me.

ADAM

I didn't mean to, Rachel.

Adam glares at her. Rachel gently hands off a basket to Anna.

RACHEL

(to Anna)

Anna . . . Meryl, please gather the eggs.

We follow Anna and Meryl as they walk beside the house where the chicken nests are. Anna reaches in and pulls out several eggs; they are a deep shade of blue. Meryl reaches in and gets another blue egg. WE HEAR THE SOUNDS GETTING LOUDER FROM RACHEL AND ADAM, THOUGH WE CAN'T MAKE OUT WHAT THEY'RE SAYING. Meryl and Anna peer back at them. The children are scared. We are not sure why. Adam walks over to the children. Adam smiles; he bends down to their eye level. He places his finger over his mouth with a motion to shhh them. With their attention he takes off his gloves. WE SEE HE HAS BLACK FINGERNAILS. HE REACHES BEHIND ANNA S EAR AND PULLS OUT A TOY. THE TWO GIRLS LAUGH. WE HEAR THE SUDDEN THUNDER OF HORSES. TIGHT ON THE EGGS FALLING ON THE GROUND. TIGHT ON ADAM REACHING FOR HIS GLOVES. Adam reaches for his ax. RACHEL LOOKS CONFUSED. Rachel and Adam look around at the empty forest. The children look at their parents. The sound disappears.

9. EXT. SOMEWHERE IN THE FOREST—DAY

Meryl is sitting with her doll across from her.

MERYL

(in a motherly tone)

You must wear your mittens and you mustn't talk to anyone.

(in a baby voice)

But I don't want to wear my mittens!

(in a motherly tone)

You must! You have black fingernails.

She puts the little mittens onto the doll's hands. Anna jumps out, grabs the doll, and holds a stick like a sword at Meryl.

ANNA

What do we have here? She doesn't want to wear her mittens? Well, don't believe the King would like that!

(to Meryl)

You can't be trusted!

(in baby voice)

Kill her at once. . . .

Anna takes the doll and runs off with it. Meryl follows in fast pursuit. WE FOLLOW AS THEY DASH THROUGH THE WOODS. THE CAMERA FOLLOWS THEM AS THEY DART THROUGH THE LEAVES AND BRANCHES. Meryl almost catches up, only to fall. Anna gains some distance; once again, Meryl gains on her. Meryl stops to catch her breath and loses sight of Anna, then catches sight of her dress. Off she runs.

10. EXT. SOMEWHERE IN THE FOREST—DAY
Meryl is out of breath. Anna is still in the lead, staggering ahead. They approach a group of five children at play. They have not seen other children in a long time. They stand statuesque for a moment and then are lured in by the children's game.

11. EXT. THE SHACK—DAY
Rachel is taking down the linens. The sound of children laughing is in the background. WE HEAR THE CLANGING IN THE WIND OF A BELL. Rachel looks up. TIGHT ON RACHEL. HER STARE GOES FROM CALM TO HORROR.

12. EXT. SOMEWHERE IN THE FOREST—DAY
They are playing King of the Mountain. The sun slightly begins to set. As Meryl is about to reach the top, WE FAINTLY HEAR THE SOUNDS OF HORSES. The children continue to play. The children stop playing. They look up at MERYL and stare in terror. THREE DARK KNIGHTS ARE ON HORSEBACK BEHIND MERYL. The children look down at ANNA's hands and back away.

13. EXT. THE SHACK—DAY
Adam comes upon the house. He sees the ramshackle remains of the shack. The windows of the house have all been smashed. Rachel is nowhere to be seen. He shakes his head in denial. Adam frantically calls out Rachel's name. WE HEAR EVER SO FAINTLY THE SOUNDS OF HORSES. He screams for Anna and Meryl.

14. EXT. CASTLE ON AN ISLAND—DUSK

NIVY

(V.O.)
The Evil King did not destroy all his subjects; for some he had other plans.

The castle is dark and sinister. The sunset ripples off the water.

15. INT. DUNGEON
Anna and Meryl are now dressed only in flimsy burlap uniforms and clogs. WE SEE A DEEP SPACE WITH ONLY A

HINT OF LIGHT COMING FROM A TINY CRACK WAY UP ABOVE. As they walk into the dungeon, the sounds of moaning are present. Anna and Meryl are bothered by the foul odor. Other prisoners walk past the girls. Anna and Meryl almost get separated, but cling to each other.

MERYL

(whispering)

Anna, why are we here? Is it because we're bad?

Anna motions to Meryl to be quiet. Anna takes Meryl's hand and holds it.

16. INT. DUNGEON ENTRANCE TO WORKERS' ROOM
Anna and Meryl stand next to each other in a line. WE HEAR THE BELL SOUND. Girls are to either side of the little girls.

MERYL

I like sugar . . . and I like strawberries.

ANNA

I like rainbows and . . . I like chocolate.

MERYL

I like ponies . . . and. . . .

A light from a doorway flashes a crimson glow on the girls.

MERYL

I like . . . snowmen . . . and I like unicorns.

ANNA

and. . . .

DISSOLVE:

17. INT. DUNGEON WORKER ROOM

NIVY

(V.O.)

Little Anna and little Meryl toiled in the King's dungeon. The days grew into nights, the nights into weeks.

A red glow flickers in the room. A small girl comes towards the camera. She has a shovel in hand; her face is covered with sweat. She lifts the shovel and dumps the coal in towards the camera. Anna comes up and does the same thing. Meryl walks up and dumps the coal in towards the camera. Another little girl follows in the same motion. A bell sounds, everyone leaves frame.

18. INT. DUNGEON

NIVY

(V.O.)
That night the King's guard entered the dungeon.

WE PULL BACK AND SEE THAT TIME HAS PASSED. ANNA AND MERYL HAVE RATTED HAIR, PALE SKIN, SUNKEN EYES, AND ARE MUCH THINNER. A tall man in black enters.

GUARD

(in NIVY's voice)
Anyone who will work all night to dig ditches will receive . . . a bowl of soup.

Meryl looks at Anna who looks frail and weak. Meryl goes with the man. Anna slumps back.

NIVY

(V.O.)
Only Meryl had the strength.

SLOW DISSOLVE:

19. INT. DUNGEON
Anna lays with her eyes closed, and the camera slowly rises above her.

20. INT. DUNGEON—UNKNOWN
Meryl is covered in mud. She staggers in, carrying a tin bowl of soup. She is so exhausted that she can barely make it to Anna. Anna appears even paler than when Meryl left her. Meryl places the bowl of soup in front of Anna. She shakes Anna several times to wake her up. Anna leans up, looks at the soup, then looks at Meryl. Anna lies back down. Meryl shakes her again; Anna doesn't get up.
Meryl hands Anna a spoon. Anna dips her spoon in and Meryl dips hers in. Anna brings her spoon to her lips and, just before she puts it in her mouth, ever so carefully spills the soup back into the bowl so Meryl doesn't see.
Meryl brings her spoon to her lips and, just before she puts it in her mouth, ever so carefully, so Anna doesn't see, spills her soup back into the bowl.
Again Anna dips her spoon into the soup and again she carefully spills it back into the bowl. Again Meryl dips her spoon into the bowl and again she too spills it back into the bowl. This continues again and again; the spoon drops the soup back into the bowl. The soup's level in the bowl stays the same.

Meryl stares at Anna and sees what she is doing. Meryl smiles. Anna sees that she has been found out. Meryl dips her spoon in and places it at Anna's lips. Anna opens her mouth and eats the soup. Anna then dips her spoon and feeds Meryl. Meryl and Anna feed each other until there is no more soup.

MERYL

(V.O.)

(impatiently)

So, what happened to them?

21. INT. LIVING ROOM—DUSK

THEY ARE SILHOUETTED BY THE FIRE. Meryl and Anna are moved. Anna stares at her fingertips, then looks at Meryl who is staring back at her.

NIVY

Many say that it was that simple little bowl of soup that saved Meryl and Anna. But I say it was also their hope. For the Evil King that had caused so much misery was overthrown. And the dark and sad dungeons were open and people with black fingernails no longer had to cover their hands.

MERYL

Grandma, that sounds like a real story. Just like a movie.

Meryl gets up and hugs Nivy. Anna hugs them both.

ANNA

Grandma, where did you hear that story?

Nivy leans back to turn off the reading lamp behind her. The light is on long enough to reveal the numbers that are tattooed into her arm.

NIVY

That's another story. . . .

THE LIGHT IS SWITCHED OFF—FADE TO BLACK

ROLL CREDITS

THE END

THE LADY IN WAITING

by Christian Taylor

1. EXT. FORTLEY MANOR. EARLY MORNING 1.
All is quiet as the first rays of sunlight hit FORTLEY MANOR. At the front gate is a large sign which reads:
"Bartle and Johnson of London announce the sale of Fortley Manor, an extensive country estate." Across the bottom is plastered SOLD.

2. INT. FORTLEY MANOR. MORNING 2.
Large rooms lie empty of furniture, everything is spartan and clean, and nothing moves save the morning light that gradually increases throughout the building. A distant RUSTLING is heard.

3. INT. DINING ROOM. MORNING 3.
A pair of woman's hands sifts through a packing box filled with newspaper-wrapped objects. A small bundle is added, and the box is closed. A sticker is placed on the box which reads AUCTION. There is a sigh from the owner of the hands, MISS PEACH. Miss Peach is a grey-haired, formal-looking woman m her late fifties. She sits awkwardly on a suitcase in the middle of the dining room, which is bare of furniture save a few packing boxes and the odd piece of newspaper. Miss Peach is conservatively dressed in a drab woolen coat and unassuming hat. Miss Peach lifts a cardboard box from the floor in front of her and places the box on her lap. Carefully, she opens the box and reveals inside an array of letters and correspondence. At the top lies a faded postcard of New York skyline. Miss Peach turns over the postcard and it reads: "Dearest Walter, I Miss You, New York Misses You. Oh how stubborn you British are! Love Always, Catherine."

Miss Peach replaces the postcard and closes the box. SARAH, a plump rosy-cheeked maid, enters; she too is dressed in a coat and hat. She carries a box.

SARAH

I believe this is the last box from his Lordship's study.

MISS PEACH

Thank you, Sarah. This box contains Lord Walter's private correspondence. They can be destroyed.

Miss Peach places the box on the floor.

3. INT. DINING ROOM. MORNING (CONT.)

SARAH

That lawyer in charge of the will, Mr. Case, came by earlier; he brought this.

Sarah withdraws from her coat pocket a white envelope and hands it to Miss Peach.

SARAH

He said you would know what it was.

Miss Peach takes the letter and examines it. It reads: "Catherine Spencer, 356 Park Avenue, Penthouse, New York, NY 10022." She pauses and then places it in her handbag. STEVENS, a young butler, enters.

STEVENS

Will that be all, Miss Peach?

MISS PEACH

Yes, yes. I believe our jobs are finished here.

SARAH

Miss Peach, I'd just like to say you ran a beautiful house. It was a pleasure to work on your housekeeping staff.

Miss Peach gathers her things.

SARAH

If his Lordship was alive I'm sure he would have said the same.

MISS PEACH

Indeed. When you've finished closing up the house, Stevens, drop the keys at Mr Case's office.

4. INT. HALLWAY. MORNING
Miss Peach exits the dining room and walks down the marble hallway.
CUT TO:

3. INT. DINING ROOM. MORNING (CONT.)

STEVENS

Where she going?

SARAH

I think Miss Peach may be travelling to meet her rival.

5. EXT. FORTLEY MANOR. DAY 5.
Miss Peach exits Fortley Manor, and, carrying her suitcase, she walks down a quiet country lane.
THE TITLE: THE LADY IN WAITING appears on the screen.
CUT TO:

6. EXT. NEW YORK CITY SKYLINE. NIGHT 6.
Seventies MUSIC builds over a BRIDGE view of New York City, glistening and alive. Cars whiz along avenues, and a myriad of lights shine from an array of windows. This is New York in its heyday—vibrant and energetic.
Over the view comes the title card:
Wednesday, 13 July 1977.
9:15 p.m.
CUT TO:

7. EXT. CAB. NIGHT 7.
Miss Peach sits in the back of a cab as it enters the city. She peers out of the windows, mesmerized as the lights of the city flash past.
CUT TO:

8. EXT. APARTMENT BLOCK. NIGHT 8.
A taxi drives up and stops outside an apartment building. Out steps Miss Peach dressed similarly as before. She looks up at the high-rise block (#8A) and then enters the building.
CUT TO:

9. INT. APARTMENT BLOCK LOBBY. NIGHT 9.
A doorman wrestles with a large bouquet of flowers, which are being delivered by a young man on roller skates. The young man holds out a receipt card, which the doorman struggles to sign. Miss Peach enters the lobby and walks right past the busy doorman. Arriving at the elevators, she presses the button and waits. From her purse she withdraws the letter, takes a quick look, and then quickly returns it to her bag. The elevator arrives and Miss Peach enters.
CUT TO:

10. INT. ELEVATOR. NIGHT 10.
Miss Peach enters the elevator and presses the button for the penthouse. The doors close, and Miss Peach stands alone. Miss Peach presses the penthouse floor button again, a DOORBELL sounds. The sound of a DOOR OPENING and. . . . Miss Peach begins to mumble to herself as the numbers of the floors flick past.

MISS PEACH

Oh hello . . . Miss Spencer?

Miss Peach pauses.

Miss Spencer? Miss Catherine Spencer? I am Miss Peach. I have a letter from Lord Walter. Could I come in?

The elevator continues to rise, 25 . . . 26 . . . 27 . . . 28, and, PING, it comes to a stop. Miss Peach is jolted from her day dream as the doors open, and there stands SCARLET, a stunning and heavily made-up black woman. She boasts a pair of sunglasses, a large wig, a fancy theatrical dress, and a large leather zipper bag. She rushes in, ignoring Miss Peach, and presses the lobby button. The doors close and the elevator continues to RISE.

SCARLET

I don't believe this.

Miss Peach stares at the dramatic and chaotic figure of Scarlet who now stands slumped against the wall. Miss Peach is silent but continues to stare. Scarlet stares back.

10. INT. ELEVATOR. NIGHT (CONT.)

SCARLET

I know. It's like a crash on the highway—you can't lock at it and you can't look away.

Miss Peach attempts a smile, but Scarlet stares blankly back. Miss Peach quickly turns away. There is a moment of awkward silence as the elevator continues to glide up. Suddenly the lights in the elevator begin to flicker, and there echoes a loud SOUND of energy being drained.
CUT TO:

11. EXT. NEW YORK CITY. NIGHT 11.
A traffic signal goes blank.
A DON'T WALK signal stops blinking.
A street light fades.
Blocks of apartment buildings go dark.
The Empire State Building switches out. . . .
SOUNDS of a chaotic city echo out.
CUT TO:

12. INT. ELEVATOR. NIGHT 12.
The DRAINING SOUND CONTINUES; the lights in the elevator become dimmer and dimmer and dimmer; there is a loud ZAP; the elevator comes to an abrupt halt, followed by a bright flash . . . and then BLACK.

MISS PEACH

What's happened?!

Silence in the dark. A lighter is lit revealing Scarlet.

SCARLET

Lady, we've broken down.

12. INT. ELEVATOR. NIGHT (CONT.)

MISS PEACH

Oh dear . . . we can't do that . . . what now.

Miss Peach stares at Scarlet utterly nervous and mesmerized. Scarlet reaches down into her large leather bag, which is on the floor.

MISS PEACH

Wait! What are you doing?

Scarlet ignores Miss Peach and crouching over her bag continues her search. Miss Peach opens a panel and removes an emergency telephone.

MISS PEACH

Hello. . . . I'm trapped in the lift. . . . anyone there?

There is no reply. Miss Peach fiddles with the telephone and then replaces the receiver. Scarlet continues to rummage in her bag.

MISS PEACH

How long do you think . . . how long are we going to be stopped?

SCARLET

I don't know.

Scarlet continues to rummage in her bag. An emergency light flickers on.

MISS PEACH

Oh. We might be trapped for hours.

Scarlet finds some cigarettes and looks up frustrated.

SCARLET

Lady, I'm aware of that!

12. INT. ELEVATOR. NIGHT (CONT.)

MISS PEACH

I wish you would stop saying that. I'm not a Lady. No Lady this, Lady that. Just Miss Peach. My name's Peach.

Scarlet stands.

SCARLET

Scarlet. How do you do?

Scarlet lights a cigarette. Miss Peach gives a disapproving cough.

SCARLET

I have to smoke!

MISS PEACH

Scarlet is that . . . a stage name?

SCARLET

You could call it that.

MISS PEACH

I knew it. My mother was a theatre person. And what do you do in the theatre, Miss Scarlet?

SCARLET

People . . . hire me for private parties and things. I sing mostly.

MISS PEACH

All that excitement . . . never saw the point really.

Scarlet notices an ornate diamond broach on Miss Peach's lapel and removes her sunglasses to make a closer inspection.

SCARLET

No room for glitter maybe, but give me diamonds anytime.

12. INT. ELEVATOR. NIGHT (CONT.) 12.

Miss Peach makes a small protective gesture to check her broach.

MISS PEACH

Yes . . . it was my mother's. It's glass I'm afraid. Rather fancy, I thought.

SCARLET

Going somewhere special . . . special visit?

MISS PEACH

Yes . . . an old friend.

SCARLET

This was my mother's.

Scarlet outstretches her hand upon which is a small, delicate diamond ring. Miss Peach puts on her glasses.

MISS PEACH

It's very beautiful.

Miss Peach makes a closer inspection of the ring peering at Scarlet's outstretched hand.

Large hands. You've got wonderfully large hands. Miss Scarlet. Rather like a . . .

Miss Peach is about to take Scarlet's large hand in hers when . . . Miss Peach looks up at Scarlet who stands still. Quickly Miss Peach withdraws her hand and steps back. She is silent but has become most distressed and nervous.

SCARLET

What is it?

Miss Peach remains silent and tidies herself.

MISS PEACH

Nothing.

12. INT. ELEVATOR. NIGHT (CONT.) 12.

There is a PAUSE, and the two exchange glances. Miss Peach remains silent, then she blurts out.

MISS PEACH

Pardon me but can you do that in public?!

SCARLET

Do what?

MISS PEACH

There are laws!

SCARLET

Not anymore.

MISS PEACH

What one does in one's private life is one's own affair, but to flaunt it in public . . . it's not right.

SCARLET

Why don't you mind your own fucking business?

MISS PEACH

Please!

CUT TO:

13. INT. MACHINE ROOM. NIGHT
A large cog lets out a loud CREEK and moves slightly.
CUT TO:

14. INT. ELEVATOR. NIGHT
There is a sudden jolt as the elevator drops down.

MISS PEACH and SCARLET

AHHHHhhhh!

CUT TO:

14. INT. OPEN ELEVATOR. NIGHT
The inner door opens slightly to reveal that the elevator is trapped between floors.

SCARLET

Looks like we've outstayed our welcome.

Scarlet withdraws from her bag a small crowbar. Miss Peach looks nervous as Scarlet skillfully inserts the crowbar between the outer doors and begins to lever. Scarlet levers the doors open and pulls them apart. Miss Peach stares mesmerized by Scarlet's performance.

SCARLET

Let's just say . . . it's not easy being a woman these days.

Scarlet slips the crowbar back in her bag and smiles sweetly. She grabs her bag and stealthily slips between the doors and out to the darkened floor below. She disappears into the darkness leaving Miss Peach alone. Miss Peach waits . . . and waits . . . and waits. CUT TO:

15. INT. OPEN ELEVATOR. NIGHT
In the distance we hear a RADIO REPORT echoing down the corridor. Suddenly an odd looking MAN holding a drink in one

hand and a small radio in the other pops his head through the elevator doors. He rests the drink and the radio on the floor of the elevator. He switches the radio off. He is obviously drunk and stares at Miss Peach. Miss Peach stares at him. He stares at Miss Peach.

MAN

Hi there.

MISS PEACH

Oh hello. . . . I don't suppose you re the repairman?

MAN

The way I look at it. It's dark . . . there's me looking for company . . . there's you up there all alone. Like strangers in the night. How about it honey?

Miss Peach stares at the man horrified. She is frozen in disgust and holds tightly onto her handbag.

16. INT. STAIRWELL. NIGHT
Scarlet opens the door of the stairwell and scans up and down. In the distance there echoes a SCREAM from Miss Peach. Scarlet looks back and reenters the corridor. CUT TO:

17. INT. OPEN ELEVATOR. NIGHT
Miss Peach screams. The man raises his hands defensively.

MAN

Ok . . . ok . . . your loss.

The man turns to leave. Miss Peach sighs, clutching onto her bag.
CUT TO:

18. INT. CORRIDOR. NIGHT
The man stands faced with Scarlet who is lit ominously by her lighter. She stares at the man sternly. Quickly the man gathers his things and scampers away.
CUT TO:

19. INT. OPEN ELEVATOR. NIGHT
Miss Peach waits. Scarlet reemerges lit only by the elevator light. Scarlet outstretches her arms to Miss Peach.

SCARLET

Afraid of the dark? The whole building is out. Coming?
CUT TO:

20. INT. APARTMENT CORRIDOR. NIGHT.
Miss Peach hesitates and then cautiously sticks out her leg.

Awkwardly together the couple pry Miss Peach out of the elevator and onto the floor.

20. INT. APARTMENT CORRIDOR. NIGHT (CONT.)

SCARLET and MISS PEACH
Oh wait . . . Ok the floor . . . wait . . . I'm trying . . . where's the floor . . . Ahhhm slipping . . . waaaiit . . . aaahhhh

Miss Peach slips and both Scarlet and Miss Peach fall to the ground.

SCARLET
Are you all right?

MISS PEACH
I thought men were good at lifting things.

SCARLET
Yeah well, I'm not the lifting kind.

Scarlet stands while Miss Peach grips onto her ankle.

MISS PEACH
I've broken my ankle.

SCARLET
What! Are you sure?

Miss Peach flashes a look of malice at Scarlet.

MISS PEACH
Sure? How could I be sure. I need a doctor.

SCARLET
Well, can you move your toes?

In pain Miss Peach squinches up her face.

20. INT. APARTMENT CORRIDOR. NIGHT (CONT.)

MISS PEACH
Just.

SCARLET
It's not broken then. I can help you walk.

The corridor stretches ahead ominously dark.

MISS PEACH

But there are no lights.

Scarlet rummages in her bag, which has fallen to the side of Miss Peach.

SCARLET

I almost forgot.

Scarlet withdraws a large candle sculpted like an erect penis and moves it toward Miss Peach.

SCARLET

Salvation.

Miss Peach sits frozen in horror and confusion faced with the penis. Timidly, Miss Peach takes the penis and clasps it in both hands. With her lighter, Scarlet touches the tip of the candle and light floods out. Scarlet moves to lift Miss Peach. Miss Peach continues to stare at Scarlet.

MISS PEACH

You're possibly the most alien person I have ever encountered in my life.

SCARLET

Lady, that talk could get you cut up and dumped in a black plastic bag.

CUT TO:

21. INT. STAIRWELL. NIGHT

The door to the stairwell bursts open. Miss Peach limps, one arm is wrapped around Scarlet, the other carries the candle. They begin to climb the stairs, HUFFING and PUFFING. A group of three PEOPLE come charging down the stairs. They have party blowers in their mouths and carry balloons. They rush past TOOTING and YELLING. One of the people, a WOMAN, stops and blows a party horn in Miss Peach's face and runs on. Scarlet struggles with Miss Peach.

SCARLET

Well at least someone's having fun.

MISS PEACH

Why are we going up?

SCARLET

To visit your friend.

MISS PEACH
No! We can't go there. Not like this.

SCARLET
If you wanna talk options. We're forty flights up and you've crippled yourself. She's a friend; she'll help you.

MISS PEACH
No wait . . . you don't understand.

CUT TO:

22. INT. APARTMENT DOORWAY. NIGHT
Miss Peach and Scarlet stand outside the apartment. Both are very disheveled and sweaty. Miss Peach holds the candle. Softly she knocks on the door. They wait. No answer. Scarlet then knocks on the door. They wait. No answer. Scarlet knocks again. They wait. No answer.

MISS PEACH
Oh well, no one seems to be home.

Scarlet drops her bag and kneels on the floor. From her bag, she withdraws an array of delicate tools. Scarlet lifts the tools and inserts them individually into the lock. Miss Peach whispers.

22. INT. APARTMENT DOORWAY. NIGHT (CONT.)

MISS PEACH
What are you doing!?

SCARLET
I told you. . . . I'm not carrying you down forty flights of stairs.

Scarlet delicately fiddles with the lock.

MISS PEACH
Stop. You can't. What if she comes back?

Scarlet adjusts one of the tools and there echoes a loud CLICK.

SCARLET
She's your friend; she'll understand.

Scarlet twists the door handle and the door swings open. Scarlet smiles sweetly.

SCARLET
Besides, the door was open. Coming?

Scarlet enters.

CUT TO:

23. INT. APARTMENT HALLWAY. NIGHT
The two enter the apartment. Miss Peach hesitates at the door. Scarlet tries the light switch. All remains dark. Miss Peach limps in protectively.

MISS PEACH
Don't touch anything!

Scarlet comes across a side table in the hallway upon which are two candlesticks. Scarlet lights the candlesticks. Miss Peach continues to limp.

SCARLET
That ankle isn't going to get any better with you limping all over the place.

23. INT. APARTMENT HALLWAY. NIGHT (CONT.)
Miss Peach sits down on a chair as Scarlet searches the drawer of the side table. Scarlet discovers a flashlight and hands it to Miss Peach. Taking one of the candlesticks and the penis candle Scarlet wanders up the corridor.

SCARLET
Nice place your friend has.

MISS PEACH
Don't touch anything.

Scarlet disappears into the bedroom leaving Miss Peach alone. Miss Peach switches on the flashlight and uses it to scan the HALLWAY and distant LIVING ROOM (#23A). Everything is tidy, delicate, and feminine. The odd piece of furniture and painting can be glimpsed. Scarlet reemerges carrying only the penis candle. Scarlet moves to lift Miss Peach and begins to carry her down the corridor.

SCARLET
You can rest your foot in here.

CUT TO:

24. INT. BEDROOM. NIGHT
They enter the bedroom. There in the middle of the room is a beautiful double bed, bedside which Scarlet has set down the candlestick. Scarlet carries Miss Peach over to the bed. Miss Peach hesitates. Scarlet gently pushes Miss Peach down on to

the bed. Scarlet goes into the bathroom. Miss Peach scans the bedroom.

MISS PEACH

You really don't have to stay. I'd hate to keep you if you have places to go.

CUT TO:

25. INT. BATHROOM. NIGHT

Scarlet has set down the penis candle and is faced with an array of expensive makeup and lotions. She caresses them, lifting a crystal scent bottle to her nose.

SCARLET

No, I have no place special to go.

26. INT. BEDROOM. NIGHT

Miss Peach caresses the silk bed cover and turns to the bed side table upon which are several silver-framed photographs. The photos are a decadent array of fun times through the ages. Miss Peach carefully studies the photographs.

Miss Peach searches and finally comes across a picture of CATHERINE SPENCER and LORD WALTER. She then lifts a single picture of Lord Walter and examines it closely; across it is written "To Catherine, my love always, Walter." For a moment she caresses the picture of Lord Walter. Scarlet reemerges carrying some bandages and a glass of water. Miss Peach quickly replaces the photograph. Scarlet hands the glass of water and two pills to Miss Peach. Miss Peach hesitates.

SCARLET

Painkillers.

Tentatively, Miss Peach takes the pills and swallows them, never losing eye contact with Scarlet. Scarlet then kneels at Miss Peach's foot and takes off her shoe. She then unravels the bandages and begins to bandage her ankle.

MISS PEACH

Thank you so much, but I think I can manage now. I'm really quite capable.

Scarlet continues to bandage Miss Peach's foot rather clumsily.

MISS PEACH

No, no, you're doing it all wrong.

SCARLET

I'm sorry. I'm only trying to help.

MISS PEACH
Well you're not helping . . . you're making things far worse. I think it would be best if you left.

SCARLET
That's nice. I help you out of the elevator . . . carry you up here, bandage your foot.

26. INT. BEDROOM. NIGHT (CONT.)

MISS PEACH
Well it's all wrong. Everything you're doing is wrong.

SCARLET
Well I'm terribly sorry . . . I didn't realize I was with an expert.

MISS PEACH
When you've spent the better part of your life in the service of others, you become very particular about such things.

Scarlet finishes bandaging.

SCARLET
Well maybe it's time to take a rest!

Swiftly Scarlet puts down her things, gets up, and leaves. Miss Peach gets up to follow her but winces in pain as she puts weight on her foot. She hesitates and then sits down on the bed. Hot and exhausted, she decides to rest. She lies down clutching onto the flashlight, which she rests protectively on her stomach.

DISSOLVE TO:

27. INT. LIVING ROOM. NIGHT
Scarlet's hand withdraws from her bag a small transistor radio which she switches on.

RADIO
Due to a thunderstorm upstate, four separate power lines were struck by lightning earlier this evening. Within half an hour the utility suffered a massive loss of some 2,000 megawatts. At precisely 9:34 p.m., New York City experienced a total electrical blackout. As the Consolidated Edison Company struggles to restore power to the city, reports of widespread violence and looting have been flooding in.

27. INT. LIVING ROOM. NIGHT (CONT.)
Whiskey is poured into a crystal glass. Scarlet sits alone and loses all her polish; spreading her legs in a very masculine way. She goes over to the window and looks out across the dark skyline. A distant SIREN is heard.

DISSOLVE TO:

28. INT. BEDROOM. NIGHT
The bedside candlestick has burned down considerably. Miss Peach is jolted awake and briskly switches on her flashlight pointing it toward the doorway. The light hits Scarlet's face as she stands in the bedroom door holding a candlestick. She stands proud like the Statue of Liberty. She wears a large mink fur coat, costume jewelry, and a large decadent hat.

SCARLET
Nice huh?

MISS PEACH
Where did you get those? Take them off immediately.

SCARLET
I'm not going to hurt them. Please, I need them for five minutes.

MISS PEACH
What do you mean, need? I don't think you quite know what you need.

SCARLET
What makes you so sure! You don't know the first thing about me, Peaches.

Scarlet gives a large vivacious smile as Miss Peach looks on hopelessly. Miss Peach stands up and begins to leave the bed room.

MISS PEACH
We should never have come; we can't stay here.

CUT TO:

29. INT. HALLWAY. NIGHT
Miss Peach walks briskly with her limp.

SCARLET
It's a blackout for Christ's sake. It's chaos out there.

MISS PEACH
And what if she comes back? She'll be angry that you broke into her house, touched all her things.

SCARLET
WE . . . WE broke in, honey. No one dragged you through that door.

Miss Peach is frozen.

SCARLET
You told me she was your friend.

MISS PEACH
Well she is . . . sort of. A friend of the man I dedicated my life to. I couldn't turn my back on that.

SCARLET
You lied then.

MISS PEACH
You lied to me first. With all your . . . glitter.

SCARLET
Glitter?

MISS PEACH
Why exactly do you dress like that!?

Miss Peach motions at Scarlet's attire. Leaving Scarlet behind, Miss Peach wanders toward the living room.

29. INT. HALLWAY. NIGHT (CONT.)

SCARLET
Because I like it. I love the attention.

MISS PEACH
So you're just a performer; it's fancy dress.

Miss Peach turns to Scarlet who stands confused.

MISS PEACH
You may be very striking, but look at yourself. What are you being now. You don't even know. She finds us here, I'll be a laughingstock. We both will be, but in your case it scarcely matters.

Miss Peach looks at Scarlet who stands still.

(PAUSE)

SCARLET
Excuse me, I need to take a shit!

MISS PEACH
You're totally uncivilized!

CUT TO:

30. INT. LIVING ROOM. NIGHT
Miss Peach enters the living room, which is now bathed in candlelight. Scarlet has beautifully arranged candles all around the room; it is a breathtaking sight. Miss Peach stands in awe. On the table, Scarlet has laid a beautiful dinner set for two, the food is simple but inviting. Two place cards sit on each plate. In beautiful italics on one is written "Lady Peach" and on the other "Lady Scarlet." Miss Peach turns back to Scarlet who has now disappeared. She turns back to the table and sits down. Miss Peach observes the place settings, and surreptitiously, she rearranges the incorrect silverware arrangement.

CUT TO:

31. INT. BATHROOM DOOR. NIGHT
Miss Peach taps on the bathroom door. Timidly, she whispers.

MISS PEACH
Scarlet. Scarlet.

There is no response.

I'm sorry Scarlet.

CUT TO:

32. INT. BATHROOM. NIGHT
Scarlet sits in front of the mirror. She removes her wig and sits bald. From a large jar Scarlet scoops some cream and smears it on her face, drastically her thick makeup is loosened.

MISS PEACH
You're so colorful, my dear, so full of color. . . . I probably appear as rather a grey person to you . . . and you're right.

CUT TO:

31. INT. BATHROOM DOOR. NIGHT
Miss Peach stands close to the door.

MISS PEACH

You see, I've been a housekeeper to a man for over thirty years. Our relationship was overwhelmingly professional in tone . . . though naturally we might discuss informal topics . . . from time to time.

Miss Peach pauses.

MISS PEACH

I came to deliver his love letter. I don't know this woman . . . you see. All I know is that . . .

32. INT. BATHROOM. NIGHT

With a sponge Scarlet rubs and rubs and gradually removes all the makeup. Scarlet stops and begins to listen to Miss Peach. Scarlet takes a drag on her cigarette and stares at her bald reflection. She remains effeminate in features, but without all the makeup, all the glamour is gone.

MISS PEACH

I gave him the best years of my life. The very best and he didn't even notice. I suppose you could call me a coward. So you see, I'm in no position to judge your actions. . . . I simply envy your courage.

Gently and slowly Scarlet removes her loud and glitzy ear rings.

31. INT. BATHROOM DOOR. NIGHT

Miss Peach leaves, taking her candle with her. The candle is blown out.

CUT TO:

33. EXT. MANHATTAN SKYLINE. EARLY MORNING

The sun gradually rises over the building tops. A RADIO UPDATE echoes out. Pull back to reveal Scarlet standing at a window.

DISSOLVE TO:

34. INT. LIVING ROOM. MORNING

Scarlet stands at a window. The room is lit by the blue light of morning. Miss Peach lies on a sofa fast asleep. Scarlet sits down opposite her; she is dressed simply, but beautifully. Her outfit and hairstyle are feminine, but she has shed all her flamboyance. Her beauty now stems from her pure precision and simplicity. She smokes a cigarette. Miss Peach wakes up. Spread on a chair in front of Miss Peach is a beautiful outfit and an elegant pair of shoes.

SCARLET

People used to tell me how I could be straightened out. What I needed was a good woman. I said fine, since a woman is the best there is. . . . I want to be one, the most beautiful one.

34. INT. LIVING ROOM. MORNING (CONT.)

Scarlet looks at Miss Peach and smiles.

SCARLET

You must realize what you have . . . and enjoy it. If it was up to the rest of the world, they wouldn't let you.

DISSOLVE TO:

35. INT. LIVING ROOM. LATE MORNING
We move through the apartment. The dull light of morning highlights the odd object here and there. Candles stand burnt down. All is still. Someone SINGS in the distance. We enter the living room. A dressing table has been set up. Miss Peach sits in front of the mirror. Scarlet stands above and SINGS while she tends to Miss Peach.

DISSOLVE TO:

36. INT. LIVING ROOM. DAY
Nail polish is placed on some nails. They are filed and trimmed. Eyeliner is placed on some eyes. Mascara on lashes. Lipstick on lips. The tight curls of Miss Peach's hair are brushed out. Powder on the face. Shoes are slipped on some feet. A dress is put on. Earrings are clipped on. A necklace is delicately wrapped around a neck.

DISSOLVE TO:

37. INT. LIVING ROOM. DAY
Scarlet continues to tend to Miss Peach. She then goes over to get a scent bottle. Miss Peach reaches for her bag and out falls the letter. She withdraws the envelope and it reads "Mrs Catherine Spencer." She holds it closely and then looks up at her reflection in the mirror. She is now complete—beautiful and elegant in both style and makeup. She pauses and stares at the letter. She remains silent. Scarlet returns and stands close by. Miss Peach remains silent. She then takes the letter and replaces it.

37. INT. LIVING ROOM. DAY (CONT.)

MISS PEACH

I'm not Catherine Spencer, I would have liked to have been, but I'm not. Had I been anyone worthy of respect at all, I dare say I would have left Fortley Manor long before this letter was ever written.

Miss Peach smiles and puts the letter away. She stands up straight and is a picture of refined beauty.

SCARLET

Miss Peach your carriage awaits.

Miss Peach gives a curtsey and then twirls to show off her attire. She twirls and twirls and twirls and twirls. . . .

DISSOLVE TO:

38. INT. APARTMENT. NIGHT
Classical MUSIC can be heard. Miss Peach continues to twirl and is dressed beautifully and Scarlet simply, as before. Miss Peach's formal hair is now loose and relaxed, and both Scarlet and Miss Peach have a content expression on their faces. Delicately and tentatively the pair waltz elegantly around the room. Miss Peach limps, but hardly. Miss Peach and Scarlet continue to dance. The music finishes, and they come to a stop. They hesitate and then move closer together. Behind them we see the city lit up. They hesitate as if they're about to kiss. Suddenly there is a sound of energy being CHARGED. The lights in the apartment flicker on, and then off, and then on again. Under the bright lights Miss Peach and Scarlet break their embrace. The spell ends and all is revealed. They shift awkwardly, embarrassed by their intimacy.

CUT TO:

39. INT. HALLWAY OF APARTMENT. NIGHT
Miss Peach and Scarlet begin to leave the apartment. Scarlet gathers her bag, and before exiting Miss Peach removes the letter from her purse and places it in the frame of a mirror. Miss Peach pauses with her hand and then looks up at her reflection, which is youthful and content. She smiles.

40. INT. ELEVATOR. NIGHT
The HUM of the elevator as it glides down. Miss Peach and Scarlet stand side by side. They are SILENT and do not communicate in any way. It's as if they are total strangers to one another. The elevator stops and in gets an ELDERLY MAN.

OLD MAN

They promised us back in '65 that it was the last time. Well twenty-seven hours I was trapped in my apartment. It's a disgrace. I say hang the lot of them.

The elevator comes to rest on the ground floor. The old man gets out, followed by Scarlet and Miss Peach.

CUT TO:

41. INT. LOBBY. NIGHT
The lobby of the apartment block is busy with postblackout activity. Miss Peach turns to Scarlet. For a moment they smile. Scarlet's expression changes as she observes something of interest over Miss Peach's shoulder.

SCARLET
Goodbyes were never my thing.

Scarlet smiles and walks past Miss Peach and wanders toward a handsome-suited man across the lobby. Miss Peach watches as Scarlet introduces herself, asking the man for a light. Miss Peach decides to leave and walks slowly toward the exit.

DOORMAN
(calling)
Miss Spencer! Can I help you.

Miss Peach swings around, responding to the name Catherine Spencer and is faced with the back of an elegantly dressed WOMAN who carries some luggage. Miss Peach freezes and watches as the woman stands waiting for the doorman. Miss Peach begins to approach and then stops herself. She looks up and sees Scarlet watching her. The doorman picks up the woman's luggage and begins to carry it toward the elevator. The woman hesitates, tidies herself, and follows the doorman. Scarlet gives Miss Peach a wave of her hand. Miss Peach smiles and turns away, briskly walking out the front door.

FADE OUT

SLEEPING BEAUTIES

by Karyn Kusama

FADE UP—sound of a MOTORCYCLE starting and revving.
FADE DOWN.
FADE UP on TITLES. FADE to black.
FADE UP—overlapping voices of TWO TEENAGE GIRLS. One cries out.

VOICE

Ouch, that hurts!

Cut to interior BEDROOM, night. IRIS, sixteen years old, is standing and brushing LUCY's hair. LUCY is seated in front of her. They speak to the reflection in the MIRROR in front of them. IRIS hits the tangles in LUCY's hair. LUCY, fifteen years old, winces.

IRIS

I'm sorry, I'm sorry . . . it would help if you conditioned it.

LUCY

But it makes it look greasy.

IRIS

Not if you use the right kind.

LUCY

I kinda like it this way.

IRIS

I guess you always had the prettiest hair.
(IRIS finishes the last strokes and slightly pats LUCY's long hair.)
Okay, all done.

LUCY

Tomorrow I'll do yours.

IRIS

Okay.

LUCY rises from the VANITY TABLE, and both girls remove their thin SUMMER ROBES. Underneath they are wearing long, lightly flowered cotton NIGHTGOWNS. IRIS jumps onto her BED. Meanwhile, LUCY positions a FAN toward the window and turns it to the "high" setting. IRIS reaches for the small drawer beneath the NIGHT TABLE, fishing around and then pulling out a pack of CIGARETTES and a small ASHTRAY.

LUCY arranges herself cross-legged on the opposite BED and faces IRIS. They are silent for a while, looking at each other. IRIS gets up and begins to pace. She lights a cigarette as if she's fatigued by the rigors of her day-to-day routine. Both girls share the cigarette, careful to exhale toward the window fan.

IRIS

(looking at the CLOCK)

Okay, it's time.

LUCY

Let's go.

IRIS

(still pacing)

So we know this: tall, not too tall. And thin. Pale . . . shouldn't he be pale?

LUCY

. . . Oh yes, very pale, see-through almost. . . .

IRIS

Long, dirty blond hair . . . fine, fine, fine. . . .

LUCY

So fine it falls through your fingers . . . (pause) . . . Dark eyes. . . .

IRIS sits abruptly on the bed, crossing her legs and facing LUCY. She gestures widely with her cigarette, as if aggravated.

IRIS

No, I thought we talked about this. His eyes should be light and clear and spooky. . . .

LUCY

But. . . .

IRIS

Oh, let's not argue. . . . (pause) . . . We should figure the rest out.

LUCY raises her eyebrows.

IRIS

His mouth, what about his mouth?

LUCY

The best part. . . .

Both girls pause, lost in thought. IRIS begins tentatively.

IRIS

His lips will be full . . . a sort of wide Iris mouth. (pause) Right?

LUCY does not reply.

IRIS

You . . . you can't look at his mouth for too long. . . . It's almost too dangerous, you know?

LUCY lays on her back and hugs herself as if chilly.

LUCY

Okay, I guess. . . . Gosh, we've almost finished him.

IRIS stabs out her cigarette and rests her elbows on her knees, hands cupping her face.

IRIS

Soon we'll have to find him.

LUCY

Soon we'll have to give him a life.

IRIS gets up and wanders around the room, first toward the window, then to the vanity table. She picks up the large, ornate HAIRBRUSH, pulls out loose strands, then sets it down.

IRIS

(while walking)

But he has one . . . all that open road, that huge cycle . . . the dust flying off his wheels . . . (looking at her reflection) . . . you and me . . . (pause, turning to LUCY) . . . he's true because we want him to be.

LUCY

(puzzled)

Iris, the time. . . .

IRIS

Right, it's late. . . .

Both climb under their covers and get comfortable before saying anything.

LUCY

Goodnight, Iris.

IRIS

Goodnight, Lucy.

LUCY

I love you.

IRIS

Love you too.

LUCY

See you in the morning.

IRIS looks at LUCY, then turns off the old LAMP on the night table.

IRIS

(whispering)

Sweet dreams.

The room is dark. The fan continues to hum, the clock ticks, and occasionally an insect buzzes against the screen window. A breeze blows the gauzy CURTAINS. IRIS and LUCY are holding hands from across their beds. The MOONLIGHT is thick on their faces.
A popping sound is heard coming from the window, as if someone is throwing a pebble at the SCREEN.

CUT to a CLOSE-UP of LUCY and IRIS's locked fingers as they fall from each other.

DISSOLVE to a CLOSE-UP of IRIS's face as she sleeps.

DISSOLVE slowly as IRIS, in a WIDE SHOT, gets out of bed and goes to LUCY's side. She rouses LUCY. In groggy agreement, they walk to the window, standing side by side and peering out. The breeze is blowing their long nightgowns as if they're liquid sheets of light.

LUCY

Look.

IRIS

I know.

On the thick green lawn, three stories below them, is a MAN leaning against the seat of a beat-up Harley-Davidson MOTORCYCLE. His hair is long and thin, his face is pale, his build is lanky.

MAN

(offscreen)

Which one of you girls wanna take a ride?

LUCY and IRIS stare out at the MAN, then turn to look at each other. They are dazed.

IRIS

But . . . he's not finished. It's too soon. . . .

LUCY

Someone has to go down. . . .

(panicked)

Yes, but we never decided which one of us would actually . . .

LUCY

I know, I know. (pause) You choose.

IRIS looks out the window. She turns to LUCY and straightens LUCY's hair.

IRIS

It's you. . . . You go.

LUCY

You don't want to ride?

IRIS

No, not tonight. . . . You go, and I'll wait here for you.

LUCY

(dreamily)

All right.

LUCY lifts the screen window. IRIS helps her out onto the TRELLIS as if in a trance. The MAN continues to lock up at both of them, humming "Wild Horses" to himself. LUCY climbs slowly down the trellis. Her nightgown gets caught in the wood grating; she still moves smoothly and without hesitation. IRIS closes the screen window and sits in the LARGE WINDOWSILL, watching the action below and humming "Wild Horses" softly.

LUCY walks toward the MAN. CUT to a CLOSE-UP of her face.

FADE UP on IRIS in VOICE-OVER: "Dirty blond hair-fine, fine, fine. . . ." FADE UP on LUCY in VOICE-OVER: "So fine it falls through your fingers. . . ."

DISSOLVE to a MEDIUM TWO-SHOT as LUCY touches his hair and lets it fall through her fingers. The MAN laughs. CUT to LUCY, looking at the man.

LUCY

Your eyes . . . they're so dark.

DISSOLVE to a CLOSE-UP of IRIS.

FADE UP on IRIS in VOICE-OVER: "Light and clear and spooky—we talked about this already."

IRIS

I was wrong—his eyes are dark.

DISSOLVE to a CLOSE-UP of the MAN as he takes a drag on his cigarette, exhales slowly, then pulls some stray tobacco from his tongue and lips.

FADE UP on IRIS in VOICE-OVER, discussing with LUCY: "Would he smoke Luckies?" "Maybe, yeah . . . ," etc.

DISSOLVE to IRIS's POV as LUCY and the MAN walk into the dark and leave the motorcycle in the middle of the lawn. CUT to a CLOSE-UP of IRIS.

IRIS

Wait—where are you going. . . . I can't see you anymore. . . . Lucy, this isn't fair.

IRIS cries silently.

DISSOLVE to a TWO-SHOT, as the MAN puts his hand on LUCY's bare arm, then runs his fingers over her shoulder. She is still. He moves his fingers to her neck.

DISSOLVE to a CLOSE TWO-SHOT of LUCY and the MAN. He leans toward her; she backs away slightly, then steadies herself.

DISSOLVE to an EXTREME CLOSE-UP of IRIS's eyes. She blinks slowly.

CUT to a MEDIUM CLOSE-UP of LUCY and the MAN, as he leans forward and moves her hair off of her shoulders. He slowly breathes the scent of her neck and face.

DISSOLVE to IRIS, twirling her hair in her fingers lazily.

CUT to a CLOSE-UP straight on of LUCY's face. She closes her eyes.

DISSOLVE to a straight-on CLOSE-UP of IRIS. She closes her eyes. CUT to MEDIUM SHOT from the side of IRIS standing at the window. Her hands are splayed on the sore en. She sways back, then steadies herself.

DISSOLVE to a CLOSE-UP of LUCY. The man suddenly fills the frame. He is kissing her.

DISSOLVE to a CLOSE-UP of IRIS touching her mouth.

CUT to a CLOSE-UP of the MAN's hand as it pulls on the fabric at LUCY's waist.

DISSOLVE to a CLOSE-UP of his other hand as his fingers run through her hair. He pulls it back slightly.

CUT to IRIS standing at the window, breathing evenly, eyes closed.

DISSOLVE to a CLOSE-UP of the clock.

FADE UP on the sounds of PULSES and TICKING.

CUT to an ECU of LUCY's fingers as they find the belt hooks of the MAN's jeans.

CUT to a MEDIUM TWO-SHOT of LUCY and the MAN. His hands move up the length of her nightgown.

DISSOLVE to an ECU of the MAN's teeth as they hook on LUCY's lower lip.

CUT to a CLOSE-UP of IRIS, "waking" abruptly.

(breathless)

Lucy, it's time to come home . . . it's time. . . .

CUT to a WIDE SHOT, at ground level, of LUCY standing on the dark part of the lawn. She is serene and unruffled. She wanders around the lawn until she recognizes the trellis. The MAN and the MOTORCYCLE are gone. She starts to climb the trellis. IRIS lifts the screen window and helps her into the room. Their movements are extremely slow and fragile. LUCY cradles herself in IRIS's long, thin arms.

IRIS

(after long pause)

What happened?

LUCY

Hmmmmm?

IRIS

You know what I'm asking.

LUCY

You know . . . only you can know.

IRIS

Stop. . . . tell me.

LUCY

But you know. (pause) We can't share everything.

IRIS

Not even him?

LUCY

No, not him. . . .

They slowly get up out of the windowsill and walk to their beds. LUCY and IRIS get under their covers. They are still for a while. LUCY then gets up and goes to IRIS's bed. She lays down next to her, on top of the covers. Both are on their sides, like spoons.

CUT to a CLOSE-UP of their faces on the bed. Their long hair flows and clutters the frame.

LUCY

Goodnight, Iris.

IRIS doesn't reply. She is sound asleep.

FADE to black.

FADE UP on TITLES.

END

CAST OF CHARACTERS

IRIS—a sixteen-year-old girl. Iris is still a bit awkward, a little uncomfortable with her developing body. She is remarkably mature in some ways, a girl with a detailed imagination and a feverish sense of her future. She is a talker.

LUCY—Iris's fifteen-year-old sister. Lucy is very fresh looking and has an unusually mature beauty for her age. She and Iris look much alike, but somehow Lucy seems more at ease with her appearance. Lucy respects Iris's opinion of everything. Lucy is the less articulate of the two girls, but is comfortable letting Iris be the "leader."

MAN—a very nebulous character in some ways. Between the age of nineteen and twenty-five years old. He must have strong features. It would be preferable if he was pale and of a medium height. He must have longish and finely textured hair. He is the type of person who wears nothing but jeans and John Deere t-shirts. He wears cowboy boots because they are practical. He probably worked in a gas station at one point in his life. He may have committed some small-scale crimes as well, but nothing worthy of a major newspaper. He is from a small town—there isn't a single clear-sounding radio station for miles and all the kids hang out at the 7-Eleven off of the interstate. Until he was about eighteen, he had never seen a James Dean or Marlon Brando movie. He has, however seen almost every Elvis movie, somewhat by default. His voice is low, with a slight drawl. He doesn't talk much, unless he's got a six-pack with him, and then he's always got a story and needs to prove that he saw it first.

DESCRIPTION OF LOCATION

Large three-story house in a quiet suburban area. Spacious backyard with high, full trees and a large open area in the center. Iris and Lucy share a room on the top floor, preferably at the very side of the house. The only apparent light comes from their room; no one else seems to be home. From their large bedroom window they can hop onto a wooden trellis that runs down the side of the house.

The bedroom itself is relatively large, with two parallel beds, a large windowsill, a cluttered vanity table with a huge round mirror, a small night table, a lamp, an overhead light, and a chair or two. The room should not look especially contemporary at all, there should be a strange sense of isolation from the outside teenage world. There are no posters on the wall, and no fan magazines on the floor—only odd antique knickknacks, cheesy souvenirs from cheesy midwestern and southern towns, and a small old radio. Maybe a couple of yellowing photos lying around.

Before the man appears, the light should be very rich in golds and orange overtones. The pacing is slow, and the film should have a lush, almost smoky look. After the man appears, the lighting will be mostly for a night scene. The tones will be deep blues and reds. All the time though, I want the girls' white nightgowns to have a milky luminous quality. Other than parts of the performances, nothing about this film should be very naturalistic.

THE WOUNDING

by Susan Emerling

DG

1. ECU DOLL HOUSE

A girl's hand comes in and out of frame.

JULIE

They have to set up the table for dinner. His parents are going to come home after they come back from the movies.

Well, what are we having for dinner tonight? Chicken, ham. No, put the chicken over here. Dad likes the chicken. Dessert of course. And a beer.

Oh tomorrow's his birthday. He's going to have a birthday present.

Oh look, the kitty cat; the kitty's obviously going to try and eat it. Chicken—yeah. It doesn't look like he's eating it though. Well, he'll just be looking at it. Drooling.

Baby's asleep, yeah asleep. Let's clean up. What a mess it is. Put the choo-choo train back together.

SLOW DISSOLVE TO:

2. INT. FOYER/DINING ROOM—NIGHT

A Victorian dollhouse. Pull back to reveal SHEILA, 35 and voluptuous, passing in front of the dollhouse carrying a tray of dirty glasses. Jumbled sounds of a PARTY.

SHEILA

Well, hi there, sweetheart.

JULIE

Hi, mommy.

SHEILA

When did you get in? Come talk to me. . . .

JULIE

Mom, the coolest thing happened today. . . .

3. INT. BATHROOM—NIGHT

Sheila goes into the bathroom and pauses a moment in front of the bathroom mirror to inspect her face for signs of age. She takes out her lipstick and puts some on. She turns and tries to put some on Julie as she speaks, but Julie resists.

JULIE

. . . well, you know Mr. Connor's cat? the one that I took care of . . .

SHEILA

Oh yeah, I remember that cat.

JULIE

Mr. Connor said that when he went into the barn this morning he couldn't find her. . . .

SHEILA

Really. (She tries to put lipstick on her daughter.) No?

JULIE

So he looked everywhere.

Sheila exits and touches Julie's shoulder to encourage her to follow. Julie pauses a moment, then follows.

4. INT. KITCHEN—NIGHT
Buckling her belt, Sheila enters the kitchen and crosses to the refrigerator. Julie tags along behind her. Sheila opens the freezer and takes out several ice trays. She turns away with both hands full; Julie tags along behind her.

JULIE

So anyway . . . so he went into the loft and . . . he dug into the hay . . .

Sheila crosses back to the counter, knocks the cubes from the trays into the bucket. One falls on the floor, and Julie picks it up and drops it into the sink.

JULIE (cont.)

finally he found her. . . .

TOM, late thirties, once handsome, but dulled by alcohol, enters after them and goes to the sink to add water to his drink.

SHEILA

You remember Tom?

JULIE

Hi.

SHEILA

(drops ice into his drink)
Looking for this?

TOM

Thanks.

Julie waits for a moment to get Sheila's attention back.

JULIE

(shows the size with her hands)

. . . and there were these three tiny little furry things! She was already pregnant when I was taking care of her!

SHEILA

(smiling, finally realizing the point of the story)

Oh, so she had kittens.

JULIE

(deflated)

Yeah.

SHEILA

Hear that Tom? I don't think you should let Julie babysit your daughter!

Tom laughs with Sheila. Julie looks hurt and then smiles too.

SHEILA

Oh hey, c'mon. You want to take that out to Bill in the living room? Thanks, sweetheart.

Julie exits past Tom and Sheila to enter the dining room.

5. INT. DINING ROOM—NIGHT

A long table set with an elaborate fall meal. BILL, late fifties, is playing with a dog.

BILL

Oh, I love you, that's right, go on go on. . . .

Julie enters the dining room and sets the bowl down and pokes over the food.

AL, middle-aged, serves himself from the buffet. Sheila and Tom can be seen through the doorway to the kitchen. Their HUSHED VOICES and LAUGHTER fill the room.

SHEILA (O.S.)

How'd I sleep last night? Like a baby as usual.

TOM (O.S.)

Yeah.

SHEILA (O.S.)
I woke up every hour.
(laughter)
God, how awful.

An awkward moment is shared by Bill, Al, and Julie as they listen. Nothing is said. Bill scrapes the meat off the knife onto Julie's plate. Julie looks away from Bill nervously as they listen to the laughter off-screen.

BILL
Your mother was worried about you.

JULIE
No she wasn't.

Al and Julie glance at each other. Al smiles. Julie, uncomfortable, turns away and wedges herself between the chair and table.

SHEILA (O.S.)
I'm going to go check on the table.

TOM (O.S.)
Hey, c'mon, just a moment, c'mon. . . .

Laughing, Sheila enters from the kitchen and circles the buffet table.

SHEILA
Hi there. Mind if I steal this?

BILL
Go right ahead.

She picks something up from the cutting board and drops it into her mouth, wiggling her bottom to show the sensation of the good flavor. She exits to the foyer. AL tears a leg off a chicken.

6. INT. FOYER/STAIRS—NIGHT
Through the rails of the staircase, Julie sits alone, balancing a plate on her knees. She arranges a small grouping of doll house furniture displaying a living room and holiday dinner around her plate as she eats. SOUND of ice TINKLING in glasses is unnaturally loud; the soft indistinguishable patter of CONVERSATION.

SHEILA (O.S.)
I'd love to get a picture of that. I'd love to get a picture of that.

AL (O.S.)

So just who is Julie's father anyway? So who's Julie's father? That's what I never understood. Headless and footless adult figures pass in and out of the frame in front of her obscuring and revealing Julie.

7. INT. DEN—NIGHT

A bar. Amber liquid pours into frame as Tom's hand fills a tumbler with scotch, ice, and a touch of water. Sheila leans very close to Tom and lets her breast brush against his arm as she lifts the glass out of his hand.

Julie enters unobserved from the darkness of the corridor behind them to witness the exchange. Sheila stirs her drink with her finger and licks her finger. Tom and Sheila stand close together and SPEAK under their breath. AD LIB.

SHEILA

Hi, is that for me? You know what Julie asked me?

TOM

What?

SHEILA

If you were the same Tom she met at her birthday party years ago.

TOM

You're kidding.

(They laugh.)

SHEILA

(laughing)

So how's your wife?

Bill enters unobserved for a moment. Sheila notices Bill and crosses to him.

SHEILA

(turning toward Bill)

Thanks for the drink, Tom. Can I get you anything, sweetheart?

BILL

No thanks. I'm all set.

Bill swirls the alcohol in his glass, forces a smile, and pulls away and heads to the bar. With Tom and Bill in the background by the bar, Sheila steps away and lights a cigarette, inhaling deeply.

TOM

Great scotch, Bill.

BILL

That's nice.

8. INT. DEN/CORRIDOR—NIGHT (intercut with sc. 7)
Al comes from the corridor behind Julie and surprises her. He performs a simple magic trick offering her a cigarette. Julie takes it. He lights it for her. Julie tries to look natural smoking the cigarette but is made uncomfortable by Al's proximity to her.
From the living room, Sheila watches Julie smoking with an air of surprise but does not reprimand her. Instead she smiles at her daughter and blows smoke rings with her own cigarette. They exchange smiles.

9. INT. LIVING ROOM/DEN—NIGHT
Delirious montage of details of the room and the movement of the guests as the party wears on.

10. INT. LIVING ROOM—NIGHT
Sheila and Julie dance as Julie hammers away on the organ. She plays very badly. The mother and daughter improvise a raucous R 'n' R tune. Bill and Al are off to the side in quiet conversation. Sheila dances across to Bill.

SHEILA

Come dance with me.

BILL

(smiling, pushes her away)
C'mon, c'mon.

Sheila dances back across toward Julie, and Tom joins her in a sloppy dance.

BILL

Just knock that off; you're making me crazy. Turn it off. Shut that thing off.

Julie lifts her hands off the keyboard and the organ dies.

JULIE

It is off.

SHEILA

Take it easy, Bill.

BILL

Stop that dee-dee-dee shit.

Julie gets up and leaves.

TOM (O.S.)

Hey, Jules, c'mon play for us.

11. INT. STAIRWELL/FOYER—NIGHT

Julie stomps up the stairs. A needle drops sharply on the turntable.

From the base of the stairs, Al watches Julie's foot disappear around the banister.

12. INT. LANDING/MASTER BEDROOM—NIGHT

At the top of the stairs, a light is burning in the large master bedroom on the bedside table next to a bottle of whiskey and a tumbler; the bed is unmade. An informal wedding portrait of Sheila and Bill is on the nightstand. A rifle rests in the corner of the room.

Julie lingers in the doorway a moment. She enters and closes the door behind her. She pushes over the photos on the bedside table and jumps on the bed where she discovers her mother's nightgown.

BILL (O.S.)

Just a little while ago you were nothing, you know, you were nothing. Just a woman in a bar with a little snotty-nosed kid, a little snotty-nosed kid.

SHEILA (O.S.)

What is this story you're telling me? A little Biafra here.

Sheila and Bill laugh.

SHEILA (O.S.)

I was perfectly fine.

BILL (O.S.)

I understand it was a hell of a job. That was real—working for the president. One hell of a job. I mean it was fine, I'm not saying anything—c'mon—you were working in a bar. Give me a break.

SHEILA (O.S.)

I happened to grow up five blocks from that bar. I know all the people. It's not a sleazy place.

BILL (O.S.)
I'm just saying that it's not exactly brain surgery, that's all.

SHEILA (O.S.)
Good Lord! I wouldn't exactly call yourself a brain surgeon.

She pulls her shirt over her head and holds the nightgown up.

13. INT. BATHROOM—NIGHT
SOUNDS of the PARTY continue downstairs: MUSIC, VOICES, GLASSES CLINKING mingle with the rushing WATER. Water pours from the tap; bubbles form on the surface of the water. Julie's foot plays with the tap as it fills the tub.

SHEILA (O.S.)
One invention and you're sitting pretty.

BILL (O.S.)
That's right, we're sitting pretty.

SHEILA (O.S.)
Oh yeah, well, we'll just see about that. You're getting pretty tight, aren't you? Counting every penny.

Julie sits in the bubbles up to her neck. Her dry hair hangs over the edge of the tub. She picks up a lipstick from the edge of the tub and applies it using the side of the tube as a mirror. She admires the fractions of her face that she can see in its reflection.

14. INT. DEN/BAR—NIGHT
Sheila leans against the hearth framed by a rack of rifles. She lets out an exasperated sigh over the sound of her own voice arguing with her husband.

BILL (O.S.)
It's not every penny. It's thirteen hundred dollars. I have a right to ask my wife.

15. INT. BATHROOM—NIGHT
Julie slowly slides herself into the water. She thrashes around under water blowing bubbles to the surface. Underwater the argument turns to mush.

BILL (O.S.)
I'm just asking. I have a right to ask my own wife about the goddamned money.

16. INT. LANDING—NIGHT
A bottle is knocked over.

SHEILA (O.S.)
I resent, I resent that you call my daughter. . . .

17. CONT. INT. BATHROOM—NIGHT
Julie reemerges from underwater and the sound returns to normal.

BILL (O.S.)
What did you call me that for . . . just think of who you're talking to.

SHEILA (O.S.)
You're drunk.

BILL (O.S.)
Oh yeah, so what are you the Virgin Mary you're so sober?

17. A S/FX SHOT OF GLASS tumbler with ice fills with scotch.

18. INT. BATHROOM—NIGHT
In a three-way mirror, apricot satin shimmers as Julie slides a luxurious nightgown, several sizes too large, over her head. The voices downstairs vanish as she is enraptured by her own sensuality. A loud CRASH is heard downstairs.

19. HARD CUT TO:
A tumbler of ice and scotch CRASHES to the ground.

20. INT. BATHROOM—NIGHT—continued
Julie turns sharply at the SOUND.

21. INT. FOYER—NIGHT
Julie comes out of the bathroom and runs to the landing. Seen from high above through the bars of the staircase. Tom is between Sheila and Bill. The figures pass in and out between the rungs of the banister. Bill taunts Sheila.

SHEILA
Get your stomach out of the way.

BILL
Fuck you.

TOM
Don't, Bill, c'mon. . . .

SHEILA
I still have a few good years on you.

BILL
Fucking few, baby, few fucking years, baby. . . .

Sheila spits in Bill's face and laughs.

BILL
Fucking whore.

SHEILA
(shrieking)
Get out of my way.

BILL
Come back here, come back here.

Bill lurches toward her. Julie watches the fight from the landing. The FIGHT swirls up the stairs. AD LIB. As Sheila and Bill approach, Julie moves quickly away from the door of the room to the stairwell of the third floor.

22. INT. JULIE's BEDROOM—NIGHT
Julie backs into her own bedroom and stands in the semidarkness. Sheila and Bill can be seen running up the stairs.

SOUNDS of Sheila and Bill SCRAMBLING into the master bedroom. The door SLAMS shut.

SHEILA (O.S.)
Stay away from me, don't touch me!

BILL (O.S.)
Put that gun down, put it down.

SHEILA (O.S.)
I said stay away from me. . . .

Sheila SCREAMS.

A shotgun BLAST is heard.

23. INT. DOLL HOUSE—NIGHT
The miniature chandelier swings in the doll house and a large armchair is overturned. The SOUND of tinkling GLASS.

24. INT. JULIE's BEDROOM—NIGHT
Julie remains frozen and glazed, clutching the bundle of clothing. Her breath rasps slightly as she holds it in. She

strains for sound. For a few moments SILENCE pervades the house. Finally, a DOOR OPENS and SLAMS shut, BOUNCING OPEN again from the force. Sheila lets out a long SIGH.

BILL (O.S.)

I can't believe you.

SHEILA (O.S.)

You fat ugly thing that I married. You're a piece of shit, you know that. You're a piece of shit.

Julie's eyes blink and shift toward the direction of these sounds.
Julie takes a few steps forward and listens as STEPS bound quickly down the stairs, a dog YELPS in pain.

TOM (O.S.)

Hey, Bill, what's going on?

DOOR OPENS and SLAMS shut. FOOTSTEPS crunch on GRAVEL. a CAR DOOR OPENS and SLAMS shut, and a dog BARKS, a car DRIVES away up a long GRAVEL drive.
After several beats, Sheila lets out a LONG SLOW SOB. Julie very slowly lets out her breath in an extended sigh. She moves slowly toward the stairs, stopping first to place the laundry in her hamper, and then descends.

25. INT. LANDING/MASTER BEDROOM—NIGHT
Tom's FOOTSTEPS bound up the stairs; near the top, his pace slows.
Julie watches from the third floor landing as Tom slowly approaches Sheila's room. Tom enters and sees Sheila holding the smoking rifle in front of her.

TOM

Put the gun down, baby, put the gun down, baby.

SHEILA

Get out of my room. Get out of my room. Get out of my room.

Tom strides up to her and grabs it out of her hands, overpowering her with no difficulty. He catches her off balance and hurts her hands.

AL (O.S.)

Sheila, Tom, what's going on?

With the rifle in one hand, Tom backs out of the room. Sheila throws an ashtray at him.

Tom turns and sees Julie behind him.

TOM

(voice quivering but in command)

Everything's fine . . . go to bed.

He pushes past her and hustles down the stairs.
Al, hanging back from the scene, stands midway on the stairs.
He hangs his eyes on Julie as Tom pushes past.
Al pauses a moment staring at Julie, then follows Tom down the stairs.
Julie, standing in the open doorway, in embarrassment notices that she is still in her mother's nightgown and pulls it close around her.

TOM (O.S.)

C'mon, let's get out of here. Al, c'mon move it.

Julie stands silent and contorted, tears filling her eyes, but she does not cry.

SHEILA

Julie, Julie.

Julie turns and walks slowly toward her mother. The music box begins to play.

26. INT. MASTER BEDROOM—NIGHT
Julie embraces Sheila and lays her into bed. Julie sits quietly on the edge of her mother's bed, and softly and out of key, she sings her to sleep.
DISSOLVE TO:

27. INT. DINING ROOM—NIGHT
Passata la musica finita la festa. The guests have gone home, and this is what remains. Wax drips from smoldering candles, the carcasses of the turkeys are picked bare. Bottles and wine glasses are tipped on their sides. A broken flower vase spills forth, and the water makes an incessant drip into a puddle on the floor. The fruit has rotted in its bowl.
FADE TO BLACK.

DEAD LETTERS DON'T DIE
(Originally "Thomas Fupper")

by Anais Granofsky and Michael Swanhaus

BLACK SCREEN

White calligraphy text appears on the screen. "Once upon a time, just a Christmas ago . . .

INT. MAILBOX—DAY
Darkness.
The creaking of rusty hinges.
A rectangle of light creeps open, and the face of AMANDA CARSON appears in the lit frame. A French chapeau rests on her flaccid brown hair. Hiding behind nervous squirrel-like features are scared, world-weary eyes. She glances around, tenderly marks the envelope with a kiss and drops it into what we now discover is a mailbox.
The letter lazily floats downwards and lands atop a hill of waiting letters.

CUT TO:

EXT. DEAD LETTER OFFICE—DAY
A plaque reading "U.S. POSTAL SERVICE-DEAD LETTER OFFICE" is bolted to a closed side door.

INT. DEAD LETTER OFFICE
Mountains of jaundiced Santa letters. Long-forgotten packages line the aged brick walls. The depths of the Dead Letter Office. Christmas cheer hangs limp from every over-packed shelf. A pathetic Post Office–issued tree struggles to hold its last two remaining bulbs. The camera PANS past discarded presents. A snow shaker, two dancers eternally whirling in an afternoon snow storm. Lacy red panties. A huge rotting teddy bear, two bags resting under its arms.
We finally stop on THOMAS FUPPER, a middle-aged postman with a thin, nondescript face. He's intently reading a weathered copy of *Cyrano de Bergerac*. Beside him sits CHUCK SLATES, the only other worker in this office of lost dreams. Chuck reads a Christmas edition of *Playboy*, while sucking on a Pepsi through a red twizzler.
A loud CRASH echoes throughout the room as the doors are flung open by BOSS, a grossly overweight man with the face of a bulldog. He huffs and snorts with the exertion of carrying two large mail sacks.

BOSS

Hey piss ants! Why don't you get your hand off your chub and help me out!

Thomas and Chuck grapple with the bags, dragging them to the sorting table.

BOSS (cont'd)
Goddamn Santa Claus is gonna give me a bleedin' hernia!

Boss sits down with a rush of air.

BOSS (cont'd)
All these kids do today is take. Take. Take. That's what you get with a world full of backseat produce. When I was a kid, a smack across the head did me just fine. Hell, I'd go to the sack with a grin on my face, thinkin' I'd had a damn good Christmas.

CHUCK
I think that's referred to as child abuse.

BOSS
It's more than I get now. (He glances over to Thomas.) You talkin' today Fupper?

Thomas stops his sorting and looks up.

THOMAS
Sure I am, Boss.

BOSS
Too bad. Get this crap sorted by three.

Boss heads back out the door.
There's a CLUNK in the walls. Thomas falters in his sorting and looks at the clock. It's four. The faint sound of a letter wisping down the chutes.

INT. CHUTE
A letter tumbles and soars downward in a type of stationery ballet.

DEAD LETTER OFFICE
Thomas stares at the chute's opening.

CHUCK
That her?

THOMAS
Yeah.

CHUTE
Arching and dipping, the letter makes its way toward the dim opening.

DEAD LETTER OFFICE
Thomas waits. Not breathing. The letter approaches. The far-off sound of a typewriter.
SWOOSH
It soars out of the chute and lands directly in front of him. The lipstick kiss marks the letter as Amanda's. Thomas stares. Unable to move.

CHUCK
So, what doth the fair maiden have to say this week?

Thomas reaches out and picks up the envelope. Gingerly he tears it open and begins to read. His voice blends with Amanda's and continues over into the next scene.

AMANDA (V.O.)
My dearest Joshua. As always, I miss you with everything I am.

EXT. AMANDA's HOUSE—AFTERNOON
Thomas sits on his trusty 1940 Schwinn Classic bicycle, his brown-bag lunch sits in the plastic basket hanging above the front tire. A speedometer and mileage counter are attached to the handlebars, and two "U.S. Postal" saddlebags hang from the seat. Thomas takes a bite out of his sandwich, his eyes never leaving Amanda's front door.

AMANDA (V.O.)
Christmas is coming, as it tends to do each year, and I am still in solitude. This time of year holds no joy, only loneliness.

Amanda stands on her front porch, completely unaware of Thomas's watchful eyes. She is trying to hang a wreath on her door, but just can't seem to get it.

AMANDA
Darn it!

Thomas looks on with an aching love. Her frustration is not hers alone. He cringes as she tries . . . and fails.
STEVE, another mailman, comes walking down the sidewalk. Thomas jumps at the sound of his voice.

STEVE
Hey, Tom. Whatchya doin'?

Thomas quickly glances at Amanda. His foot kicks the pedal.

THOMAS

I was . . . was just eatin' my sandwich, here.

STEVE

Awful far for lunch ain't it?

THOMAS

I was . . . just, here, on the route.

STEVE

Aw yeah, I didn't think you delivered here no more.

THOMAS

I, ah, yeah, I had myself transferred to the office.

STEVE

The office?

Thomas starts the bike in motion.

THOMAS

It was good seeing you, Steve.

Steve smiles uncertainly.

STEVE

Yeah, you too.

Thomas makes like a tree.
Amanda finally hangs her wreath and, with a last glance, walks inside and closes the door.
The wreath hangs as a delicate symbol of Christmas, then falls to the ground with a loud SMASH.

CUT TO:

INT. DEAD LETTER OFFICE—AFTERNOON
Thomas sits reading the last of Cyrano. The brown-bag lunch finished and crumpled in front of him. Chuck appears from the back of the room.
He holds up a very tacky, see-through negligee.

CHUCK

Deb's secret Santa gift. What do you think?

Thomas looks up from his readings.

THOMAS

You bought that?

CHUCK

Naw, it was in the back. Package didn't have a return address. Saved myself five bucks.

THOMAS

I guess it's the thought that counts.

CHUCK

Damn right. What'd you get for your ole' lady?

THOMAS

Oh, I . . . I wouldn't even know what to. . . . She deserves more than I could give her.

Chuck shoves his lacy gift in a drawer and begins to throw letters into their appointed boxes.

CHUCK

Still haven't talked to her, huh?

THOMAS

Uh, not yet.

Chuck faces Thomas.

CHUCK

Fupper, you gotta take the bull by the balls.

He crumples the letter he is holding into a ball.

CHUCK

This Stevie Wonder, secret lover crap has gone on for much too long.

THOMAS

It's still too early.

CHUCK

It's been two years! She writes to her dead husband for God sakes; you can't tell me she doesn't need a friend.

THOMAS

I don't want to rush it.

Chuck shrugs his shoulders.

CHUCK

Hey, it's your day at the track, but if you ask me, no one likes to bet on a horse that shows.

The SOUND of Thomas's bicycle.

CUT TO:

EXT. AMANDA's HOUSE
Thomas sits on his bike across the street straightening his bow tie. A suit that appears to be one size too small rests on his bony frame. A single daisy sits in his basket.

THOMAS

Hello, my name is Thomas Fupper. I'm a mailman at the . . . uh, post office, and I've been reading. . . .

He takes a deep breath, smoothes his eyebrows, grabs the flower, and dismounts his bike.

EXT. AMANDA's FRONT WALK
Thomas approaches the cement walkway.

THOMAS

Hello, my name . . . is Thomas Fupper. I've been . . . I mean I work at the Dead Letter Office. . . .

Thomas's footsteps falter. His last remaining words sink in, and he halts, his foot near the edge of the path. He stares as if seeing the house for the first time.
Go! Go, Goddammit! Nothing. Thomas wilts, he can't go through with it. He gingerly lays the daisy down on the cement slab of the walkway. He retraces his steps, a beaten man. Thomas speeds away just as Amanda rounds the corner and comes to her walkway. A daisy. She picks up the abandoned flower and looks around. No one. Must have fallen out of a bunch. She moves toward her house, cradling the flower.

CUT TO:

INT. AMANDA's HOUSE—NIGHT
The daisy sits in a glass on Amanda's T.V. dinner stand. She's eating a Swanson frozen dinner "Beef Surprise." The television blares some nonsensical movie of the week, in which Amanda is deeply involved.
We PULL OUT to reveal a set of men's clothing neatly laid out as if someone was sitting there. Beside the suit is a small child's outfit, propped under the invisible man's arm. It looks like a normal family at rest, minus the family. Amanda reaches over and takes the empty sleeve in her hand, as if taking the arm of a loved one. A distracted smile remains on her face.

CUT TO:

INT. THOMAS'S APARTMENT—NIGHT
The dingy little room is lit by a single lightbulb hanging from the cracked ceiling. Thick, floral print wallpaper clings to the sheet rock. A Charlie Brown Christmas tree slouches in the corner.
A picture of Fred Astaire and Ginger Rogers dancing in the snow is taped to the wall.
Rudolph the Red Nose Reindeer laments from the television.
Thomas sits in an overstuffed armchair. (The next sequence of shots will be done as we dolly behind Thomas's head.) He raises a cup of cider to his lips. Drinks. Lowers the cup. Drinks again. The cup disappears from sight. He raises his hand and places a gun in his mouth.
Christmas lights blink. The steel barrel knocks against his teeth. A tear rolls down his sallow cheek. Rudolph. Thomas yanks the gun out of his mouth and sinks down onto the orange shag rug. The gun slips from his fingers.

GRAPHIC MATCH:

INT. DEAD LETTER OFFICE—DAY
A child's drawing of Santa lying in a pool of blood. Below, in the hand writing of an eight-year-old, are the words:
SANTA LIES.
Chuck shakes his head as he examines it.

CHUCK
Merry Christmas. Jesus.

Thomas sorts through hundreds of letters. Boss comes busting in. More letters, and he's not pleased.

BOSS
I wish I was packing. If I was packing, I'd blow some heads clear off their necks.

Thomas gingerly takes the sacks from his boss. Resigned to being unarmed, Boss sinks into a chair.

BOSS
At least it's the last day of this holiday horseshit.

CHUCK
That's more in the spirit, Boss.

BOSS
You can suck my spirit.

Chuck drops his bag and faces Boss.

CHUCK
Now, did the good man from the North Pole person really piss in your Corn Flakes? Or does being an ass hole just die hard?

BOSS
You have a problem with me, Mr. Slates?

CHUCK
In fact I do. Tom and I were wondering why people like you find it necessary to puke on everybody else's parade?

BOSS
This true, Fupper?

Thomas looks up, dazed.

THOMAS
Yeah, sure.

CHUCK
You'd think you were the only guy ever to get his ass kicked by a holiday.

Boss stands up.

BOSS
You want to know the last time I ever celebrated Christmas? December 24, 1959. That's the last time my mother ever brought home a stinking pair of orange jogging pants. Every year she'd come home from that stinkin' pants factory and every year she'd have that brown paper package. Three pairs of extra-large orange jogging pants. You know what that does to a kid, havin' to go back after every Christmas break wearin' oversized, polyester orange pants. Let me tell you, it teaches you that Christmas good tidings don't last much past the twenty-fifth of the month.

Thomas and Chuck stand silent.

BOSS
So I decide I'm not gonna do it no more, not this year. She walks in with this big ham-hock-eatin' grin on and hands me that package. I flung that orange bomb so hard across the room I could hear it tearin' in mid-flight, "I'm not wearin' those fuckin' orange pants no more!!! I hate 'em and I hate you!" Well my mother, she starts to cry and she doesn't stop, in fact she

keeps cryin' right out the front door. I looked over at that torn brown package and there they were, pretty as could be, a pair of spankin' new blue jeans. That's the last time I ever saw the woman who gave me this rat trap of a life. See, I'm not pretending my life isn't an empty piece of crap. So if it pleases you to eat your turkey and shove a couple of potatoes down your gizzard, then be my guest. Just leave me the fuck alone.

Boss turns and leaves the room. Chuck and Thomas are speechless. Chuck reaches into his drawer and pulls out a plastic bag.

CHUCK

I guess I won't give him this.

THOMAS

What is it?

CHUCK

Jogging pants.

(shrugging)

No forwarding address.

Chuck tosses them to Thomas.

CHUCK

Here, use them with passion.

Thomas looks down at the bag.

THOMAS

Things aren't so good, are they Chuck?

CHUCK

No, my friend, they're not.

Chuck throws down the letters in his hand.

CHUCK

Well! Screw this, I'm gettin' outta this hell hole. I got a mildly attractive wife and two bug-eyed kids waitin' for me. You comin'?

THOMAS

Naw. Her letter comes today.

Chuck throws on his coat.

CHUCK
Wanna see what I found today?

He holds up the drawing of the dead Santa.

CHUCK
Nice, huh?

THOMAS
Who sent that?

Chuck crumples the picture into a ball and throws it onto the sorting table.

CHUCK
A very misdirected child.

There's a CLUNK from above.

CHUCK
I'll leave you two alone.

A pat on the back and Chuck's gone. Silence.
The letter travels its whispering path and lands in front of Thomas. He rips open the envelope.

AMANDA (V.O.)
My dearest Joshua. I am writing to you for what may be the last time. The little hope I've been clinging to is gone.

CUT TO:

EXT. STREET—AFTERNOON
Thomas rides down the street between two long snow banks. He notices nothing. The world does not exist.

AMANDA (V.O.)
Once, I could believe that a miracle could fall from the sky. But as the season becomes colder, I now know that I can't stay in a life that doesn't need me.
Amanda's letter flaps inside the plastic basket.

CUT TO:

EXT. STREET
We follow a scruffy pair of shoes making tracks down the sidewalk. A black bag bounces against his knees. Shouting and police sirens can be heard.

CUT TO:

EXT. STREET
Thomas's wheels crunch through the cold winter air.

CUT TO:

EXT. STREET
The scruffy pair of shoes, now attached to a scruffy looking man round the corner and SLAM!!! Right into Thomas. Police round the corner.
The man untangles himself and flees, dropping the black bag on the road. Police pound past.
Silence. Bicycle wheels spinning. Thomas reaches over and pulls the bag close to him. He slowly unzips it and looks in.

CUT TO:

EXT. SHOP—AFTERNOON
Thomas's bicycle slides to a stop in front of a small second-hand shop. In the window, a Santa suit stands glowing in the cold afternoon light. Thomas cuffs the kickstand and dismounts.

CUT TO:

EXT. STREET—CHRISTMAS EVE—LATE AFTERNOON
Christmas decorations droop across the street top, smothering the air with Christmas joy. Snow pours out of the sky. The faint sound of Booker T & the MGs playing "Santa Claus Is Coming to Town."
Then, out of the snow, barreling down the street is Thomas. His bicycle is decorated like a Mr. Magoo version of a Norman Rockwell Santa sled. A plastic Rudolf the Red-Nosed Reindeer with a glowing cherry red nose is wired to the front. A transistor radio propped up in his basket blares Booker T. Thomas sits decked head to waist in the Santa costume from the store window. On his legs are the orange jogging pants from Chuck.
The black bag sticks out of his mail sack.
Madly, he steers his bike through the snow. He cuts sharp right down the next block.

CUT TO:

EXT. EMPIRE STATE BUILDING—NIGHT
A Salvation Army Santa Claus stands in the cold next to his empty money pot senselessly ringing his bell. Thomas buzzes up past him and curbs his bike. He steps onto the pavement, grabs the bag and pats Rudolf on the head.

THOMAS
Don't go away, I'll be back in a zip.

He approaches the entrance.

DARREL (O.S.)
Yo, Santa!

A group of young black kids rouse Thomas from behind. DARREL, the leader of the boys, struts up to Thomas and pushes him in the back. Thomas turns in confusion.

DARREL
Santa, I'm talking to you.

His friends walk up and surround Thomas.

DARREL
Yeah, I was just wondering if you got any presents in that bag for me.

The boys laugh.

THOMAS
What?

He pulls a knife from under his jacket.

DARREL
Let's get this over with. Give me your money.

The kids pull in tighter. Thomas looks over to the Salvation Army Santa and back to the kid.

DARREL
Come on, man. I don't need this crap tonight.

THOMAS
Can I ask you a question?

Darrel's thrown back by his sincerity.

DARREL
(looking around to his boys)
A fuckin' crazy man.
(back to Thomas)
Yeah, OK. What?

THOMAS
You ever believe in Santa Claus?

All the boys laugh.

THOMAS

As a kid?

DARREL

I don't believe in no fairy tales, and I sure as hell never expected no handouts. I got schooled pretty quick that what you take is what you get. So to answer your question, I never had a chance to believe in no Santi Claus.

THOMAS

I'm sorry.

DARREL

Yeah, so am I.

Thomas grabs a couple hundred dollars from his pouch.

THOMAS

(dropping the bills into Darrel's open hands)

That's all I can give you.

Thomas disappears into the Empire State Building. As he trails off down the hallway, satchel in hand, the camera PANS UP to the top of the Empire State Building.

DISSOLVE TO:

INT. AMANDA'S HOUSE—NIGHT

CLOSE-UP on a framed postcard of King Kong scaling the side of the Empire State Building. SCREAMS and HOWLS blare from off-screen. The camera DOLLIES OVER to Amanda, who stands at the kitchen sink, plate in hand, carefully listening to an old transistor radio which rests on the window sill. A NEWS CASTER continues:

NEWSCASTER

The police don't seem to know what to do. Nothing like this has ever happened on Christmas Eve. . . .

EXT. AMANDA's HOUSE

Thomas sits on his bike across the street watching Amanda through the window. A pile of Amanda's letters neatly tied under a red velvet bow sits in his basket. Thomas straightens his eyebrows and readjusts his beard.

THOMAS

Hello, my name is Thomas Fupper. I know you don't know me, but I . . . (he inhales deeply) I am in love with you.

He grabs the letters and dismounts his bike. Swiping his hand along Rudolf's body, he gives him a quick pat on the head and moves toward the house.

EXT. AMANDA'S FRONT WALK
Long strides. Slowing as they approach the door. Smooth yellow paint surrounds the buzzer. Thomas's long bony finger reaches in. He pauses. Moving closer, now shaking. The door bell shrieks. He beckons the dreaded buzzer.

THOMAS
Hello, my name is Thomas. . . .

From inside he hears the VOICE OF THE NEWSCASTER.

INSERT RADIO:

NEWSCASTER
The riots started shortly after a man apparently dressed as Santa Claus threw approximately forty thousand dollars off of the top of the building. . . .

CUT BACK TO:
The voice trails off. Loud screams and police sirens are heard from inside the transmitted world.

Thomas stands stunned.
Fire. Howling sirens. It can't be real.
He falters back, unable to comprehend the repercussions of his actions. Suddenly the door opens. Thomas jumps and drops the letters. They tumble and spill across the front steps. He glances down at the letters and back to Amanda, who quickly recognizes them as hers. Embarrassment contorts in her saddened eyes.

THOMAS
I, I. . . .

He slowly backs away as Amanda looks down at the letters.

THOMAS
(continuing to back up)
I. . . . I'm sorry.

He turns and bolts right into his bike, causing it to come crashing down with him. He stumbles to his feet and takes off down the block.
Amanda stands alone on her front porch with the last few years of her life thrown at her feet. Ever so gently, she crouches down and reaches for the precious papers. Her eyes well up as she's left to collect her innermost thoughts.

CUT TO:

INT. DEAD LETTER OFFICE—NEXT MORNING
Thomas lays amongst bags of letters, sound asleep. Sunlight streams into the office. Particles of dust highlighted like crystal.
He pries each eye open with some difficulty, rolls his head to one side, and scuttles backwards. He quickly smoothes over his eyebrows.
Amanda sits on a pile of letters, calmly watching him.
Thomas's bike is parked behind her.
They say nothing, merely contemplating each other's presence.
Thomas opens his mouth but Amanda speaks first.

AMANDA
I followed you. From my house.

Silence.

THOMAS
It was an accident. Everything that happened was a mistake.

AMANDA
How did you get my letters?

THOMAS
I work here . . . in the office. I didn't mean any harm. Everything just happened so quick, I wasn't ready.

AMANDA
Who are you?

THOMAS
My name's Thomas.

AMANDA
OK, Thomas. Tell me, what's happening?

Thomas lets his hands drop.

THOMAS
It went all wrong. They didn't understand. I just wanted to give them something to believe in.

AMANDA
It was you.

THOMAS
I was giving it to them. Everybody needed something and . . . it was all I had to give you.

AMANDA

What does that have to do with me?

Thomas shifts in his pile of letters and looks down.

THOMAS

I've always had this dream, and it's ridiculous because it's a direct rip-off of an old Fred Astaire film, but it's mine . . . because you're there. We're dancing in the sunlight of a snowstorm. And, I, I couldn't let that die.

Amanda timidly looks at his face.

AMANDA

How do you know me?

THOMAS

I used to deliver to your house. I tried so hard to speak with you, but when I saw what he did to you.

Amanda looks away.

THOMAS

I hated coming there; I hated not doing anything when I saw him hurting you. But when I left, you started writing.

AMANDA

You were reading them.

THOMAS

It was the only way I could know you. I wanted to give you your miracle. But they didn't understand what it was supposed to be.

Amanda crawls over and removes Thomas's beard and hat.

AMANDA

My husband didn't die. He took everything and disappeared.

A letter shoots out of the duct and soars into the air.

THOMAS

I know.

The faint strings of an instrument.

AMANDA

He took my life.

Five more letters fly into the air. In seconds, hundreds of letters are shooting out of the duct. CLASSICAL WALTZ MUSIC slowly fades in.

THOMAS

I just want to try.

AMANDA

I don't know how to start.

THOMAS

You already have.

Amanda takes Thomas's hand. He inhales her clean scent.
They slowly embrace.
Letters fly everywhere, like snowflakes.
Step by step, they begin to waltz across the floor like Ginger Rogers and Fred Astaire. Two people who have never known love just found it.
In the background, the sound of POLICE SIRENS can be heard.

THE END

INDEX